To Hoyle

Bob Lindberg

FINDING PERSONAL HAPPINESS

Three Magical Paths

Robert E. Lindberg, Ph.D.

FINDING PERSONAL HAPPINESS

Three Magical Paths

Robert E. Lindberg, Ph.D.

Psychological Insights Press
San Antonio, TX 78229

© 1996 Robert E. Lindberg, Ph.D. Printed and bound in the United States of America. All rights reserved. No part of this book may be reproduced or transmitted in any form or by any means, electronic or mechanical, including photocopying, recording, or by an information storage and retrieval system—except by a reviewer who may quote brief passages in a review to be printed in a magazine or newspaper—without permission in writing from the publisher. For information, please contact Psychological Insights Press, 7500 Callaghan Road, Suite 145, San Antonio, TX 78229.

Although the author and publisher have made every effort to ensure the accuracy and completeness of information contained in this book, we assume no responsibility for errors, inaccuracies, omissions, or any inconsistency herein. Any slights of people, places, or organizations are unintentional.

First printing 1996

ISBN 0-9652118-0-0

LCCN 96-69797

Editing, design, typesetting and printing services provided by About Books, Inc., 425 Cedar Street, POB 1500, Buena Vista, CO 81211, (800) 548-1876.

ATTENTION CORPORATIONS, UNIVERSITIES, COLLEGES, AND PROFESSIONAL ORGANIZATIONS: Quantity discounts are available on bulk purchases of this book for educational purposes. Special books or book excerpts can also be created to fit specific needs. For information, please contact Psychological Insights Press, 7500 Callaghan Road, Suite 145, San Antonio, TX 78229 or call (800) 694-8060.

DEDICATION

*I dedicate this book to my three wonderful children,
Todd, Julie, and Brent.*

• ACKNOWLEDGMENTS •

There are so many people, too numerous to mention, that I want to thank for their contributions to this book.

- All my clients who so enriched my life. If they had not had the courage to share their struggles and successes, this book would never have been written.

- My friends who read parts or all of this book and gave their supportive comments.

- The university professors, religious leaders, and professional colleagues who so enlightened me on the three magical paths.

I would especially, however, like to thank:

- Nancy Trimble, my wonderfully loyal and efficient secretary, who spent hundreds of hours working on the manuscript.

- Marie Simpson and Susan Gee for all of their encouragement and editorial suggestions.

- Marilyn and Tom Ross and their staff at About Books Inc. for the creative cover design, insightful editing, and expert advise on all aspects of this book.

• TABLE OF CONTENTS •

    1. An Introspective Look   1
    2. The Three Magical Paths   9

PART I–A Loving Relationship: The First Magical Path   13

    3. The Magic of Love   15
    4. The Five C's   19
    5. Chemistry   23
    6. Sex After Forty   41
    7. Caring   45
    8. Handling Arguments With Care   51
    9. Communication   61
    10. Communication and Criticism   73
    11. Commitment   85
    12. Commitment and Unreasonable Expectations   95
    13. Competency   103
    14. Competency and the M.E.   123
    15. Summary to the Relationship Section   133

PART II–Career: The Second Magical Path   135

    16. How Was Your Day?   137
    17. Job Stress   143

18.	Creatively Coping With Stress	149
19.	Good Career Matching	157
20.	Positive Relationships on the Job	171
21.	Establishing Positive Relationships	175
22.	Stress Strategies	187
23.	Self-Talk and Job Stress	193
24.	The Endorphin Fix	205
25.	What Is My B?	211
26.	Summary to the Career Section	217

PART III–Mission: The Third Magical Path — 219

27.	Mission	221
28.	What Is a Mission?	225
29.	Mission and the Midlife Transitions	231
30.	Selecting a Mission	237
31.	Setting Mission Goals	247
32.	The Power of Imagery	251
33.	Retirement and the Mission Path	255
34.	The Spiritual Force	261
35.	Summary to the Mission Section	275

PART IV–Overcoming Obstacles — 277

36.	Another Introspective Look	279
37.	The Three Magical Questions	283
38.	Finding a Competent Counselor	293
39.	Persistence	299

References and Helpful Reading — 301

Index — 305

• CHAPTER 1 •

An Introspective Look

"My marriage is not that bad. In fact, I know most people have it much worse. I just thought it would be more exciting."

"I sure wish I had a different job. I start dreading going to work by Sunday afternoon, and I spend all week counting the days until Friday gets here."

"I used to go to church, but somehow I drifted away when we moved. Sometimes I miss it, but I am not even sure what I believe anymore."

"I really don't have any reason to complain. The marriage is okay, the job is okay, my personal life is okay. It is just that I used to be a lot happier."

Happiness in one's heart, happiness in one's mind, happiness in one's soul, or just an overall happiness in one's life—this is the yearning I hear from people on a daily basis. As a psychologist and marriage therapist in private practice, I have had the unique and wonderful opportunity to spend more than twenty-five years listening to people find happiness and fulfillment in their personal lives.

I have had the privilege of learning from corporate heads, full-time mothers, attorneys, ministers, salesclerks, elected city officials, secretaries, physicians, school teachers, and people in hundreds of other careers. They were married and single, male and female, old and young, eager and apprehensive, successful and struggling. But one thing they all had in common was a desire to feel better.

During these counseling sessions, my clients have taken the adventurous risk of exploring their inner thoughts and feelings with me. They have invited me into their private worlds and given me the opportunity to understand their emotions and, to some degree, walk in their psychological moccasins.

Most of the people I see in my private practice have struggles or issues common to most people. They are facing situational concerns created by a strained relationship, a personal disappointment, excessive job stress, or simply a realization that "surely there must be more to life than what I am currently experiencing."

Sometimes these situational concerns are complicated by personal struggles such as low self-esteem, codependency, or unresolved emotional issues, but the underlying psychological profile is usually the same. My clients are basically emotionally healthy people looking for ways to feel better about themselves and their situations. They want more personal happiness!

How do these individuals find personal happiness in their lives? More specifically, how can *you* find personal happiness in *your* life?

First, let's define happiness. Happiness can be artificial (getting high on drugs or alcohol), transitory (sexual orgasm or winning a prize), or external (praise or recognition from another person). But for happiness to be sustaining, it has to be genuine, ongoing, and internal.

One of Webster's definitions of happiness is "a state of well-being and contentment." Let's use this as the official definition. The definition of happiness I really like, however, comes from Joseph Addison: "The grand essentials to happiness in this life are something to do, something to love, and something to hope for."

Rather than spend pages defining happiness and giving inspiring quotations, let me tell you what my mother used to say about self-help books.

My mother, at age eighty-four, was still an avid reader. She regularly took the bus to the Santa Barbara library to pick up one or two new books. When we had our weekly long-distance telephone chats, the conversations were spirited because my mother was sharing what she had just learned. Her favorite topics were biographies of famous political figures, religion, and (you have probably already guessed) self-help psychology. The conversations were fascinating because every time I talked to her, it was like having just read a good book.

One of my mother's pet peeves, especially in the self-help area, was a book that had too much introduction. "The book took too long getting to the main points," was her frequent criticism.

I dare not make the same mistake!

Listed below are sixteen powerful psychological strategies for coping with many of the normal pressures and stresses of daily living. All of these strategies are widely recognized by experts as effective psychological tools for finding happiness. Take this informal quiz to see how many of these strategies you currently use to ensure your psychological happiness.

If you take this quiz by yourself, circle the number 1 under the "Me" column for each strategy you feel you are using less effectively than most people, a 2 for each strategy you use about as well as the average person, and a 3 for each strategy you use more effectively than most people.

A more engaging way to take this introspective look is to do it with a friend. Take the quiz together, and each of you circle a 1, 2, or 3 on the first strategy. (Your friend can use the "Other" column.) Before you go on to the second strategy, however, have a sharing discussion about how well the two of you apply this strategy in your personal lives.

If you are ready for a bit of introspection, proceed with the self-assessment quiz (1 is below average, 2 is average, 3 is above average).

Me   Other

1-2-3   1-2-3   1. I rely primarily on *myself* to provide the positive feedback about my appearance, personality, character, and accomplishments

                  as opposed to

        relying primarily on *others* to give me this positive feedback.

4 • **Finding Personal Happiness**

Me   Other

1-2-3   1-2-3   2. I give myself permission to escape temporarily when I feel the need to get away from all the stresses and pressures

>   as opposed to

> needing to wait until I am emotionally exhausted or physically ill before I can take time off.

1-2-3   1-2-3   3. I do not take myself too seriously. I can laugh at my little mistakes, miscalculations, and misperceptions

>   as opposed to

> every mistake becoming a big deal, something of earthshaking consequence.

1-2-3   1-2-3   4. I make the automatic assumption that other people like me until I get data to the contrary

>   as opposed to

> assuming that other people do not like me until they have proven otherwise.

1-2-3   1-2-3   5. I stay *focused* by concentrating on what I am doing at any given moment

>   as opposed to

> frequently distracting myself by reliving the past, worrying about the future, or dwelling on other things I should be doing.

1-2-3   1-2-3   6. I do an aerobic, thirty-minute workout at least three times a week to obtain "the endorphin fix" (an emotional high)

>   as opposed to

> being a couch potato who limits the workout to a stretching exercise which involves reaching for the TV remote-control device.

Me   Other

1-2-3   1-2-3   7. I give any ambiguous situation (a teenager is ten minutes late, a boss wants a conference) a positive interpretation rather than a negative twist until I obtain more information

>> as opposed to

filling in the ambiguity by assuming the worst possible scenario has happened (a teenager has been in an accident, the boss is going to fire me).

1-2-3   1-2-3   8. I have good "change-of-pace" activities to add variety to my life (tennis, toy trains, painting, reading, mountain climbing)

>> as opposed to

being a workaholic who is limited to work, work, and work and who, when not working, is thinking about work!

1-2-3   1-2-3   9. I give myself more positive self-talk than I do negative self-talk. It is easy to give myself self-enhancing pep talks and "warm fuzzies"

>> as opposed to

more frequently giving myself negative self-talk as I dwell on my shortcomings and inadequacies.

1-2-3   1-2-3   10. I am an initiator. I assertively ensure that positive things are happening in my life

>> as opposed to

passively waiting for others to initiate the good ideas, activities, or events.

Me Other

1-2-3   1-2-3   11. I am very forgiving. I do not harbor grudges, and I let the past truly become the past

as opposed to

holding on to all the negative things that other people have done to me in the past.

1-2-3   1-2-3   12. My initial reaction, when criticized, is to ask other people to more fully explain what they mean and how they are feeling

as opposed to

immediately beginning to defend myself by quickly pointing out (a) how their perceptions are wrong or (b) how my behavior was caused by something they did.

1-2-3   1-2-3   13. I expect things to change—it is a natural part of life. (The car will break down; people will leave me; the economy will shift.) My goal is to flow with the normal changes

as opposed to

expecting everything to remain status quo and thus becoming excessively upset when changes do occur.

1-2-3   1-2-3   14. I am quick to praise other people and let them know they have done something well

as opposed to

not praising other people because I am concerned they might think that my compliments are insincere or too flattering, or that I merely "want" something.

Me Other

1-2-3   1-2-3   15. I share my feelings. I let people know my inner thoughts, and I reveal the intimate parts of my private self

        as opposed to

    only telling people things that will create a favorable impression. Only a public self is disclosed.

1-2-3   1-2-3   16. I feel I have control over my life. Most of my decisions and emotions are under my direction

        as opposed to

    my life being mainly determined and directed by what others want and need. They have primary control over what happens to me.

Now total up your points and interpret your results using the following scale.

16–24 = You have a *low* score. You have not adequately developed many of the psychological tools necessary to sustain a high level of personal happiness. Your chance of finding personal happiness, unless you change, is *low*.

25–36 = You have an *average* score. You have adequately developed many of the psychological tools necessary for a good level of personal happiness. Using these tools, your chance of finding personal happiness is still *low*.

37–48 = You have a *high* score. You have an excellent repertoire of psychological tools for finding a superior level of personal happiness. Relying on these well-honed strategies, your chance of finding personal happiness is still *low*.

Okay, I admit it, I set you up. But the point I wanted to make, in a dramatic enough way to capture your attention, is that these powerful psychological strategies do not create personal happiness.

The sixteen strategies may create the psychological climate and personal potential for happiness, but even a perfect score of forty-eight will not create a sustaining force for personal happiness unless *you are on one of the three magical paths.*

• CHAPTER 2 •

The Three Magical Paths

There are three ways to find a deep, sustaining happiness. The bad news is that there are only three paths to deep happiness, but the good news is that you have to successfully negotiate only one of these psychological paths through life in order to have a sustaining personal happiness. Two out of three or three out of three simply add to this happiness.

As pointed out in chapter 1, most of the standard psychological strategies do not ensure that you will find personal happiness. This is not to minimize the contribution of the sixteen strategies (and each of these will be expanded on throughout the book), but they are merely tools to help you stay on one or more of the magical paths.

Positive self-esteem is not the answer. Negative self-esteem increases the odds that you will not even start the journey, but positive self-esteem becomes a wasted gift unless it is actualized in one of three ways. There are millions of people who have a positive self-image but never truly find happiness.

The same thing is true with physical health. I once heard a minister say, "Good health is a major source of wealth. Without it, happiness is almost impossible." I thought that was a strong statement for a person who is primarily concerned about your soul.

Good health is not the answer, however. Bad health may preclude one from finding happiness, or at least make the struggle much more difficult, but good health does not ensure personal happiness. It is not, by itself, one of the three personal energizers. I know many people who annually receive an excellent health report from their physician, but they do not feel good about their lives—or about themselves.

Even a positive attitude toward change, standard advice for people going through a midlife crisis, does not make it happen. A positive response to change is necessary to survive all the changes that will be thrust upon you, that is, you will get older, children will leave home, careers will be altered, people will die. But even if you make all sorts of outstanding adjustments, you will not find happiness if you are not on one of three psychological paths.

Positive self-esteem . . . good health . . . a healthy attitude toward change . . . the sixteen psychological strategies . . . these may be essential elements for giving you the potential for finding happiness, but they, in and of themselves, will not give you personal happiness. There are only three paths, three options for truly finding a sustaining inner sense of genuine happiness.

What are these three psychological paths? The three magnificent avenues all involve essential elements of your being. One primarily involves your heart . . . one your mind . . . and one your soul.

The heart plays its major role in a loving *relationship*. Although I will focus primarily on this being expressed through a marital relationship, the principles would apply as well to any intimate, loving relationship.

The mind finds expression through productive, perhaps even creative, achievements. Since time and financial constraints usually require this to be expressed through a *career*, this will be the focus in this book.

The soul is most energized through having a *mission* for your life. It encompasses having a deep meaning or purpose for your existence . . . a purpose that moves beyond mere philosophical contemplation and finds itself expressed in some tangible, behavioral ways.

I have observed in twenty-five years of listening to people that they need fulfillment in only *one* of these three areas to find a high level of happiness. For example, when people have a truly loving relationship with their mate, they are able to tolerate a dull job or lack of mission. Likewise, the individuals who are involved in an engaging career better tolerate a bland marriage and make fewer demands to "change or else." I even find that people who have a consuming mission in their life make smooth adjustments to both a flat marriage and a boring career.

If a person is locked into an abusive marriage or hates his or her job, the success in one of the other areas may not be enough to override this psychologically destructive experience. But if the marriage is only dull or the career merely unchallenging, the success on one of the other paths is often enough to override this deficiency.

Section one will look at the intimate relationship in your life, section two will explore how well you like your career, and section three will focus on your mission for your life. Section four will examine alternatives if you are psychologically unable to begin your journey down one of these three positive psychological paths for finding personal happiness.

Before you begin your journey, however, please pause for a few minutes and carefully reflect on the awesome impact one of these journeys can have on your life. Consider how the relationship path, career path, and/or mission path could be your path to personal happiness . . . or if totally neglected, a journey to personal unhappiness.

The Relationship Path

Marriage can be magic or madness. This is not surprising because marriage creates such an intimate closeness . . . an intimate closeness that intensifies all emotions. The good relationships become better and the bad relationships become worse! Many people prevent this process by developing a peaceful coexistence or hiding behind busy routines, but often the truth surfaces. The intimate relationship either grows or dies. The marriage surges toward magic or it slides toward nothingness.

If you still have the potential for love in your marriage, go for the magic of love!

The Career Path

A career can be ecstasy or agony. This is true because no other personal pursuit demands so much time. If this time is spent in a rewarding challenge that stimulates interest and creates a sense of accomplishment, a person experiences deep surges of personal satisfaction. Likewise, if this time is wasted in mindless routines or experienced as a stressful tour of duty, a person will have a constant struggle with emotional unhappiness.

If your job offers you the opportunity to fulfill some of your personal needs, celebrate your good fortune ... and do what it takes to hold this positive emotional edge.

The Mission Path

A life's mission can be compelling or nonexistent. People who have a deep sense of mission experience a unique feeling of well-being that is rarely matched by any other pursuit or relationship. Some even call it the celebration of the soul. People who totally lack a sense of mission do not suffer the intense pain created by a destructive marriage or highly stressful career, but they can suffer an emotional flatness, a lack of meaning, and a loss of purpose ... psychological states that take the positive edge off of life's triumphs and add a depressive deadening to life's tragedies.

If you have a compelling mission for your life, you have already experienced the unique high that this path can provide. Prize it and jealously hold on to it.

My deep desire is that you find a personal happiness through one of these three paths!

· PART I ·

A LOVING RELATIONSHIP

The First Magical Path

• CHAPTER 3 •

The Magic of Love

There is little magic in this world, much less than what people believe. Some people wait at home hoping for the magic phone call to rescue them from their loneliness. Others look for the super pill to cure their psychological ailments or seek the perfect solution to solve all their personal problems. Usually they are disappointed. There is one area, however, where there still seems to be some magic left; this is the magic of a loving relationship. This loving bond between two people still seems to transform people—it creates positive changes. You realize this because you have seen it happen, perhaps even experienced it yourself.

Can you recall a time in your life when you were really in love? Even now you may sense the energy, the aliveness, and the fullness you felt during that special time. You may recall how you woke up more excited in the morning, how you approached all of your tasks with more enthusiasm, and how the daily problems of life suddenly were "no big deal." This is the power of a loving relationship with a special someone.

People write about love. Kahlil Gibran in his book *The Prophet* beautifully describes love:

Love has no other desire but to fulfill itself. But if you love and must needs have desires, let these be your desires:

To melt and be like a running brook that sings its melody to the night.

To know the pain of too much tenderness.

To be wounded by your own understanding of love; and to bleed willingly and joyfully.

To wake at dawn with a winged heart and give thanks for another day of loving.

To rest at the noon hour and meditate love's ecstasy.

To return home at eventide with gratitude.

And then to sleep with a prayer for the beloved in your heart and a song of praise on your lips.

But even these words can seem empty rather than exhilarating if they do not reach in and capture deep emotions within you. Love is experienced not described!

Experience this love as you focus on a time when you were really in love with another person (perhaps you currently are). Recall the loving feelings and emotionally experience them. Recapture the tenderness, the closeness, the excitement, and the way the world faded into the background as the two of you connected. Remember how it brought out the best in you ... the caring, the interest in each other's welfare, the commitment, and the tapping into your best essence, even when it heightened the old struggles with jealousy, envy, and insecurity caused by the vulnerability of being so much in love.

Remember the spontaneity of the sexual connection, the bonding of the emotional connection, the stimulation of the intellectual connection, and the completeness of the spiritual connection. Recall the little things such as the special message that was sent as your eyes met and held the glance; the excitement even in doing routine things together; the anticipation just before you were going to see each other; and the desire to want to share your thoughts and feelings, overshadowed only by the desire to listen, really listen to each other's thoughts and feelings.

This is the ecstasy of a loving relationship with another human being. Love is the human emotion that causes all other emotions to pale, and this is most psychologically appropriate. Love keeps everything else in perspective. Without love, even the celebration of successful children, financial wealth, outstanding accomplishments, and social standing become less fulfilling. With love, even the tragedies of life are experienced with an optimistic personal resolve.

This is love! This is a unique emotional experience ... an emotional experience that appropriately adds a most significant dimension to your life.

How can you retain (or regain) this magic of love in your marriage? The couples who have this magic tell me they create this love through the five C's.

• CHAPTER 4 •

The Five C's

There are millions of people who are currently seeking and finding personal happiness in an unmarried relationship. They may be (a) dating and still exploring the possibility of marriage, (b) engaged but delayed in finalizing their marriage vows, (c) divorced and waiting until their children are older before they remarry, (d) in love but fearful, because of previous pain, of making a marital commitment, (e) wanting to be married, but only finding people who fall slightly short of what they want in a marital partner, or (f) older and reluctant to remarry because of financial and/or health considerations. These loving individuals may be missing some key marital elements, but they are currently seeking happiness through an unmarried relationship with a "significant other."

Most people, however, believe that the best way to maintain an intimate relationship, an intimate relationship that reaches for the magic of love, is through the commitment of marriage.

I agree. A marital commitment is the best way to *sustain* "the spontaneity of the sexual connection, the bonding of the emotional connection, the stimulation of the intellectual connection, and the completeness of the spiritual connection."

My clients have helped me understand there are five C's that are the cornerstones of a successful marriage. The couples who have the five C's in their intimate relationship are happy, and the couples who do not have the five C's are unhappy.

The more I listened, the more I realized the key role that the five C's play. When I started pointing out the five C's to my clients, I noticed that we had an easily identifiable set of labels for discussing their relationship. We instantly had a common language for clarifying what was currently missing in the relationship and for developing strategies to improve this intimate connection.

I noticed the same insightful "aha" when I discussed the five C's in noncounseling settings. My graduate students easily conceptualized the five C's, and whenever I mentioned the five C's on my radio and TV shows or in my speeches, I received immediate acknowledgment. They also saw these five C's as key factors in their intimate relationships.

Throughout this first section, I will focus on the five C's that are the essential ingredients of a successful marriage. As a preliminary teaser, however, consider how potential magic or madness is present in each of these five C's.

1. ***Chemistry.*** The magic of good chemistry creates joy; the hugging, holding, touching, and kissing are shared pleasures. The madness of no chemistry makes each sexual encounter a deadening and depressing experience.

2. ***Caring.*** A genuine concern creates an encompassing sense of well-being. A lack of caring fosters a feeling of "being used."

3. ***Communication.*** A close, in-depth sharing can create a magic of such intensity that even great sex pales by comparison. The lack of intimate sharing creates an emotional "dry rot."

4. ***Commitment.*** With the magic of commitment, marital problems are viewed as challenges, concerns to be resolved. The madness of no commitment creates anxiety; each problem raises the silent question, "Does this mean you want to leave?"

5. ***Competency.*** A personal competency allows a person to be open to deeper and deeper love. A lack of competency smothers love under the blanket of jealousy, insecurity, and poor self-esteem.

Chemistry, caring, communication, commitment, and competency are the qualities that make an intimate relationship sparkle. The five C's are also the factors that create emptiness, hurt, and frustration when they are missing. The five C's are critical components of your walk down the first magical path because no human connection seems to create so much joy or cause so much agony as the emotional bond between two lovers who have promised to love and cherish until "death do us part."

Explore your marriage (or unmarried relationship) with respect to each of the five C's in the next ten chapters, and you will be taking a major step toward creating more magic in your marriage. Use chemistry, caring, communication, commitment, and competency as points on a compass to help you navigate your course to a successful relationship.

• CHAPTER 5 •

Chemistry

Chemistry is the flow of electricity between a man and a woman. Chemistry is the tingle, the sudden surge of feelings, the exciting emotional abandonment that lovers feel for each other. There is a "turn-on," a special sensation in the body, a piquing of interest. Chemistry is sexual, but it is not always limited to a sexual expression. There may be an exchange of other chemistry factors such as an intellectual clicking, an emotional excitement, and/or a spiritual union, but it is more. The intellectual, emotional, and spiritual aspects can be experienced without any romantic overtones, but chemistry, as defined in this book, always includes a romantic attraction.

Chemistry creates the desire for close sexual contact—you want to touch your mate and feel his or her body next to yours. Chemistry makes sex a pleasurable experience, a time for establishing intimacy and specialness in the relationship. The absence of chemistry makes sex a thing to be tolerated or even abhorred; it becomes an empty, negative experience. Of course, relationships can survive without chemistry, but it requires a special adjustment. There has to be the quiet acceptance of the consequences of being in a "no-chemistry" relationship.

Chemistry is not always intense. The overt intensity may wane as the relationship matures—a simple touch no longer creates the overwhelming desire to tear off your clothes and rush into the bedroom. But the chemistry, even though less dramatic, is still there.

Chemistry makes the end of the day special, a time for hugging and holding.

Lack of chemistry means wishing for twin beds or separate bedrooms.

Chemistry keeps conflicts in perspective; fights have a way of ending abruptly.

Lack of chemistry prolongs conflicts; fights linger on for days.

Chemistry reduces the boredom and humdrum of daily routines.

Lack of chemistry creates dullness and nothingness in the relationship.

Chemistry pulls a couple together.

Lack of chemistry pushes a couple apart.

Listed below are five descriptions of sexual chemistry in a marriage. On the line in front of each description write out the percentage of the time that this illustration best describes how you feel in your relationship.

____% 1. The sexual magic is still there. The turn-on has its natural highs and lows, but you always sense a little buzz when you touch, hug, and look at each other. You say a quiet "thank-you-God" prayer when you hear your friends say that the sexual attraction always fades after a couple of years. Granted, there is not always the intense I-want-to-make-mad-passionate-love-right-now feeling, but you still enjoy the excitement you feel as you watch your mate play tennis, socialize with other people, or walk through the front door after a short business trip. And you enjoy making love!

____% 2. You feel a lessening of excitement toward your partner. You inwardly know this is caused by your consuming pursuit of your career (or other responsibilities). The competitive stress, the long hours, and the tremendous outpouring of energy leave you emotionally and mentally exhausted. When you come home, you simply want to collapse. When you do occasionally put your career aside, however, you find it easy to "light the fire again."

____% 3. You have a constant struggle to overcome some of your early sexual attitudes. Sex was never mentioned in your home; nice people did not think about such things. You now reject these restrictive attitudes, but your body still has not gotten the message. Your early mental pictures about how a nice person responds are in conflict with your desire to be sexually responsive to your mate.

____% 4. You would like to have a positive sexual relationship with your partner. But how can you feel sexual when there is nagging, criticism, and complaining 90 percent of the time? You end the workday with the eager anticipation of seeing your mate, but the dialogue within the first five minutes causes you to wonder why you were excited. The chemistry is there but has few opportunities to express itself. Either there is a new interpersonal conflict or the atmosphere is still charged from the negative emotions of the previous one.

____% 5. You are simply turned off. There really is nothing your partner could do that would make any difference—the chemistry has been permanently destroyed. Any attempts at creating a turn-on only make things worse. The best you can hope for is a casual brother-sister type relationship. Despite your potential for having a good sex life, you will never turn on to your mate.

As you can see, sexual chemistry comes in many different packages. It can range from exciting to a deadening nonexistence. The good news is that I have seen many couples sustain a high level of chemistry for ten, twenty, even thirty years of their marriage. (And it does not even stop after thirty years.) They have dramatically exploded the theory that chemistry always fades after a couple of years and is blandly replaced with comfort, caring, and security.

How do these couples keep the chemistry alive? They naturally rely somewhat on the other four C's: a communication that combines the sexual intimacy with an emotional intimacy; a caring that makes one feel valued, prized, and accepted; a commitment that creates a safe security as one becomes increasingly vulnerable; and a competency that suggests a person enters a relationship with a positive self-image and no excessive personal insecurities. But they do not limit themselves to these four C's. They do not assume that chemistry "just happens" or is beyond one's control.

One way they enhance chemistry is to make a distinction between love and lust.

Love is a prizing of the other person. There is an emotional bond, a connection. Love creates a respect, a liking, an acceptance, a wanting to be with; but more uniquely, there is a special depth to these emotions. Poets and writers try to describe these emotions for us, but they are truly understood only by people who have felt them.

Love is essential for a happy marriage. Couples who have love become best friends as they connect on many levels. They enjoy having fun together, and they enjoy getting old together. Most couples rank love the most important quality in a marriage; without love it becomes difficult for two people to spend a lifetime together.

Lust is a feeling. Perhaps chemistry is a better word because lust carries a negative connotation for many people. Chemistry is the excitement, the inner urging, the passion that inflames the sexual closeness. Chemistry creates a desire to touch, to feel the passion. A high degree of chemistry makes sexual contact intense rather than quiet, consuming rather than satisfying, and passionate rather than comfortable.

Chemistry is not as important as love. Most people rank chemistry somewhere between third and fifth on the list of qualities essential for a good marriage. No! This is not totally true. Couples *who have chemistry* in their marriage give chemistry this lower ranking. Couples *who do not have chemistry* often move chemistry to first in importance. In other words, chemistry assumes a higher priority when it is missing than when it is there.

Love and lust (chemistry) are two qualities essential for most marriages to be truly happy; two qualities that have inadvertently created deadly assumptions—assumptions that are tearing apart the same relationships the double L's are designed to hold together.

The assumptions are:

1. If there is chemistry, this is proof that there is love.

2. If there is love, the chemistry will automatically follow.

Love and lust are more mutually exclusive than most people realize. It is possible to have intense chemistry for someone without ever loving him or her . . . *and* to love someone deeply without ever experiencing chemistry. It is a mistake to depend on chemistry to create love *or* to depend on love to create chemistry. The best relationships have both, but they are created more independently of each other than most people realize.

Most agree intellectually that the first assumption is incorrect. They know that there can be a turn-on for someone without being in love. But when chemistry is intense, it becomes harder to separate chemistry and love. The sexual passions and the emotional intensity feel like love, and it becomes easy to overlook major incompatibilities or qualities that preclude a truly loving relationship. Often it is only after the marital conflicts have crushed the chemistry that one makes the distinction between lust and love.

The second assumption also creates marital problems. I wish I had a hundred dollars for every client I have heard say, "I really respect, admire, and like my mate. Yes, I knew the intense romantic feelings were not there when we married, but I figured they would develop later."

Love does not automatically create sexual chemistry. The absence of love soon dulls the importance of chemistry, and the presence of love greatly intensifies chemistry. *But love does not automatically guarantee chemistry.* Chemistry has a unique quality apart from love. It is complimented by love, enhanced by love, but it is not synonymous with love. In other words, do not rely on love to be the sole creator of chemistry. You have to work at keeping love alive, *and* you have to work at keeping chemistry alive.

Without love, chemistry usually dies, even in the confusing cases where intense chemistry keeps the couple together long after the love and respect have disappeared. Unfortunately, *chemistry can die even when the love remains.* People need to work on the chemistry as well as the love.

In studying high-chemistry couples, I have found they use four sexual strategies to a greater degree than couples who do not sustain a strong sexual interest. One word of caution, however, as you study these strategies: They are designed for couples who still have a spark left. They will not work if chemistry is totally dead or, as is true in some cases, was never there to begin with.

A Dating Mentality

Start watching how young lovers treat each other when they are dating. (Better yet, remember what you did.) Notice how they do the little things designed to heighten the other person's sexual interest. There are the romantic gestures: the flowers, the unexpected gifts, the candlelight dinners with long conversations. There are the special surprises, the doing something out of the ordinary. It may be a special event or merely sneaking a kiss at an "inappropriate" time. Holding hands and touching become a way of life. And there is the extra effort to be attractive: the freshly showered body, the perfume or cologne, the stylish clothes, and the special attention to one's appearance are telltale signs that this person is in love (and lust).

Then they marry. Within a few years a Saturday night date means picking up a home movie for the VCR; showering and fixing up on the weekend means company is coming over; touching means, "I am getting horny;" and a dozen roses, at any time other than the obligatory Valentine Day's gift, trigger the concern, "What has he done that he is ashamed of?"

The couples who keep the chemistry alive never lose the dating mentality. They continue to treat each other with that "new love" attitude. Without ever realizing it, they follow the powerful psychological concept of cognitive dissonance. Cognitive dissonance, according to Leon Festinger, postulates that there is always a stress (a dissonance) created when one's behaviors and beliefs are in conflict. If people want to reduce this dissonance, they have to either change their behaviors or their beliefs.

The unthinking assumption by most people is that the behavior is usually the element that shifts to match one's beliefs. Dr. Festinger's classical research demonstrated that most often the opposite occurs. It is the beliefs that one alters to match the current set of behaviors. For example, a person cheats slightly on his or her income tax (behavior) and feels guilty because his or her belief system is that one should be honest. What happens to this newly created dissonance? Does the behavior shift to match the value system, and the person never again tries to gain a slight advantage on the 1040 . . . or does the belief shift to match the behavior? ("I do this only because the government is so wasteful, and besides everyone else is doing it.")

The couples who keep the chemistry alive have discovered that the "lovers" type of behavior does not stop because the chemistry fades. Instead, it is the chemistry that starts fading because there are no loving acts! Put in more positive terms, the couples who continue to celebrate an exciting chemistry know that the loving acts (behaviors) are a powerful way to keep the chemistry feeling (belief) alive!

Some of the creative ways they have used their actions to keep the chemistry fires burning are listed here:

1. They never stop doing the little romantic things. There is the unexpected surprise gift, the single rose that so powerfully says, "I am still in love with you," and the romantic card which creatively expresses loving feelings. They are constantly thinking of ways to please each other, and the focus is on the romantic not the practical.

2. They have at least one date each week, an evening or afternoon reserved for just the two of them. They religiously block out a time when they can enjoy each other's company without the distractions of friends, parents, coworkers, or (and make note of this) their children. This date is not for grocery shopping; it is a time for intimate sharing, fun, togetherness, and handholding.

3. They do not get sloppy around each other. They maintain a dating mentality throughout their marriage. They are comfortable with each other, but they never become too comfortable. If their dry skin forces them to choose between an evening shower for each other and a morning shower for coworkers, they automatically choose the evening shower. They also (a) sneak out of bed in the morning to freshen up and then quietly slip back into bed, (b) select the stylish weekend outfit over the one that was rejected by the Salvation Army, and (c) clean up immediately after the yard work/housework, not six hours later. I could go on but I think you get the picture.

4. They have psychological cocktails. A psychological cocktail occurs when people sit down to chat, but the intoxicant is praising not alcohol. They take turns giving each other "warm fuzzies" (positive compliments about how much they enjoy, appreciate, admire, and like each other). They continue doing what they did during that wonderful dating phase.

5. They follow the adage that "variety is the spice of life" by regularly disrupting the marital routines with new activities (and this chemistry strategy is not limited to new sexual positions). They have surprise dates, try new foods, meet new people, and expose themselves to new ideas.

6. In summary, the couples who keep the chemistry alive throughout the various stages of their marriage have the attitude, "How would I behave if I were in the initial phase of a very special relationship?" The couples who lose the chemistry laugh at this attitude. They say it is silly . . . right up to the time that their chemistry is declared dead!

Sexual Turn-Ons

When I speak to audiences on the topic "Marriage: Magic or Madness?" I often talk to them about the different sexual turn-ons for men and women.

With a smile on my face, I ask, "What are the main sexual stimuli for women?" The answers are things auditory (a soft voice saying "I love you") and tactile (a gentle loving touch). Then I ask, "What is the main sexual trigger for a man?" The answer is a visual (a mental picture of an attractive woman).

I suggest both the men and women become victims of their own projections. They erroneously assume that the sexual stimuli for their mates are the same as it is for them.

The woman, when she wants to turn on her mate, whispers, "I love you" and gently touches him. And the man, in trying to pique her sexual interest, goes to the gym and works out. He wants his body to look great.

With the same amused smile on my face, I suggest that we need to reverse these strategic moves. The man needs to learn how to do more gentle touching and give the reassuring words of love, and the woman needs to go to the gym and pump iron. I never fail to get a laugh with this last statement.

This became a good speech line, but it is sexist and somewhat inaccurate. The couples who keep the chemistry alive for years do not make this male-female distinction: They *both* use all three turn-ons. Both are very free with saying "I love you," and it is never perfunctory! The "I love you" is accompanied with a nonverbal message that says this feeling is deep, bubbling to come out, and enthusiastically shared.

Both of them are also very free with the gentle touches. These loving caresses are not limited to times when they "want something." The touches send a variety of messages ranging from, "Have I ever told you how much I prize you?" to "I have a 'plan' for us this evening," and from "You turn me on," to "I really care for you."

Finally, they keep their bodies in shape. Their physical appearance is attractive, there is an athletic look to their walk, and their weight is normal. They are committed to a physical workout routine; perhaps they even make this a time of togetherness.

They look great and they look great to each other! Many look better than friends who are fifteen years younger.

If you want to keep chemistry in your relationship, I would strongly suggest that you, like the couples who do keep the chemistry alive, use all three sexual turn-ons faithfully.

Imagery

Couples who keep the chemistry fires burning use a high-energy sexual fuel called imagery. This concept will be discussed in more depth in chapter 14, but allow me to introduce the topic now to explain how it relates to sexual chemistry.

Briefly stated, the theory behind imagery is that whatever we visually imagine (mental pictures with matching emotions) goes into the subconscious mind with the same impact as if it had actually happened to us. This psychocybernetic concept postulates that our conscious mind easily distinguishes between vividly imagined thoughts and actual reality, *but our subconscious mind does not*. If we "see" ourselves doing things, it has a powerful impact on future performance.

World class athletes use this concept all the time. They "see" themselves accomplishing the outstanding athletic feat, and their subconscious minds are programmed to have peak performances. They have the mental permission and proper programming to excel.

Imagery plays a critical role in sexual chemistry. Picture a newly married couple who are in love and in lust. What do they think about as they are anticipating their next "time together?" Among the other pleasurable thoughts is a flood of sexual fantasies. They replay recent pleasures, they recall the tender touches, they relive the excitement. And they have an energized anticipation of what the next encounter is going to be like. They can already feel the closeness and sense the aliveness in their bodies. They are programming their subconscious minds for the anticipated sexual excitement.

Now it is five years later! This same couple focuses on the eight hours of work, the three hours of housework, and the two hours of hassles with the children. They escape from this by being mesmerized with two hours of a powerful drug called TV.

At 11:02 P.M. they roll over in bed and accidentally touch each other. It is the first sexual imagery that they have had that day, and they wonder why the sexual chemistry fires are not lit.

Most people attribute this weak sexual response to, "It just happens after you have been married for a few years. The chemistry 'naturally' fades, and if you are lucky, it is replaced with enough communication and caring to make it okay." But the couples who sustain the sexual interest do not accept this "natural" occurrence. They know it is not too much togetherness nor the deadening routines of marriage that kill the chemistry.

It is, among other things, a dramatic change in sexual imageries. A change that goes from twenty times a day to zero times a day. If a person would think of imagery as foreplay, it would mean going from extensive foreplay to no foreplay before lovemaking. In other words, chemistry may not "just naturally fade." It fades because there is not the mental foreplay that piqued the sexual intensity during the initial phase of the relationship. The couples who have the chemistry after years of marriage still have rich sexual fantasies. It is not surprising they are in the mood as they snuggle up at day's end (if they wait that long).

Ready to put imagery into action? Program some of the following thoughts into your subconscious via imagery fifteen to twenty times a day. Don't be shocked by the number of times; this is what you did earlier in your relationship. Vividly see some of the following pictures.

1. Recall two of the most passionate sexual encounters that you have had with your partner. Relive and pleasure on these memories.

2. Feel your partner touching some of your erogenous spots . . . sense the excitement that is created in your body.

3. Mentally touch your partner in some of his or her especially pleasurable areas. Notice the subtle sexual response that this creates.

4. See your partner at his or her loving best. Hear the whispered "I love you;" feel the tender, loving touch; see the look in his or her eyes.

5. See yourself having playful foreplay and then stopping without having sexual intercourse, thus holding the excitement until a later time.

6. Practice turning your negative sexual imageries into positive sexual imageries. Every time a negative thought comes on your mental movie screen (they are programmed into your subconscious mind with the same impact as the positive ones) quickly replace it with a positive sexual picture. For example:

   - You recall a negative sexual encounter. Block it out with a red stop sign. And then substitute one of your best sexual encounters.

   - Your partner looks tired and haggard. Block this picture and replace it with a picture of your partner at his or her sensuous best.

   - You have a sudden flash of concern about your sexual adequacy. Shift the picture to a time when you were, in all modesty, great!

7. See your sex becoming more playful. Visualize the teasing, fun, smiles, and little pleasures.

8. See you and your partner, five years from now, having the best communication, caring, *and chemistry* that you have ever had in your relationship.

9. Picture yourself on a romantic island. All the cares of the world have evaporated in the ocean mist. The focus is on the loving intensity that you feel for your partner . . . an intensity that increases with the sound of each wave crashing on the rocks.

10. See the two of you making love after a soul-to-soul communication, a sharing that turns the intense excitement into an indescribable ecstasy.

Sexual Security

Couples who sustain the chemistry over the long haul highly prize their sexuality and are totally comfortable with it. Sex is simultaneously a critical part of their intimate life and not *that* important. This dual attitude allows for a natural flow, a comfortable swing of sexual emotions. They make easy adjustments to each other's shifting sexual moods and have a smooth transition through the sexual stages they will experience in a lifetime.

This comfort level surfaces in several positive ways. They (1) comfortably accept that one's sexual response fluctuates, (2) never try to force a sexual response, and (3) treat sex as an emotional and sexual expression, not a performance.

1. Comfortably accept that one's sexual response fluctuates. Some couples expect sex to be great every time. Anything short of a "bell ringer" becomes an immediate concern. One or two mediocre experiences invalidate a long series of excellent sexual encounters. Rather than simply writing off a so-so experience as a temporary situation, an immediate concern develops. Haunting questions quickly surface:

"What is wrong?"
"Has something changed?"
"Is our relationship in trouble?"

Other couples have a relaxed attitude toward their sexual expectations. They allow the same swing of emotions in the sexual area that they do in other areas of their lives. They subscribe to the advice given by one sex therapist who said, "Remember, you do not always have to go from A to Z."

What she meant was that every sexual experience does not have to reach the highest sexual and emotional peak. Sometimes you will stop at F or M or T. The sexual encounter may be (a) a lustful sexual taking, (b) giving to please another, (c) simple gratification of a sexual drive, (d) expression of loving and caring, or (e) peak emotional and sexual experience.

Couples who are comfortable with their sexuality accept each sexual expression for what it is at that moment. What it is one time does not detract from what it was last time nor does it indicate what it will be next time.

2. They do not force a sexual response. Sex and breathing have a lot in common. A person's breathing is natural and flowing unless there is too much tension. People do not make breathing happen; at best they allow it to happen. If they were to try to forcibly alter their breathing there would be a disruption in the rhythmic pattern. People do not do this, but if they treated their breathing the way they do their sexual response, many would suffer from respiratory dysfunction.

The same principle applies to sex. The absence of concerns about one's sexual performance allows the most natural and spontaneous sexual expression. People can prevent a sexual response, but they do *not* make it happen. Their sexual response is involuntary; it occurs as a natural reaction to erotic stimuli.

When people have concerns about their sexual performance, they often develop what Masters and Johnson call the "spectator" role. Rather than enjoying the erotic stimuli that create a spontaneous arousal, they step back and watch themselves like spectators at a baseball game. They start wondering whether they will reach orgasm, maintain an erection, hold back long enough, or create enough excitement in their partner. This spectator role lessens their spontaneity, creates additional concerns, and inhibits the sexual responsiveness.

The couples who have a comfort level with their sexuality easily spot when they are slipping into a spectator role. If this happens, they do not try harder. They know that "trying harder" only creates more anxiety, concern, frustration, and tension, which inhibits rather than enhances their likelihood of having a successful response.

Instead, they immediately step back and reestablish a loving contact with their partner. They focus on the pleasant erotic stimuli that their partner presents. They wait for the positive sexual stimuli to spontaneously trigger the natural desire for sexual intimacy, rather than being an apprehensive spectator who deadens sexual spontaneity. They wait for the relaxed natural responses . . . ones that wonderfully happen when things are right.

They also discuss any concerns they may have. This sharing lessens any doubts that a partner may have (anxiety over performance is not confused with a lack of desire or love), and frees the partner to give a loving reassurance . . . a reassurance that (a) sends an "I do not think less of you because we did not have a complete sexual response" message, and (b) provides a relaxed atmosphere that conveys the loving thought that there is no expectation for perfection every time. This reassurance can give lovers tremendous relief. It dramatically lessens anxiety and reduces the fear of future sexual "failures." They can simply take pleasure in what was good, because all intimate contact between sexually secure lovers is good.

3. *Sex is an emotional and sexual expression, not a performance.* The publication of sex manuals and popular books on sexuality has done much to give people a better comfort level. These publications have provided needed information and have given people a greater acceptance of their sexuality.

Unfortunately, this emphasis on sexuality has inadvertently created a new problem. Some books treat sex as an achievement that can be rated good, better, and best. They make spectacular orgasm the goal and imply that the gauge of one's sexuality is being ready and willing to try all types of sexual experiences. Only the multiorgasmic person who has sex in seventy-two different positions really has it together.

One of the unfortunate by-products of this attitude has been a preoccupation with sexual response. For some, sex has become a performance rather than an expression of love. "If enough buttons are pushed in the proper sequence, there will be a guaranteed sexual explosion" is the new goal of lovemaking. Some people approach sex as if they were receiving a grade in school rather than sharing a special expression of intimacy.

Couples with a good comfort level remember the obvious individual differences among people in terms of their emotional responses. The person who explodes with anger is not necessarily more upset than the person who channels that anger; the person who openly cries at a funeral may not be grieving more than the friend who holds his or her composure; and the parent who is demonstrative with his or her children does not necessarily love more than the less demonstrative parent.

The same is true of a sexual response. It cannot be judged only on external signs. After all, an explosive orgasm for one person may be no more pleasurable than a quiet orgasm for another. Any truly satisfying relationship has an intimate emotional component. When this intimate emotional component is communicated through sex, the sex becomes special—a specialness that the most sophisticated of sexual techniques could not come close to approximating. Sex is an expression of feelings not a performance.

Let's look at one couple and how they handled performance pressure.

Brent and Stacy had a loving relationship and their sex life was satisfying. After they made love, they often held each other, feeling the tenderness and warmth of their bodies. Of course they had their problems, but their difficulties clearly were not in the area of physical intimacy.

One day Brent casually picked up a new best-selling book on sexuality at a local bookstore. He spent the next four evenings reading *the* book.

The next time they made love, Stacy noticed Brent seemed a little tense, but she thought, "He probably is just tired or concerned about his job." After they finished making love, rather than just holding and relaxing as they normally did, Brent suddenly sat up and asked, "Did you?" A startled Stacy replied, "Did I what?" Brent answered in a mildly irritated manner, "You know what I mean. Did you?" While Stacy was still puzzling over what he meant, Brent reached under the mattress and pulled out the book. He quickly turned to the section entitled "Female Orgasm" and handed it to her. This section described what a female orgasm should be like. To use a medical analogy, this book implied the female orgasm should be similar to a grand mal epileptic seizure.

After she finished reading the section, Brent repeated the question, "Well, did you?" Stacy patiently tried to explain to her husband that it was not necessary to have this exact reaction. She assured him that she was very satisfied with her sexual response—it was very special. Just when she thought she had her husband reassured (fortunately, these sex manuals do not discuss the ideal *male* sexual response), he suddenly looked at her and said, "Well, on a scale of one to ten, where do . . . ?"

That evening neither of them slept very well. Brent was wondering if his wife was really satisfied since she did not respond exactly as described in the book. ("Maybe it is my faulty technique.") Stacy also became concerned. ("Maybe there is something wrong with me since I do not respond the way the book describes.")

The next time they made love, they were somewhat worried and apprehensive. Predictably, the tension limited the spontaneity of the sexual encounter. This experience only heightened their concerns. This negative pattern continued and within two months it was a major concern.

Fortunately, our loving couple took quick and decisive action. They went for counseling. By the end of the first session, they realized what had happened. They laughed and made plans for a book burning. Within one week, they were back to their satisfying lovemaking.

• CHAPTER 6 •

Sex After Forty

Jack, a forty-nine-year-old successful businessman, had been married to Sue for twenty-six years. It was a good marriage; in fact, many of their friends described it as an ideal marriage. They had similar interests, were best friends, had successfully raised three children, and were still in love with each other. The previous year they celebrated their twenty-fifth wedding anniversary with a ten-day vacation in Hawaii.

But then the trouble began. One night, Jack failed to sustain an erection. It was the first time this had ever happened to him, but it still created apprehension. He tried again a few minutes later with the same results. Nothing was said, but it was an hour before Jack finally fell asleep.

Three weeks later it happened again. This time his concern heightened. "Is something wrong?" was the thought that kept flashing through his mind.

When it happened a third time, his apprehension was replaced with a subdued panic. Jack started wanting intercourse as soon as he was erect (so he wouldn't lose it), often backed away from lovemaking (one more "failure" would be too difficult to handle), noticed that he was having a harder time ejaculating even when he did maintain the erection (or was the erection softer?), and even scheduled a secret appointment with his physician (everything checked out okay physically).

Lovemaking with Sue quickly moved from a time of joy and pleasure to a time for proving adequacy. Jack reverted to the spectator role discussed in chapter 5. Rather than enjoying the loving sexual responses of his wife and using these stimuli to light his own sexual fires, Jack was in the bleachers observing his performance. The thought, "How wonderful it is making love to Sue," was replaced with, "Will it stay hard? Will I lose it? Will I complete the act?" It is not surprising that his sexual response started to short-circuit. Even at work, the sexual concern was frequently on his mind. He cringed every time he heard a locker-room joke about someone being "over the hill."

Phase two escalated the problem. Jack started blaming his wife for his sexual response. It was because she had put on weight, was too critical, and was not as loving as she used to be. It was easier to ask, "What is wrong with the marriage?" than "What is wrong with me?"

But the concerns about his sexual inadequacy lingered and made him vulnerable to what happened next. Almost as if it were a script for a daytime TV soap opera, Jack started flirting with his partner's attractive thirty-five-year-old secretary. Within three months it had turned into a sexual affair. The affair did not last long, but it did "prove" that he was adequate and "confirmed" that it must be his wife's fault.

Then he met Carol. Not only was there a second sexual affair (which appeared to further confirm Jack's adequacy), but this one also connected on an emotional level. Of course by this time, Jack had totally pulled away from Sue sexually and emotionally.

What happened next? You can put one of two endings to this case because both frequently happen. One ending is that Jack decides that he no longer loves Sue, and the twenty-six years of happy marriage are discounted. Jack moves out, and their friends are shocked. They cannot understand what happened. Most blame the divorce on a vague midlife crisis, but it really was just a simple fear of sexual performance which, when not adequately dealt with, triggered an avalanche of disguised marital problems. The "I am too tired to make love" became "I am tired of the marriage."

The second scenario is that Jack confronts his sexual concerns and takes steps to reduce his understandable fear. Fortunately, this is what Jack did. The sad thing is that he did not do this before Sue had to go through the devastating pain of her husband's unfaithfulness.

Sex does go through changes after forty . . . changes that you need to be aware of in order to avoid the trauma that Jack and Sue experienced. As you enter the past-forty phase of your sexual life, you need to comfortably accept the inevitable sexual changes.

The sad fact of life is that age does take a certain toll. Most professional athletes have to retire before they reach the age of forty. Only a Nolan Ryan or a Kareem Abdul Jabbar can sneak in a couple of extra years. This does not mean that they can no longer play baseball or basketball, just not at the same level of peak physical performance.

The same thing happens sexually, especially for men. (Actually many women have an increased sexual functioning at this age.) No longer will he sexually qualify for the Super Bowl, but this does not mean that he can no longer play the game.

At midlife, most men find that they have less of a sexual "tiger in the tank." They find that sexual frequency lessens, there is a greater recovery time, the erection may not be quite as firm, the ejaculation slightly more subdued, the occasions of impotency more frequent, the time required to reach an ejaculation greater, and the occasions when sexual intensity will automatically override physical fatigue less frequent. But this natural aging process can simply be a fact of life that a man flows with smoothly, rather than creating a panic that causes a premature retirement from the sport of sex.

The good news is that the men and women who comfortably accept these changes continue to be sexually active late into life, while the ones who panic often, as the pilots would say, "crash and burn."

It is also important to keep the communication lines open. If a man will share the concerns he has about his sexual functioning (especially his concerns about occasional episodes of impotency), he will relax mentally. He does not exaggerate the problem in his mind, and his wife can give him the loving reassurance that she also is not concerned. This mutual understanding and acceptance can eliminate the stress and increase the sexual spontaneity in the relationship.

No communication, on the other hand, aggravates the situation. The man pulls away so he does not have to risk another failure, nitpicks as to why he is not as sexually excited anymore, or even subconsciously picks a fight just before going to bed to ensure that there will be no request for sexual intimacy. Soon the sexual withdrawal becomes an emotional withdrawal. There are no tender hugs, gentle caresses, or loving statements. After all, this emotional intimacy could lead to a request for sexual intimacy.

A further complication develops when the woman senses the withdrawal but does not know why it is happening. Her understandable concern is, "My husband no longer desires me." These unexpressed fears create more concern than an occasional episode of impotency ever would. And when she bottles up her concerns, just as her husband is bottling up his concerns, you have the fertile ground for a scenario similar to the one described in the beginning of this chapter.

Keep the communication lines open. Discuss any sexual concerns in a sharing and loving manner and watch the "problems" evaporate. Even better, this sharing usually draws a couple closer together.

• CHAPTER 7 •

Caring

Caring is the deep concern you have for others. It is interest in their welfare, wanting the best for them, a deep desire they have happiness and comfort. The classic example of caring is that of a mother for her child. No price is too much and no sacrifice too great if the welfare of the child is at stake.

In a romantic relationship, the caring is based, in part, on the amount of romance and love. In the best relationships, however, the caring aspect is not limited to chemistry. The caring remains high even as the romantic love vacillates between the normal highs and lows. Caring is based on an emotional bonding that rises above the fluctuations of romantic chemistry.

Caring is an emotional state that runs deep but can seem bland when compared with the excitement of chemistry. This is unfortunate because it is easier to find a relationship that has chemistry than to establish a relationship that has caring. Deep caring in a relationship can be a rare, priceless gem that should not be capriciously cast aside.

Perhaps the value of caring is captured in the case of Jim, a risk-taking entrepreneur, whose business exploits had been written up in several newspaper articles. He had started with nothing and turned a failing business into a tremendous financial success. Through all the sacrifices and struggles, Carol was loyal, loving, and supportive. They had a good marriage, and she provided a haven for Jim during his high-energy, risk-taking endeavors.

Unfortunately, at the peak of his sudden success, Jim met another woman. She was classy, sophisticated, intelligent, and socially prominent. Soon they were the main topic of conversation among the "who is having an affair with whom?" set.

Just before Jim decided to ask Carol for a divorce, he stopped and took another look at the caring factor in his marriage. He knew Carol deeply cared for him. If he suddenly were to have financial reversals or an accident, Carol would be as loyal and loving as ever. She cared for him, not for his financial accomplishments. Jim realized this was not true with his girlfriend. Despite the intense turn-on, the stimulating conversation, and the exciting lifestyle, there was no solid base for caring. She was interested in his success, money, and power. This relationship had not been established on the premise "no matter what happens, we are in this together."

Jim went back to his wife. He renewed his appreciation of the role of caring in forming a stable relationship in a very unstable world. Caring was not the only reason for going home, but caring combined with sufficient communication, chemistry, commitment, and competency made this the relationship Jim wanted.

There are many factors that can enter into the caring formula, but there is one caring component that overshadows all the rest: acceptance.

Acceptance

As you are growing up, you are told a beautiful story about how you will fall in love and get married. And sure enough, you do fall in love and you do experience all those wonderful feelings that only a loving relationship can give. Within this warm glow, it is easy to gloss over the minor shortcomings of your potential mate. You focus on the person's strengths and anticipate living happily ever after.

After the wedding, fantasy fades. The romantic bliss is replaced by reality. The thrilling feelings waver as the unpaid bills accumulate, the clothes are left in a mess in the middle of the bedroom floor, or the Monday night football game gets more attention than an intimate conversation. Suddenly, the partner's faults and shortcomings are not hidden in the shadows of the romantic candlelight dinners.

Your partner looks different in the clear light of the midday sun. Here is a person with a complex set of attitudes, behaviors, feelings, and habits. You are forced to ask the question, "Can I accept this person as he or she is, or will there have to be some changes?" The answer to this question is critical to the caring dimension in a relationship.

What is acceptance? Acceptance is captured in the answer given by three happily married couples who were asked, "What is the key to your happiness in this era of divorce and unstable marriages?" Their answers were not sexual attraction, the ability to communicate, similar interests, or emotional security. These factors were all important, but the key for all three couples was being *accepted* by their mate. The caring developed through this acceptance was essential for creating a climate of being "best friends."

The value of acceptance is often underestimated. Many counseling approaches consider acceptance the most essential factor in therapy. If the therapist accepts the client unconditionally and effectively communicates this genuine acceptance, there is positive growth within the client. This unconditional acceptance gives clients the freedom to share their emotions and express their inner thoughts. When this happens, there is a positive surge within clients to resolve their problems and to make the necessary changes in their lives. The key is genuine, unconditional, total acceptance.

Acceptance is also the cornerstone of a deep friendship. True friends accept each other's basic shortcomings and make few demands for change. A special feeling develops as you are loved for everything you are, not just for the pleasing, positive things. You are now free to drop your defenses and be *you*—an exhilarating experience. This atmosphere of acceptance frees you to like yourself. As your self-image improves, your behavior becomes more positive toward this special person.

By now, you may be feeling slightly defensive, especially after taking an honest look at the interaction with your mate. You may have even thought, "But marriage is different; it is harder to maintain a constant level of acceptance in a marriage." You are right! It is easier to create a climate of acceptance in counseling or in a friendship than in a marriage because within a marriage there is an intense involvement of one's personal needs, underlying insecurities, ego identity with the other person, and expectations for happiness.

It may be more difficult to develop this all-encompassing acceptance within a marriage, but it is also true that acceptance in a marriage will have more meaning than acceptance in a friendship or in a counseling setting. If acceptance is so special in friendships, imagine what it could be in the *ultimate* relationship. Perhaps the nicest thing you could do is to treat your mate as well as you treat your best friend. Under this umbrella of acceptance, tolerance, loyalty, and understanding, your individual personalities would flourish and the relationship would be richly satisfying. The struggle to obtain this level of acceptance within your relationship may be difficult, but the reward is great.

When there is nonacceptance, the emphasis is on changing behaviors. Unfortunately, there is a "sting" even when the requests are done in a constructive manner. To appreciate this reaction, take a look at your response to negative feedback. How do you feel when your partner corrects you? Does the correction create warm, appreciative feelings and a desire to approach the other person enthusiastically, or is there minor defensiveness and a tendency to be temporarily hurt?

The same thing probably happens to your partner. Negative feedback can lead to self-depreciation and lingering resentment. Unconditional acceptance, on the other hand, may free your partner to be more accepting of himself or herself, thus more open to change. Remember that most significant changes come from within a person rather than from suggestions from others. Perhaps a sexual analogy will capture this subtle difference.

Picture yourself after your first sexual experience with your partner. What would have been the impact of the following two statements on your spontaneity and enthusiasm during the next sexual encounter?

> "This was great! I just love being close to you, feeling your body, and getting to know you. Isn't it going to

Caring • 49

be fun exploring our sexual
relationship even further?"

or

"This was great! However,
next time I wonder if you
would be willing to do
the following three things
so it will be even better.
The first thing I would
like you to do is. . ."

Some behaviors respond better to self-discovery. With self-discovery all the spontaneity, excitement, and joy are not lost as the change is being made.

There is a prayer that says, "God, grant me the serenity to accept the things I cannot change, courage to change the things I can, and wisdom to know the difference." Unfortunately, many people make two mistakes when applying this prayer to their lives. Within their personal life, people accept too many things as they are and lack the courage to strive for personal change. With their partner, they attempt too many changes and lack the serenity to accept their partner as he or she is.

Do you truly accept your spouse? Complete the following activity as you ponder this critical question. Get a series of mental pictures of your partner. Capture him or her in a variety of settings and moods. Now take out a sheet of paper and copy down the following chart.

	1	2	3
Commitment to spouse and family			
Ability to show love and caring			
Trustworthiness			
Amount of career success			
Helpfulness with routine tasks			
Emotional stability			
Enthusiasm toward life			

	1	2	3
Ability to communicate			
Sexual spontaneity			
Moral standards			
Intelligence			
Compatible goals			
Personal habits			
Physical attractiveness			

In the first column, write a number between 1 and 10 that reflects how you honestly see your husband or wife in each of these areas (1 is low, 5 is average, 10 is high).

Is this profile acceptable to you? Can you live with what you have? To better answer this question, place in the second column a number between 1 and 10 in each area that best reflects what you would like in your relationship.

Now compare the numbers in the first two columns. What discrepancies are there between what your partner is and what you would like? How critical are these discrepancies? In which areas do you think you need to strive to bring about changes in your partner? In which areas do you think the best course of action is simple acceptance of what is? Place an A in the third column for the *acceptance* areas and a C for the *change* areas.

Acceptance of one's spouse is a key factor in caring. It is not easy to care for a person you do not accept. Keep this in mind as you evaluate your chart. Maybe your goal should be to change a few of the C's (striving for change) into A's (giving unconditional acceptance).

Couples who do this often report that even the "bland" dimension of caring suddenly creates a surge of magic. There is a prizing, a valuing, a liking of the other person that transcends what he or she has done. There is a wonderful message that says, "I always accept you—even in the rare instances where I cannot accept what you have done."

• CHAPTER 8 •

Handling Arguments With Care

The other chapters in this book are written with an optimistic mind-set. This chapter is an exception. In the other chapters, I expect (I say this with a big smile) you to be able to accomplish the stated goals. I see you having the intimacy you desire, the sharing you crave, and the closeness you seek. And in the upcoming chapters there is no reason why you cannot create a consuming mission for your life, remove most of the debilitating stress in your career, develop a personal competency in all your relationships, and execute any of the other psychological strategies to the level you desire.

I do not expect you, however, to handle arguments as well as you would like. In this area you will fall short of where you would like to be. (If you think that I am simultaneously teasing you, challenging you, and being realistic, you are both perceptive and correct!)

Few people consistently like the way they argue. When the conversations get heated, the emotions intense, and the issues inflamed, most people feel things, say things, and even do things that they are not proud of. They resolve never to do that again, but then the next argument ignites and. . . .

Case 1—Don and Bonnie are a striking couple; heads turn whenever they walk into a room. Not only are they individually attractive, but they also dramatically enhance each other's attractiveness. They look like they belong together.

Just as compelling is the way they respond to each other in social gatherings. They smile, laugh, and have fun together. It is not an act . . . they genuinely enjoy each other's company. They still have a special energy even after fifteen years of marriage.

But Don and Bonnie recently returned for more marriage counseling. Why? The impetus was a screaming, shouting, threatening, five-hour argument that ended only when both of them suddenly realized two of their children were cowering and crying in their bedrooms. It was not the first time this had happened.

Case 2–Keith and Cheryl have a special emotional bonding. They both grew up in dysfunctional families and had disastrous first marriages . . . but the second time was charmed. They have been married less than two years, but already there is a special closeness. They attend to each other's emotional needs and are best friends. When they go to Mass, they hold hands and celebrate a purpose, peace, and tranquillity for the first time in their lives.

Keith and Cheryl also recently made an appointment for marriage counseling. Why? The reason is that they had an argument that got out of control. The argument escalated to the point that Cheryl physically attacked Keith and he retaliated by hitting her. At the first appointment, Cheryl had a badly bruised left eye.

Case 3–Norm and Molly have been married for seven years and have two young children, ages four and two. One of the unique features of their marriage is their strong sense of commitment. There are no concerns about their willingness to sacrifice for each other, sexual faithfulness in their relationship, or belief that a marriage should be forever.

But Norm and Molly have also made an appointment for marriage counseling. Why? Once again, the issue is arguing. Unlike the other two couples, however, they have not had any out-of-control fights, but there is a pattern of recurring arguments that happen too often and last too long. A lengthy argument last week that solved nothing caused Molly to say, "Enough is enough. We have to do something about these fights."

Why do the arguments of Don and Bonnie, Keith and Cheryl, and Norm and Molly escalate into behaviors damaging to their relationships and potentially even threaten the core fiber of their marriages? The reasons are different in each case.

Case 1–Don had a series of extramarital affairs several years ago. When Bonnie found out, Don took the cavalier attitude, "I provide for you very well, so what is your complaint? Besides, what are you going to do about it? If you divorce me, I will leave you with nothing." When Bonnie filed for divorce, however, Don was shocked into reality. He went for extensive individual therapy, made some dramatic changes, and totally changed his lifestyle. He became a loyal, committed husband.

The deep hurt still lingers in Bonnie, however. Whenever they get into an argument, the painful memories seem to resurface and add explosive fuel to the current "discussion." Don protests that he has been faithful for years, but this does not seem to pacify Bonnie.

Case 2–Keith and Cheryl's arguments originate from two underlying causes. The first is a mutual codependency that "appears" to enhance the emotional closeness, but unfortunately, also heightens the concerns when this tenuous insecurity/dependency bond is threatened. (See chapter 13 for more on this type of bonding.)

The second source goes back to their dysfunctional, alcoholic parents. As children, they both saw vicious verbal attacks and physical abuse when their parents fought, especially when there had been heavy drinking. Keith and Cheryl both resolved that they would never treat a spouse that way, and they kept to that promise until the last argument became too intense. Suddenly, they found themselves doing exactly what they never wanted to do; they argued and fought just like their parents did.

Case 3–The underlying issue in Norm and Molly's ongoing arguing is dominance. Norm came from a home where his father was clearly the "head of the house" and his mother was a submissive, compliant wife who did everything to please her husband. Molly had the opposite situation. Her mother was the strong dominant figure and her father played a submissive secondary role.

This marked difference in modeled marital styles creates constant power struggles for Norm and Molly . . . power struggles that are reenacted every time there is a discussion on how the children are raised, money is spent, or household duties are assigned. They even have diverse expectations on who should give in when they have an argument that cannot be readily resolved. Both have said that they want a fifty-fifty relationship; but both function like it is seventy-thirty, in their own favor.

Complicating the situation even further is Molly's high-powered job and the fact that she makes considerably more money than Norm. This gives Molly more power in her assertions and causes Norm to resort to either sarcastic comments or passive-aggressive behavior.

What are the answers to the arguing issues that caused Don and Bonnie, Keith and Cheryl, and Norm and Molly to seek counseling? One obvious answer is to confront the underlying causes for these arguments. Counseling could do the following:

1. It could help Bonnie to forgive and forget the painful memories of her husband's extramarital affairs and help Don have a more empathic understanding of Bonnie's painful struggles with his previous sexual behavior.

2. It could give Keith and Cheryl additional awareness of (a) how earlier parental behaviors impact their current marital arguing, and (b) how to obtain a better balance between dependency and self-sufficiency.

3. It could enable Norm and Molly to better understand how the issue of dominance escalates many of their arguments, and how behaviors such as sarcastic comments, passive-aggressive responses, and too much raw assertion for power will elevate the arguments to a more damaging level.

Counseling can help resolve these legitimate issues for all three couples, but one danger is that by the time all of these underlying issues are worked through, the ongoing arguments will have already done extensive and maybe even irreparable damage.

Even before all the underlying psychological problems are resolved, rules for arguing in an intimate relationship should be established. This is the focus of this chapter as you take a deeper look at the caring dimension in your marriage.

You may never fully climb to the peak of the mountain (learn how to argue correctly), but this chapter will give you some mountain-climbing techniques in case you would like to give it a try. Listed below are some guidelines for preventing arguments from becoming too intense, heated, or inflamed. Let's call these guidelines the Ten Commandments for Arguing. You will never reach perfection—just as you occasionally miss the mark with the original Ten Commandments—but we can all come closer than we presently do. We could have more arguments that clarify issues rather than inflame feelings, end up with greater closeness rather than increased alienation, and solve old problems rather than create new ones. Try to follow the Ten Commandments For Arguing any time you argue. (And yes, the "sin" is forgivable if you slip.)

1. Do not bring up the past. Referring to past events is occasionally helpful to clarify current issues, but the majority of the time, bringing up the past is done (a) to shore up a losing argument (You are "losing" an argument, so you clobber the other person with a past misdeed that has nothing to do with the present disagreement.), or (b) to "justify" a current emotion (You are feeling jealous, but the other person has successfully confronted you with the absurdity of your current accusation, so you bring up an incident that happened years ago to try to legitimize your current insecurity.).

Any time the past is inappropriately brought up, a person should react as if he or she has just pulled up to a red traffic light. Stop the argument immediately and refuse to proceed until the other person agrees to stop this no-win approach. If you do not take this aggressive action, watch the argument quickly escalate into another "pull out all the stops, no holds barred" shouting match.

2. You have the right to temporarily disengage. If the argument is getting too heated, you always have the right to *temporarily* pull back. Notice the word "temporarily"; this is different from an "I refuse to talk about this anymore" attitude.

It should always be acceptable to take a break from the argument to regain composure and allow tempers to cool down. Both partners always have to respect the other person's right to exercise this option. For this to work, however, the person requesting the break has to be willing to continue the discussion within a reasonable period of time, and the other person has to give space (no hovering or hot pursuit) during this time-out. A good strategy to adopt when one person needs a time-out is to agree to a time when the two of you will continue the discussion.

3. There must be a willingness to listen. During arguments many combatants never listen. They are constantly interrupting or mentally rehearsing their next retort while the other person is speaking. This technique may work in college debate competition but never in a personal argument.

You have to be willing to listen to the other person's side. Try to walk in the other person's moccasins by paraphrasing what the other person just said and felt before you make your next point. Do this to understand the other person's feelings, to couch your ensuing comments in more acceptable terms, and to make it easier to give a little—so essential in ending a heated exchange. Remember that an argument occurs when there are differing opinions. Try to hear your partner's opinion while communicating your own.

4. *The goal is to solve a problem not to win an argument.* Often one person has better verbal skills or a superior debating technique, but this should never be the basis on which an argument is decided. This is a superficial solution and in an ongoing intimate relationship, always a step backward.

Henry Kissinger has an interesting philosophy. He reasons that "countries keep treaties only when *both* are profiting from the treaty." The same rule applies in an argument. The only good solution is one in which both gain something (a win-win solution). Never should there be a resolution where one gains a victory and the other experiences a defeat (win-lose solution). This "solution" only creates a temporary truce, and soon the battle will resume.

5. *There can be no hidden agendas.* It is essential to be open and honest about what the real issues are in an argument. Too often people will bring up one issue as a disguised way to ventilate other emotional issues: There is a hidden agenda.

For example, the couple who has an argument over the way the wife is caring for the children will resolve the issue if this is the real problem. But if the real issue is that the husband is jealous because his wife has just received a promotion that pushes her salary higher than his, there will be no resolution. The parenting issue is only solved when he admits, at least to himself, that he is wanting her to spend more time with the kids so she is less likely to receive more promotions.

Any time you are caught in an argument, you should ask yourself, "Is the issue I am bringing up the thing that is really bothering me?"

6. Do not ask questions that are implied statements. If you have a question, ask the question. If you want to make a statement, make the statement. Do not confuse the issue by asking a question when you are intending to make a statement.

The question, "Why did you do that?" could be an honest request for more information. If it is, you will welcome the response, and the argument will be one step closer to resolution. If the question, "Why did you do that?" really means, "You should not have done that!" any reply by the other person will sound like a defensive rationalization. You will react with an "I am tired of your excuses" retort.

7. Pay attention to body language. Never act as if your body language (a look, a voice tone, or a gesture) does not count the same way that words do. People often conveniently ignore what they say nonverbally. A husband screams at his wife with arms flailing in the air and eyes ablaze with anger, "Why do you spend so much time on the phone with your mother?" Later, when the incident is being discussed with a third person, this same husband in a gentle voice with loving eyes and a demure manner recounts that the long distance phone bill was $150, and all he asked was, "Why do you spend so much time on the phone with your mother?"

Your body language is a part of your conversation and should always be labeled and treated as such.

8. Intimidation is not allowed. Although the arguing sins are forgivable, this one comes the closest to being the unforgivable sin.

Couples who have a special caring do not allow abusive patterns (emotional or physical) to creep into their relationship. They reject the philosophy of some people that this is just a normal part of an intimate relationship. They know that a steady pattern of verbal abuse or any escalation to physical abuse will eventually crush the love in their relationship. These couples practice a caring that moves beyond the gentleness of concern, compassion, and kindness. They practice a caring that requires strength, mental toughness, and discipline. It is a strong caring that says, "No abuse . . . ever." If they do fall short of this goal in their arguments, they do not rationalize their behavior. Instead they use aggressive caring to get back on the no-abuse program.

One of the ground rules that should be established *today*, if it is not already followed, is the total elimination of intimidation. Never should there be threats of physical violence or threats to tell a boss, mother, children, friends, the Internal Revenue Service, or any other person about some past misdeed as a technique for winning an argument. This is always a losing proposition. It causes permanent damage to a relationship no matter what temporary advantage you gain by this approach.

9. Do not use demeaning labels. Stick with the issues. Never play the "shrink" who starts diagnosing the other person during an argument. Leave that to the professionals.

Labels such as "you are ... insecure ... defensive ... a whore ... lacking in basic integrity ... jealous ... selfish ... not a man ... frigid ... neurotic ... a loser" may momentarily stop the other person in his or her tracks. But is the damage to their self-esteem worth this momentary advantage?

10. Do not leave the other person feeling bad. You have heard the phrase, "He or she won the battle and lost the war." In any ongoing relationship (husband/wife, parent/child, boss/employee), there is no gain if either person walks away from a disagreement feeling bad. There may appear to be a winner in the argument, but the total relationship will take a step backward if this happens. This is the "greatest commandment." The only successful argument is one in which both people leave feeling better. If this does not happen, no one has really won!

What happens when all the commandments are not kept? What should couples do then? Perhaps the philosophy surrounding the original Ten Commandments also applies here. The first principle is to double the effort to keep the arguing commandments, and the second principle is to practice the grand art of a caring forgiveness.

Both Bonnie and Cheryl (cases 1 and 2) had to face the forgiveness issue directly. Bonnie had to struggle with whether to forgive Don for the multiple sexual affairs and his "men will just be men" attitude when she discovered what was happening. Cheryl, who had promised herself that she would never tolerate any man ever hitting her, had to decide whether to forgive Keith and give the marriage another chance.

Both women decided, after some careful soul-searching, to forgive and make every attempt to release the memories of the painful events. Bonnie reasoned that Don had truly changed his lifestyle, and his past sexual behavior did not reflect his current attitude toward fidelity in a marriage. Likewise, Cheryl determined that Keith was genuinely sorry for what had happened, and sincerely promised that it would never happen again.

Both women made it very clear, however, that this forgiveness was not a revolving door. The next sexual affair or the next physical attack meant the end of the marriage.

Of course, all forgiveness issues do not have the emotional loading of an extramarital affair or a physical beating. Some acts are even worse. One example is sexual abuse of a child for which there may be no desire to ever forgive. Other acts are less severe. Behaviors such as telling a lie, flirting at a party, forgetting an anniversary, insulting a mother-in-law, or violating one of the Ten Commandments for Arguing may be more easily forgiven . . . especially if it is past behavior.

Couples who have the extra caring always err on the side of forgiveness. They never use this forgiveness bias to justify unacceptable current behavior, but the past truly does become the past. Naturally there are some exceptions to this philosophy; but the general rule is to forgive, forgive, and forgive what has happened in the past and focus on the dynamic present in which the caring can become an energy source that rivals the energy of exciting chemistry and great communication.

Consider five suggestions as you contemplate the forgiveness factor. These can play a critical role in your working through the hurts that occur in any long-term, intimate relationship. You may not agree with all of these suggestions, but at least consider what would happen to the caring in your marriage if you did implement these suggestions.

1. Ask for forgiveness. If you are the one who has inflicted the pain, resolve today to ask for forgiveness. Let your partner know how deeply sorry you are, and say that you hope that he or she can find it in his or her heart to forgive you.

You may be surprised at how forgiving people are when you take the courageous step of seeking their forgiveness. Even if they initially do not respond, you have set the stage for their reassessing the lingering hurt, anger, and pain. It may be only a matter of time before they come around.

2. *Forgive your partner.* If you were the one who was hurt, the ground rules are the same. As long as it is past behavior (as opposed to *current* behavior), you should attempt to forgive your partner for what he or she did to you. This act of forgiveness does not eliminate your partner's responsibility for what was done, but it does mean that *you* attempt to release the anger and hurt. (I want to emphasize, however, that these forgiveness rules do not extend to situations where there is a pattern of physical abuse, emotional abuse, or drug/alcohol abuse. Here the best strategy is to demand counseling or to leave. Forgiveness only strengthens the abuse cycle.)

3. *Help your partner understand you.* If you are the one who has inflicted the emotional pain, try to share fully what was happening at that time. Talk about the extreme job stress, your drinking problem, your frustration over the relationship strains, your ongoing struggles with liking yourself, and so on, that contributed to your earlier struggles. This emotional understanding does not justify what you did to your spouse, but it should increase his or her willingness to reassess and to forgive you. I have known many people who more easily forgave a spouse once they understood the whole picture.

4. *Take responsibility for what happened.* If you have to err be sure to err in the direction of taking too much responsibility for the past hurts, conflicts, and misunderstandings. Blaming your partner (or even asking him or her to assume responsibility for their rightful share of the difficulties) may simply add to his or her defensiveness. Your assuming the responsibility, on the other hand, often causes your partner to say, "No, wait a minute, I also contributed to our difficulties."

5. *Be the initiator.* Stop waiting for your spouse to break down the old psychological barriers. It is not the person who is most at fault who should initiate the resolving of an old relationship conflict. Instead, it is the person with the healthiest personality and the most positive self-esteem. And naturally that is you!

Pause for a minute and take a look at your present relationship with your spouse. Do you follow the Ten Commandments for Arguing, and do you practice the grand art of forgiveness? Does your partner do the same thing?

This is the essence of a gentle, yet strong caring.

• CHAPTER 9 •

Communication

Communication is the emotional bridge in an intimate relationship. It is the way couples resolve problems, express intimacy, and add mental stimulation to their lives. Communication is multidimensional; it is the golden link between two people's minds, hearts, and souls. Communication means sharing ideas, feelings, and loving emotions. It is not surprising that couples who build these bridges develop something very special in their relationship, and couples who fail to establish these communication bridges often experience an emotional isolation.

Dynamic communication is not always measured by the amount of talking a couple does. Some couples talk all the time and never communicate. Other couples spend little time actually talking, and yet they are always communicating.

True communication is measured by the degree of honesty, sharing, and vulnerability contained in the exchanges. George Eliot captured this quality well when she said, "Friendship is the inexpressible comfort of feeling safe with a person, having neither to weigh thoughts nor measure words." This level of communication makes for true intimacy, an intimacy that helps a couple become best friends . . . and best lovers!

In order to achieve this level of intimacy, however, you must understand the critical roles that your *public* self and your *real* self play in your quest for meaningful communication.

Your public self is the impression you want to create—your social image. Often you portray the public self in an attempt to "put your best foot forward." For example, you want your favorite college professor to think that you are a bright, perceptive, creative, and insightful student. When the minister, priest, or rabbi comes over, you try to appear moral, religious, virtuous, and deeply interested in God. With your boss, you want to appear hardworking, dedicated, loyal, and productive. Later that evening at the formal social gathering, you probably find yourself trying to be stylish, poised, cultured, and refined. In other words, within each of these settings, you try to create the impression that ensures others will perceive you favorably.

Your real self, on the other hand, is the true you. It captures your essence, your soul, your inner being. It is the truthful answer to the question, "Who am I?" It is how you really perceive yourself. It includes your fears, self-doubts, concerns, jealousies, and secret desires. It also encompasses your emotional strengths, talents, admirable qualities, and other positive perceptions.

Sharing your real self means dropping your public self roles and social games. When you are your real self, you strive for a high degree of openness and allow other people to see you as you are.

The sharing of your real self is more of a risk. When you reveal the inner you, there is a feeling of greater emotional vulnerability and thus more hurt if ignored or rejected. But there is also potentially a tremendous reward for exposing the real self. The experience of having your true self accepted creates the inexpressible comfort George Eliot was trying to describe. There is the ecstasy of truly connecting with someone . . . an ecstasy that is tremendously intensified when the soul-to-soul sharing is combined with a deep romantic love.

Where do you hope to find this level of emotional connection? The answer is obvious: You hope to find it in your marriage. Within this relationship you want the special "inexpressible comfort" that comes with the intimacy of being your real self. You want the exhilarating experience of really feeling loved at this inner essence level.

The irony of marital intimacy is that the closeness you so ardently desire is often the same closeness you greatly fear. Intimacy is more than just experiencing the intense, romantic emotions. True intimacy is found only when you lower the psychological armor that protects the real you. Experiencing deep intimacy means taking the risk of *truly* sharing with your partner. He or she is allowed to see your doubts, shortcomings, and struggles as well as your strengths, positive qualities, and virtues.

Intimacy involves knowing your mate. Intimacy involves allowing yourself to be known. True intimacy means dropping the defenses and deceptions so you can celebrate a transparent disclosure of your real self. This is the royal road to great communication.

Using the 1 to 10 Scale

As mentioned previously, your public and real selves become critical parts of every dialogue you have with other people. With each exchange, you have to make an important decision: "To what extent am I going to portray a public self, and to what extent am I going to reveal my real self?" It is like an internal scale in which your totally public self is a 1 and your totally real self is a 10. At any given moment, you choose to be somewhere along this self-disclosure scale.

If you function as a 2 or 3 (public self), you will find it easier to modify your behavior in the direction that you think other people would like you to be. An implied "I really don't like this aspect about you" can be easily changed by altering your more flexible and fluid public self. Operating as a public self appears easier, safer, and less painful.

The only problem—and it is a big problem—is that this protective shield also wipes out the positive feedback. When people tell you they really like you (or imply the same by their actions), it has less meaning because you know they are seeing your public self, that somewhat superficial role you have presented. The haunting question lingers, "Would they feel the same way if they really knew me, my real self?" Since you cannot answer that question, the positive feedback is questioned and devalued.

If you communicate as an 8 or a 9 (your real self), however, everything changes. Now you are more transparent, vulnerable, congruent, and real. Other people are seeing the true you. When they give you negative feedback, you have less opportunity to modify your actions or dismiss the feedback. It hurts! It hurts because it is your inner essence they have seen and rejected. Unlike your public self, your real self is not easily modified. Since they have responded negatively to your inner essence, the impact of the message is intensified.

There are tremendous rewards, however, when you communicate at the 8 or 9 level. When you receive positive feedback, the emotional impact of the message is richly intensified. Their "I like you" messages are directed to your inner essence. Your thought is, "They are appreciating me for what I am rather than for some role I am skillfully presenting at that given moment."

In the intimate relationship with your partner, the choice becomes especially clear. If you communicate at the public self level, you may be hurt less, but you will also experience fewer positive "highs." There can be no special intimacy . . . no deep emotional connection if only the public self is revealed and shared. Sharing at the real self level, on the other hand, means occasionally experiencing more pain, but it also means experiencing a richer, more satisfying relationship. Sharing your inner being is the only way to experience the ecstasy of a true soul-to-soul communication.

Your intimate relationship demands a sharing of your real self if you want a true intimacy. There are, however, many forces that operate against your functioning in this way. One is the programming many of us received about our public image.

Frances came to me for counseling because of a general feeling of depression and nothingness. She was struggling to find more meaning in her second marriage. Counseling brought out an interesting pattern. Frances had always functioned out of her public self. As the daughter of a Methodist minister, she definitely had not been a "rebellious preacher's kid." She was a youth leader, church pianist, and model young lady. She married a judge as soon as she finished college. She quickly adapted to the role of a judge's wife and played this role with equal ease.

After her divorce, she became the perfect date who would do anything to please. Frances's whole life had been a series of roles so it was not surprising that she was continuing this pattern in an empty second marriage. Even in counseling, Frances wanted to play the role of the perfect client. I had to confront her before she would drop her public self role in therapy.

The sad thing about this role-playing was that Frances had many positive qualities. She was personable, attractive, a good conversationalist, and committed to having loving, caring relationships. Unfortunately, her choosing to always portray public roles prevented her from fully appreciating these admirable traits.

A breakthrough came when I asked her to assign a number to herself in every interpersonal situation. At any given moment within each relationship, was she a 2 (quite public), a 5 (midway between public and real self), or a 9 (quite open and real)? After she had learned to monitor her level of role-playing, her counseling assignment was to move up one number in each relationship. If she was functioning as a 2 with her coworkers, she would risk being a 3; if she was a 5 with her husband, she would try to be a 6; if she was a 7 with her most intimate girlfriend, she would try moving up to an 8. Her report after two weeks was most positive. She said she found her relationships and life more meaningful. She shared, "I feel alive again!"

It is not easy to be open. Your early parent models, past relationship hurts, and fears of being vulnerable all contribute to your understandable protectiveness. Even when you become convinced there is more to gain than lose by being transparent, it is difficult to take the risk. The following four suggestions may help you take the same exciting and meaningful steps that Frances did in her relationships.

1. Start with a positive focus. Most people have difficulty sharing positive things about themselves. You can see this happen whenever people are asked to share their positive personal qualities. The amount of nervous laughter, stammering, and hesitation clearly signals their discomfort. This occurs because we have been programmed not to say good things about ourselves. If you do not believe this, just finish the following incomplete sentence: "If I say good things about myself, I am_____."

I have asked hundreds of people to complete this sentence, and the answers are always the same:

- Bragging
- Conceited
- Egotistical
- Stuck on myself
- Vain
- Selfish
- Self-centered
- Narcissistic

No wonder you may have difficulty sharing your positive qualities. Who would choose to be saddled with these negative labels?

The risk is even greater when the positives are about one's inner being, but what an exciting way to begin the adventure of sharing your real self! As you begin sharing your positive virtues, you automatically integrate them into your marriage.

Try the following activity with your spouse. As you participate, you will begin sensing the dynamic benefits of sharing positive feelings about your *real self.*

- Look at your *inner* being. There are some qualities you like about yourself and others you may wish to alter. Today, focus on the ones you like. Select three real self qualities from the following list. Share why these qualities are a part of your real self.

Loyal	Caring
Trustworthy	Supportive
Accepting	Genuine
Warm	Energetic
Spontaneous	Persistent
Self-reliant	Enthusiastic
Loving	Virtuous
Faithful	Transparent

  This is the first step. Now complete the second step, which is having your partner share the same thing with you. Repeat this two-step process for each of the remaining six activities.

- Share two acts of generosity you have done in your life that made you feel appropriately proud of yourself.

- Recall two times when you gave yourself permission to fully share your real self. Describe the depth of those moments.

- Remember the three nicest compliments you have ever received, compliments that captured your inner soul. Share them with your partner, and tell him or her how you felt as you received these compliments.

- Describe two instances when you made the "right" decision, even though it was contrary to what you wanted to do.

- Recall two times when you were a very loving person. What was there about you at those moments that you really liked?

- Give yourself a psychological hug. Wrap your arms around your waist and give a big squeeze. What part of your "being" are you hugging? What positive qualities flashed across your mind? Share those qualities with your partner.

Work on sharing your positive qualities. Naturally you need to include the total picture as you share your real self. There are times when you will need to focus on the negatives, but avoid the danger of minimizing the positive aspects as you share yourself. This sharing of the positive helps ensure the appropriate balance, and helps you more easily accept your own personal limitations and shortcomings.

2. *Share what you are now.* When people consider exposing their real selves, many immediately reflect upon their personal "deep, dark secrets." Read the letters to Ann Landers. Many center around the theme, "Should I tell my spouse what I did five, ten, or fifteen years ago?" The thought of having to expose past indiscretions looms like a heavy black cloud.

Sharing secrets of the past may actually be a misrepresentation of your real self. Take the example of Paula, who was sexually involved with a fellow high-school student during a time when she was going through a highly stressful adolescent crisis. This brief sexual encounter ended, and her only other sexual experience has been with her husband. Should she tell her husband, who believes he married a virgin?

There is a danger in Paula sharing her ancient secret with her husband. His sexual comfort level and religious value system could cause him to place too much emphasis on this "indiscretion." He may incorrectly alter his image of his wife rather than retain the present image, which correctly reflects what Paula is *today*.

The true sharing of your real self is a "here and now" experience. Your real self is what you are at this time in your life. Past events have already made their impact on your current being. It is your current thoughts, feelings, emotions, behaviors, attitudes, and values that comprise your essence. This is what you share when you reveal your real self.

3. *Discover how your mate sees you.* You may delude yourself into thinking your spouse has a difficult time reading your true emotions, thoughts, and attitudes, but this is probably not true. Your partner likely reads you much better than you ever imagined.

These observations are not to increase your paranoia, but to show the waste involved in functioning primarily on the public self level. When you function on this level, it is only you who is being deceived.

The good news is that your partner is already reading your real self and reacting positively to it. You do not, however, benefit from this because you assume he or she is responding only to your public self, the part that you try to portray.

Start celebrating this feedback. Do not minimize the compliments by assuming your mate is only responding to your current public self. Confirm this by deliberately revealing your real self. As soon as you risk sharing your real self, you will discover that your spouse's feelings do not change. For the first time, you may be able to experience genuine joy and happiness from this positive feedback.

4. Use a systematic approach to make a change. Earlier in this chapter, you read about the approach Frances used to add more meaning to her life. She had assigned a number from 1 to 10 to each of her relationships, 1 for the total public self and 10 for the total real self. Her goal was to move up one number in each of her relationships. Try her method to develop more meaning in your relationships. Use the following five-step approach:

- On a sheet of paper, list several relationships. They could include some of the following:

Spouse	Significant other
Child	Coworker
Friend	Parent
Church member	Employee
Boss	Neighbor

- Assign a number from 1 to 10 to indicate your degree of openness in each of these relationships at the present time. Do not worry about being precise; trust your first reaction. Place the number beside the person's name.

- Decide which relationships you want to move up one number, relationships in which you want to be more real. Place the new number next to the name.

- Visualize what you have to do to reach your new number. Design creative ways to share your real self. Jot down some of these ideas next to the names.

- Start functioning in this new way in each relationship and monitor the results. You will soon begin noticing a new depth and meaning in many of your relationships.

The benefits of being your real self are special and meaningful. This does not mean, however, that you should never play a role. I do not agree with some therapists who advocate that one should *always* "let everything hang out." A person does not have to tell all nor is it inappropriate to play a role on certain occasions. If it seems advisable, give yourself permission to be your public self. But do not deceive yourself, know that it is a role.

With this awareness, you can accept the results of being a public self more easily. When you function as a 2, anticipate a predictably flat, insignificant relationship. When you understand the connection between *realness* and *meaningfulness,* you will know why meaningfulness is not forthcoming in some of your present encounters with other people. Consider the following guidelines to determine what to expect out of a relationship:

- The more I am my real self in a relationship, the more personal meaning I will obtain from that relationship.

- To the extent other people can be real with me, they will obtain meaningfulness from our relationship.

- The people with whom I can be real will be the most psychologically significant people in my life.

- People who can be real with me will see me as more emotionally significant in their lives.

Active Listening

There is another critical dimension to this intimate, soul-to-soul, real-self sharing. It is how you and your partner respond to each other's real-self sharing.

Nothing is more flattering to a person than to be really listened to; it is far more satisfying than the most positive of verbal bouquets. This is the gift you give by being an active listener.

Active listening becomes a moving, creative experience—two human beings in a deep emotional interaction. As you completely tune in to the other person, you "hear" what he or she is attempting to share. You have an "extrasensory" perception. As your partner senses your tuning in, he or she instinctively makes the extra effort to communicate. He or she wants to be heard. What it does for a relationship can be beautiful to observe.

The power of active listening was dramatically demonstrated to me by Angie, a client who came for marriage counseling when she discovered that her husband was having an extramarital affair. When confronted, he said that the other woman was "the love of his life," and he declared that he wanted a divorce. Despite all the difficulties, Angie, a loving person with a deep sense of commitment, said that she wanted to save her marriage. She came to me for counseling as the result of a speech that she heard me give on the art of listening.

After giving a rather detailed description of her marital situation, she said she would like me to teach her some active listening skills. I replied, "I am willing to do this, but I think your marital relationship is very complex, and you need to consider the total picture." (I placed additional listening skills low on the list of possible solutions.) I gently diverted her to "more important" considerations such as why her husband wanted a divorce.

At the beginning of the second session, Angie again requested that the counseling session be spent developing better active listening skills. I explained that although it was a valid request, it might be an unproductive approach given the obvious complexities of the present relationship. I tried to show her how a situation where a man professes no love, gives no indication of wanting to continue the marriage, and is involved with another woman usually requires a more comprehensive counseling approach.

When Angie came to the third session, she was mildly upset. In a gentle but insistent manner she asked, "Since I am paying for the session, don't I have some say over what we do during the session?" I was slightly taken aback by her assertive statement, but I finally did hear her. She then repeated her desire to spend the session developing better listening skills. I honored her request during the next three counseling sessions.

Within two months, Angie reported the marital relationship had taken a definite turn for the better. Her husband had broken off the other relationship, and they were rapidly developing good communication—communication that conveyed their hidden love and caring. Angie had instinctively sensed that her husband had a desperate need to be "heard." He had been searching for this understanding, and she wisely prepared herself to listen and understand more completely. While I am not suggesting that listening would be the answer in every case, active listening clearly worked for Angie and her husband.

Angie was right and I was wrong. I gently slap my counseling hands for underestimating the potential power of active listening in the hands of a loving spouse.

The master communicators know that active listening has the amazing power of freeing people to share their true feelings and to feel accepted for whom they are. And active listening is most dynamic when it contains three qualities.

1. Empathy. Empathy is losing yourself, climbing inside the skin of other people, and seeing things through their eyes. It is not feeling sorry for them (sympathy), but knowing how they feel because, to some degree, you are feeling their emotions (empathy). It is being there with them and emotionally walking hand-in-hand.

A person with empathy says, "I understand," rather than, "Why did you do that?" A person with empathy communicates the silent message, "You are not alone, I am here with you," rather than, "Come on! Get your act together!" A person with empathy responds, "I will help you seek a solution," rather than, "The trouble is that you have not acted correctly."

Have you ever been given this level of emotional understanding? If you have, you know how special, how freeing it is. Recapture the feelings . . . you were not alone . . . there was someone else there with you. This is the same quality that you can give your loving husband or wife.

2. Confidentiality. People are afraid to share their problems. They have the understandable fear that too many people will find out. Confidentiality can be a built-in safety factor. Confidentiality gives the reassurance that what is revealed stays a secret. Confidentiality allows a sharing environment where one can examine struggles without exposing oneself to the world. This is the protection professional counselors offer. This is the same safety you can offer your partner.

Starting today, make a new commitment to yourself. When your partner shares something in confidence, keep it in confidence. No exceptions... no telling anyone else... not even your best friend. If you follow the ironclad code of never violating a confidence (unless you have obtained prior approval from your partner) and communicate this attitude to him or her, you will be amazed at how approachable you suddenly become.

3. Acceptance. Acceptance is implied in the old Indian saying, "Never judge another man until you have walked a mile in his moccasins." It is also captured in the attitude, "I may not always accept your behavior, but I will always accept you." Acceptance means you truly value another person's essence—you accept them for what they are. Their feelings, emotions, thoughts, and concerns are unique and wonderful!

Acceptance is probably the most significant element in sharing your real self. In fact, you may want to reread the section on acceptance in chapter 7 with the mind-set, "How can I build acceptance into my active-listening repertoire?"

Do you want to be the most significant person in your spouse's life? Do you want your husband or wife to be the most significant person in your life? If you do, use the active-listening skills (empathy, confidentiality, and acceptance) to ensure that the greatest sharing of the real self is with each other. Do this, and you will create a magic that even magicians will envy.

You will create this magic because there is a direct correlation between the level of your sharing and the depth of your intimacy. If you share 10 percent of your real self, you will experience 10 percent of your potential emotional closeness; if you share 50 percent of your inner being, you will have 50 percent intimacy; and if you reveal 95 percent of your true essence, you will discover an indescribable ecstasy of such magnitude that you will never again think about percentages.

CHAPTER 10

Communication and Criticism

Would you like to create some instant magic in your marriage? Would you like a dramatic and quick turnaround from some current madness? The strategy is simple. Stop being so critical of each other. Curb unthinking negative comments that sound like the following:

- "The only time you show any interest is when you want to have sex."
- "Why aren't you as considerate as John is with his wife?"
- "All you do is find ways to spend money."
- "The house looks terrible."

Criticism, criticism, criticism—for many couples, criticism appears to be synonymous with marital communication. Negative messages are the main way to communicate; most conversations consist of nagging, picking, and complaining. If a hidden tape recorder were used to record their conversations, they would not believe their ears.

Criticism is also the spark that often ignites the raging forest fire of no-win, going nowhere, intense fights that can lead to mental abuse or even physical abuse. Curb the unproductive critical communication, and you will eliminate many of the truly destructive marital encounters.

Unchecked, criticism becomes a cancerous growth. It can cause a terminal illness in a relationship before a diagnosis is ever made. By the time a couple realizes the full impact of the criticisms, one of them has created thick defensive walls to ward off the barbs, found someone who is more accepting, or made a final decision to leave the marriage.

If you want to alter this cancerous growth within your marriage before it is inoperable, you need to determine the reasons for the criticism. Understanding the reasons keeps the critical remarks in better perspective and, more important, eliminates this destructive disease before too much damage is done. Four common reasons for marital criticism are discussed below.

1. A rejection of one's spouse. Some couples are critical because they dislike their mate. They wish they were not married (this may be on the conscious or subconscious level), but they feel trapped. The pressures of inadequate financial resources, religious convictions, fear of making a change, or welfare of the children force them to stay in the marriage. Criticism is a way to express this resentment over being trapped; it allows a catharsis of negative feelings. The criticism also keeps the other person at arm's length and prevents any undesired requests for intimacy or closeness.

This could be the reason there is so much criticism in your marriage. You may not accept your spouse for what he or she is, but you find it is too painful to admit. Your frequent focus on the negative aspects of the relationship is really an honest expression of your basic feelings toward your spouse.

This lack of acceptance does not automatically mean the character of one's mate is flawed. In some cases the spouse possesses many excellent traits but simply is not the type of person that the husband or wife finds desirable. In other cases, he or she is obviously lacking in qualities that are essential for a good marriage. Whether the reasons for rejection are legitimate or not, the impact is the same. The criticism merely reflects the honest condition of the marriage.

What can you do when you realize there is a basic rejection of your spouse? If this is the reason for your criticism, turn to the overcoming obstacles section of this book to confront this issue directly rather than merely continuing to throw (or receive) the deadly verbal darts.

Fortunately, the other reasons for the criticism are not so deadly. There still is hope. With awareness, you can turn the darts into bouquets.

2. An imprinting developed from models present during childhood. Modeling is a powerful teacher; much of your interpersonal behavior can be directly attributed to the models you had as a child. Parents who are physically abusive raise children who have more of a tendency to be physically abusive; parents who escape from problems through illness, drugs, or alcohol establish a pattern that often is followed by the child; and parents who demonstrate love, caring, and concern toward each other encourage their children to strive for the same in their intimate relationships.

Early models set a pattern for the role of criticism within a marriage. If a child has observed highly critical parents, he or she may adopt this lifestyle. There is a "learned" tendency to cope with the normal frustrations of marriage by being critical; it becomes the "natural" way to express one's emotions. Like any other habit, however, there are logical consequences. The criticism damages a marriage even though it is not intended to do so.

Brenda's parents loved each other, but it would have taken an expert on nonverbal communication to detect the love; it certainly was not obvious by the way they talked to each other. Brenda's father was constantly criticizing his wife for the way she spent money, kept the house, wasted time, and disciplined the children. Brenda's mother was up to the challenge. Her equally critical tongue lashed sharply at her husband's handling of family finances, obsession with football games, neglect of the yard, and weekend drinking habits. Both were always demanding changes in the other person, demands that were comfortably ignored with the same ease that water rolls off a duck's back.

Brenda learned this pattern well. She reverts to this modeled communication style whenever she is frustrated in her marriage. Unfortunately, her husband is not conditioned to ignore the verbal barbs. He interprets her critical remarks as personal attacks on him. He is starting to lose self-confidence, struggles with a mild depression, and recently asked an attorney friend about his rights if he were ever to divorce. Meanwhile, Brenda is totally missing these reactions. Her attitude that this is just part of marriage has blinded her to what is happening.

Valid criticism is an essential part of marriage. A marriage without any negative exchanges is a sterile, dead relationship.

Criticism communicates requests for changes within the relationship, changes necessary to keep a marriage alive and growing. The constant, unthinking patterns of criticism found in many relationships, however, are neither valid nor useful! The criticisms are simply old habits rather than positive requests for changes. These old habits ensure that the relationship will never experience the desired closeness, vulnerability, or spontaneity.

Stop for a moment and reflect on the style of communication in your parents' marriage. Was there a heavy ratio of negative messages? Trust me, your childhood observations have been internalized and are a part of your communication style. You will act in your intimate relationship just like your parents did, unless you make a concentrated effort to do otherwise. But this change can be made if you will carefully study the four emotional message categories discussed later in this chapter.

3. *A way to stay "protected" in a marriage.* People marry because they want the intimacy that a loving, committed relationship can give. But what does a person do when the intimacy does not develop? One approach is to make vulnerable requests for additional intimacy.

- "There are many good things in our relationship, and I would like to develop them even more. Let's sit down and see how we can make our relationship even more special."

- "I would like to work on our communication. Would you also be willing?"

- "I want to spend more time with you."

The other approach is to ask for emotional intimacy without taking a risk. The requests are indirect and couched in less vulnerable statements. Frequently the statements have a critical or accusatory tone.

- "Why are you never interested in making our relationship special? You just take what we have for granted!"

- "Why don't you ever talk to me?"

- "You spend too much time on your work."

The indirect messages provide a degree of safety. Now there is a "reason" why the requests for intimacy are ignored. Unfortunately, the disguised requests also lessen the chances of getting a positive response.

Sometimes the use of criticism to remain less vulnerable goes beyond a "safe" testing of the relationship. It is a way to create an emotional protection.

Roger has recently become concerned about his sexual adequacy. Twice within the past month, he has been unable to sustain an erection during intercourse. Very concerned, he vacillates between needing to prove his sexual adequacy and wanting to avoid another sexual failure. One more "failure" would be devastating so he starts putting off trying again.

How does Roger establish this sexual distance from his wife? He regulates the emotional distance through the use of criticism. Two or three stinging criticisms ensure that his wife will not make a sexual request. This pattern can become very confusing to his wife. She cannot understand why most of Roger's criticism seems to follow times when they have been especially close. Once understood, however, the pattern becomes quite logical. The emotional closeness could lead to sexual closeness and this is to be avoided! Roger manufactures some "justifiable" criticism that pushes them apart, and Roger's dilemma ("Should I try now or wait until later?") is temporarily resolved.

People frequently use criticism to maintain emotional distance in an intimate relationship. It protects against being too emotionally vulnerable and masks the exposure of one's insecurities. Unfortunately, the price for this protection is often high.

What happens in your relationship? Do you use an *indirect* critical approach when you ask for love, caring, and closeness? Or, even worse, do you use criticism to prevent closeness? Unfortunately, your criticism may do too good a job of protecting your vulnerability.

4. A predictable response from a person who has a low self-image. Within business circles, there is a truism that first-rate businesspeople hire first-rate associates; second-rate businesspeople hire third-rate associates. A person has to have a positive self-image in order to feel comfortable working with competent people instead of opting for the security of working with inferior people who are not a personal threat.

The same principle applies in a marriage. If a husband has a positive self-image, he is comfortable with his wife having a positive self-image. If he has a negative self-image, he can feel threatened by her positive self-esteem.

Tom is always putting down his wife in public. He is constantly pointing out her mistakes and shortcomings in a clever but cutting manner. It makes other people uncomfortable, but the criticism is laced with enough humor to make it barely tolerable.

Tom is even more clever in private. He has mastered the principles of "acceptable" criticism. He (a) saves his comments until he has a "good" reason for being critical, then lets her have it with both barrels; (b) knows that when he lacks a good excuse for being critical, he can always bring up the past; (c) interprets any defensive response to mean that she is questioning the validity of his criticism, so he repeats it; and (d) takes comfort in knowing that he can always find some justifiable reason for being critical. After all, no one is perfect.

Why does he do this? This faultfinding stems from Tom's insecurity—his low self-image is threatened. He subconsciously wants to ensure that his wife's self-image is as low as his. His humorous put-downs and persistent critiquing are disguised ways of accomplishing this objective.

At the risk of belaboring a point, I want to reemphasize that the focus on the reasons for so much criticism is not to enable you and your partner to handle the verbal barrage better. The goal is to change the pattern!

Sometimes in this age of self-help psychology, we suffer from the "curse of too much understanding." Since we "understand" why these negative behaviors are occurring, we are neutralized in doing anything about it. For example, we may rationalize that the reason he or she is so critical is because he or she is (and you can check the best answer):

_____ The adult child of an alcoholic
_____ Codependent
_____ Suffering from job stress
_____ Recovering from the partner's extramarital affair
_____ Neglected in the relationship
_____ Struggling with low self-esteem

Even when criticism is "totally justified" or not really intended to be any "big deal," the consequences usually further erode the relationship. Many people handle criticism the same way they collect trading stamps. When they have saved enough stamps (criticisms), they trade their stamp books in for a big prize (divorce, affair, or vicious counterattack). Frequently, criticism has a more negative effect on a relationship than the original incident that precipitated the criticism.

People learn to protect themselves from constant criticism. A thick protective shield is formed to reduce the sting of the critical remarks. Unfortunately, the protective shield is not discriminating; it prevents criticisms from penetrating, but it also blocks out positive messages. In time, no emotional expression is received and all intimacy is lost. Keep this in mind any time you deliver the stinging criticism. Is it really worth the risk?

Starting today, aggressively stop the criticisms that pervade your marriage. Use your awareness of the causes of criticism as a tool for making changes.

But do not wait until you are "cured" before you change the critical communication. Granted, it helps if you have forgiven the affair, found better ways to release your pent-up emotions, improved your self-esteem, or rejected the communication style modeled by your parents. But why wait? You can make a significant change, beginning today, as you adjust the four basic emotional messages that you send your spouse. The four messages that can have a dramatic impact on your future communication with your partner are as follows:

1. A *positive conditional* message is a positive message based on your partner's actions and behaviors:
   - "You look very nice in that outfit."
   - "I am proud of your professional career."
   - "I am glad that you call when you are going to be late."

2. The *positive unconditional* message is based on your mate's essence or actual "being." These messages go beyond what a person has done and respond to the basic qualities of the person. They are "warm fuzzies."
   - "I love you."
   - "You have beautiful eyes."
   - "I admire who you are."

3. A *negative conditional* message is a negative message based on your mate's actions or behaviors.
    - "I am angry at you for coming home two hours late without calling first."
    - "It was inappropriate to leave the kids home alone."
    - "I think it is wrong for you to expect me to do all the housework."
4. A *negative unconditional* message is based on something your partner is. These are "wipe out messages." Unlike the negative conditional messages, there is nothing a person can do. They contain no prescription for change.
    - "I hate you."
    - "You are stupid."
    - "You turn me off."

Examine the messages you send to your mate. Which messages do you send and with what frequency? Try an interesting experiment by making the following chart:

P.C.	N.C.
P.U.	N.U.

Every time you send an emotional message to your partner, place a mark in the appropriate box. Record your responses over several different time periods.

P.C.	N.C.
lllll ll	lllll lllll ll
P.U.	N.U.
ll	lllll

The totals may surprise you. One of the most startling surprises may be that your pattern of messages does not correspond to your basic feeling toward your mate.

As you analyze your messages, make special note of three factors:

1. Look at your negative messages. No one is asking you to be a Pollyanna who never sends negative messages. At times, it is necessary to offer a constructive criticism. An occasional valid criticism about an irritating attitude or behavior does not mean you do not like the person, nor should he or she be supersensitive about your comments. When you send negative messages, however, make them *conditional* rather than *unconditional* unless you truly intend for the message to be unconditional.

This is especially true in a marriage. You may say, "I hate you," when what you really mean to say is, "I am unhappy when you do not consider my feelings." The unconditional message damages the relationship without offering any solutions. The conditional message charts a course for changing the relationship.

2. Examine your positive messages. When sending positive messages be sure to include unconditional messages as well as conditional messages. It is easy to get in the habit of limiting your positive responses to things a person has done.

- "I am so happy you got a bonus on your job."
- "I like the way you handle the children."
- "The house looks good."

These messages enhance a relationship, but a person could wonder, "What would happen if I were not doing all these wonderful things? Would the other person still care?" This is where the positive unconditional messages provide such a beautiful compliment to the positive conditional messages. Statements such as the following have a tremendous impact on a relationship:

- "I feel wonderful around you."
- "I admire who you are."
- "I like *you*."

They establish a loving base that transcends the last transient remark.

3. Watch the ratio between your negative and positive messages. Look at the balance of positive and negative messages in your marriage. Does the ratio of positive versus negative messages accurately reflect the true relationship? If you are like most couples, it does not.

Public service announcements have called high blood pressure a silent killer. The elevated blood pressure takes a deadly toll on the heart and other vital body parts. Often the damage is done before a person is even aware of what has happened. A heavy ratio of negative messages does the same thing. It destroys a relationship with deadly efficiency.

Positive communication has the same impact in the opposite direction: It creates beautiful relationships. Positive messages have dramatic power, and yet positive communication is one of the most neglected aspects in many marriages. Strive to change this in your marriage.

Celebrate the love in your marriage as you share the following sentences with your partner. (Please note that it is more interesting and fun if you alternate your responses; for example, you give one idea . . . your mate gives an idea . . . you share a feeling . . . and so on.)

- Two physical features that you like in your partner.
- Three personality qualities that you like in your partner.
- Two talents you admire in your partner.
- Two times when your partner did something for you that you still remember as being extra special.
- Two spiritual qualities you respect in your partner.
- Two times your partner was emotionally there when you really needed him or her.
- Two times you felt especially close to your partner.
- Two ways in which your partner has been a good influence on your personal life.
- Two of your partner's achievements that you are proud of.
- Four positive feelings that you have toward your partner right now as a result of completing this positive communication activity.

Capture the feelings you have as you do this exercise. It's not necessary to point out all the positive psychological benefits of giving several positive messages for every negative message because you have just experienced this magic.

I vividly recall a counseling case that captures the miraculous benefits of giving compliments to one's partner. A middle-aged woman came into my office one day with a big ball of red yarn all twisted and snarled. (To this day, I do not know if the knots were put in to make her point or if they had accidentally occurred.) She threw the big ball of red yarn on the floor and exclaimed, "This is exactly how I feel, and it is all my husband's fault."

Her husband, an accountant, was actively involved in several community projects. Unfortunately, his busy schedule had created an "I am being rejected" mind-set within his wife. No matter what he did (and it was very apparent that he deeply loved her and wanted a close relationship), it only seemed to make matters worse. At one time he had even offered to give up most of his community involvements, but her response had been, "You are just suggesting that because I am unhappy; you really don't want to be with me." Nothing he did seemed to convince her of his love and caring.

During the joint sessions, however, I started noticing that she had an interesting response to his positive comments. For example, he would say, "Honey, you look very nice today," and she would respond with a fleeting little smile (a tip-off she really did like the feedback). But then she would abruptly shift to a negative comment such as, "What was wrong with the way I looked yesterday?" Undaunted, he would compliment her on the way she was raising their daughter, "I am so proud of our daughter, and I really feel a lot of the credit is due to your very positive influence." Again, the quick little smile, and then the negative reaction, "Are you implying there is something wrong with the way I am raising our son?"

It was obvious that her resentment over "being neglected" was causing her to be self-defeating in her desire to be closer to her husband. When he did reach out, she would instinctively rebuff him. The little smile was an encouraging sign, however. She did briefly respond positively to his comments and for a fleeting moment relished his attention. Using this as a base, I suggested to the husband in an individual session that he give his wife seven positive compliments every day. I further asked him to ignore any negative reactions she might have to his positive messages. He was to continue this pattern regardless of how she reacted.

I could sense his CPA brain whirling as a new ledger was being formed in his mind with a heading "Positive Remarks to Wife." I could see him making the entries in the ledger. I knew he was going to follow my suggestion.

Eight days later I received a call from his wife. She was calling to cancel her appointment because she felt she did not need to come. Her concluding comment in the brief conversation was priceless: "I don't know what you said to my husband during your last counseling session, but you finally got the 'son-of-a-bitch' shaped up!"

• CHAPTER 11 •

Commitment

Commitment is based in part on the amount of communication, caring, and chemistry in a marriage. Couples who have these three C's find it easier to make a total commitment to a marriage while serious deficiencies in the three C's can make any previous commitment shaky.

Commitment also has a dimension apart from the other C's. Commitment often reflects a basic value system, a value system toward marriage that can range from, "If I am unhappy or find someone who interests me more, I will leave," to "I am staying in this marriage no matter what."

Both extremes are questionable. Obviously, having no commitment ("I will leave the minute I am displeased.") provides little security, while the other extreme ("staying no matter what") can quickly move from a very admirable position to sheer stupidity if there is ongoing physical abuse or a continuous series of flagrant sexual affairs. But the attitude, "As long as there is potential for a good relationship, I am going to try to make it work," can add a positive dimension to a marriage. It gives a security that encourages taking the risks needed to improve this most intimate of relationships.

Commitment is shaped by a person's religious convictions, parental models, personal beliefs, and general attitudes toward marriage. These qualities contribute to a person's resolve to make a strong commitment to a relationship and help determine how he or she responds to marital difficulties. They create an attitude of:

- "My marriage vows are very sacred."
- "I will stay as long as there is any hope for a decent relationship."
- "Illness, financial struggles, and other difficulties will only strengthen my desire to stick with you."
- "We are now joined together as one and let no one break this bond."

Commitment is energized by a clearly defined value system, but it is not limited to this quality. Commitment is also strengthened when couples systematically set dynamic goals for their relationship—goals that give psychological energy to the commitment and goals that make commitment a positive psychological force, not merely a set of absolute standards.

The importance of goal setting has almost become an axiom. All winners declare that goals are essential to maximize one's potential and frequently point out that the absence of goals will always limit a person. There is a general consensus about the following:

- "Seldom do you exceed your expectations. Even if the opportunity arises, you generally fail to capitalize on it."
- "You get not what you want, but what you expect to get."
- "If your goal is to 'get through the day,' that is exactly what happens."

People are appreciating the importance of setting goals, and they are starting to set goals for many things in their lives. They establish goals to give up smoking, lose weight, and get in better physical shape. Others strive to make more money and climb the ladder of career success. Couples decide how many children they will have and how often they will take a vacation. But what do people do about their relationships? What are their goals for the quality of their relationships with their children, friends, coworkers, and parents? Most even neglect to set specific goals for their relationship with their spouse.

If you want a quality relationship, you need to set *dynamic goals* . . . goals that allow you to maximize your commitment . . . goals that help give you a tight emotional bonding.

Setting Relationship Goals

Take out five 3-inch by 5-inch cards. On each card write down one relationship goal, something you would like to accomplish in your relationship with your spouse. Take off the "be cautious" sign and let yourself go! Have fun fantasizing as you establish five exciting, dynamic goals.

As you write out these goals, keep three guidelines in mind.

1. *Make sure your goals are positive and constructive.* You need to state your goals in positive terms rather than negative terms. Your goal statements should describe what you want, not what you want to avoid. For example:

    - Don't say, "I won't criticize my husband anymore;" instead say, "I will be more complimentary to my husband."

    - Don't say, "I want to stop ignoring my wife;" instead say, "I want a closer, more loving relationship with my wife."

    Making a change is difficult unless there is some reward or payoff that occurs as a result. The best goals are stated in positive terms because then the payoff is built in and focused upon as the goals are stated.

2. *Make sure your goals are clearly defined, well-thought-out, and written.* There is something magical about writing out your goals. The process of committing goals to written form gives them the extra focus, emphasis, and commitment necessary to help you reach the objectives. A lasting association is formed between the goals and the written words. When you reread your written statements, you will have concrete, visual reminders that help trigger the mental processes you originally experienced. You react emotionally to the written goal statements.

3. *Do not limit your goals to ones you already know how to accomplish.* This is one of the most important concepts of goal setting. You do not have to currently possess the knowledge (method) for reaching your goals. In fact, if

you limit yourself to goals that you already know *how* to reach, you severely limit yourself.

The process of goal setting triggers several changes that show you how to reach your goals. One of the most dramatic changes is the effect the new goals have on your perceptions. Set positive goals for your marriage, and new insights for reaching your goals will automatically follow.

Now comes the exciting part! Start using imagery (see chapter 14 for a more detailed discussion on imagery) to program these relationship goals into your powerful subconscious mind. Do this by rewriting each goal statement as a personal affirmation on the back side of the 3-inch by 5-inch card. The goal becomes an affirmation as you follow these steps:

1. Write down the goal as though it has already been accomplished. Vividly imagine yourself having already changed your relationship with your mate.

2. Include in your affirmation statement the personal rewards you are receiving from accomplishing the goals, for example, intimacy, sharing, happiness, love, satisfaction, security, belonging, and so on.

3. State the affirmations in the present tense. Do not write them in terms of what you can do or are going to accomplish. State your affirmations in terms of "I am . . .," or "It is. . . ." You have to do this because the subconscious mind thinks in the present (not the future) tense.

4. Include excitement and action in your statements. Capture the feelings and emotions the changed relationship is bringing.

Study the following illustration to better understand the difference between a goal and an affirmation.

GOAL: "I would like to have a close, loving relationship with my spouse."

How does this sound? It is an admirable goal, but as it is written, it has no dynamic pizzazz. In this lifeless state, it will not

Commitment • 89

hook the subconscious mind. Therefore, you should rewrite the goal statement as an affirmation.

AFFIRMATION: "My spouse and I are on the third day of a very special vacation. We have just completed a wonderful breakfast, a time filled with many loving and appreciative glances. We are celebrating our marriage . . . a marriage that has grown from a dull, flat, humdrum relationship to one with excitement, caring, and the assurance that any problems will be eventually solved. The thought of having time alone with my loving partner is an unsurpassed pleasure."

How does this sound? Do you sense the difference between an affirmation and a goal statement?

Affirmations carry the vital components that program your subconscious mind. You have a new power for improving the commitment in your relationship because three things happen when you read your affirmations several times a day:

1. You begin revising the old attitudes stored in your subconscious mind. What you picture with emotions goes into the subconscious mind as reality. This imagery creates new attitudes.

2. Your subconscious mind starts sending you data to reach your goals. Now your perception is oriented in the direction of seeing exciting new ways to improve your marriage.

3. Your subconscious mind *automatically* provides you with the energy, creativity, and motivation needed to succeed. The subconscious mind draws on your untapped potential and charts creative new ways to accomplish your relationship goals.

Read your affirmations several times a day, and you will discover the exciting beginning of a new era in your intimate relationship—a relationship with a rock solid commitment—a marriage moving toward magic.

Creating Marital Intimacy

Goal setting with the accompanying imageries is one powerful way to create marital commitment. A second dynamic way to add energy to your relationship is to make specific commitments for each of the five C's that come from your own creative planning.

One of the real joys of therapy comes when one of my clients takes a creative step that changes his or her marriage or has a new awareness that significantly alters his or her response to a difficult marital situation.

Why do these positive things happen? It should be no surprise that the best strategies, insights, and impetus for change often come directly from the innovative person who is sitting in the chair opposite mine. My clients write the best prescriptions for their relationships. And this is as it should be, because who could possibly understand all the subtle nuances of their unique situations as well as they do?

While I am delighted to give strategies I have compiled from professional experts, clients, and personal experience, the best strategies will come, as they do in therapy, from your own creative and innovative efforts. You should *never* underestimate your ability to find extremely effective ways to make positive changes in your marriage.

Try out this process as you contemplate the five C's in your marriage. Block out a period of time when you will have no interruptions (similar to what you would experience in a therapy session) and release your creative mind. Come up with some personalized ways to strengthen the commitment in your marriage by (a) finding more time for your intimate relationship, (b) doing the little things to spark the five C's, and (c) incorporating the psychological strategies mentioned throughout this book.

1. Finding the time. I am reminded of one couple I saw in my private practice. They were the picture-perfect couple. They loved each other, had two beautiful children, enjoyed successful careers, were committed to the relationship, and even looked as if they belonged together. But they were coming for marital counseling because they "fought all the time."

It quickly became apparent that most of the intense, but seemingly minor fights, were caused by an underlying frustration of never having enough time to enjoy each other's company. When they tried to plan more time together, however, their pathetic conclusion was that by the time they bused the children to their extracurricular activities, finished all household chores, worked on their career projects, put the kids to bed, and got everything ready for the next day, there was no time left for the relationship, at least not until 10:30 P.M., when they were dead tired. They were ready to conclude that there was no quality time to be found unless they committed the "unforgivable sin" of missing a Little League baseball game.

May I confront *you* as I did *this* couple? Please take a lighthearted quiz to see how well you find the time to enjoy the relationship that was to fulfill your childhood fantasy of marital bliss, joy, and happiness. Please answer "yes" or "no" to each of the following questions:

_____ Do you take time each day for a "psychological cocktail"? A psychological cocktail is a nonalcoholic ten-minute pause when you both stop, sit down, and have an intimate conversation.

_____ Is dinner a time for sharing? Do you spend this captive time together talking with each other (This is a wonderful model for children.), or is this a time when you demonstrate your amazing physical agility as you remove all your food from your plate without your eyes ever leaving the TV screen?

_____ Do you take a walk with your mate at least twice a week? Do you use this time to relax, share, and enjoy a few uninterrupted minutes together?

_____ Do the two of you (and just the two of you) go out at least one night a week on an old-fashioned date where you even hold hands?

_____ Do you call each other at least once a day just to let the other person know that you are thinking of him or her as you actively pursue your career?

_____ Do you have a hobby that you do together, a hobby that gives you simultaneous relaxation and recreation?

_____ Do you do at least one household task *together* each day so you have forced time together despite your hectic schedules?

_____ Do you share a news article, educational program, or other learning experience at least twice a week to encourage the discussion of stimulating ideas?

_____ Do you have a three-day vacation (or even a two-day vacation) at least once every three months, just for the two of you when even the children are not included?

_____ Do you spend at least two minutes in the morning (I limit this to two minutes for the people who are not morning people.) gently chatting before you jump up to hit the track running?

If it is not too embarrassing, total up your "yes" answers. If you have six or more, give yourself a pat on the back. If you have less than six, you have just found a wonderful approach for working on the five C's. As Ron Hill, an assistant pastor at Trinity Baptist Church in San Antonio, Texas, cleverly says, "Love is a four-letter word spelled T-I-M-E."

2. *Do the little things.* There are creative little things you can do to enhance each of the five C's in your marital relationship. Each specific "little thing" will appear almost inconsequential, but they will accumulate. They will be a part of the wind on the rock that alters the contour of your marriage. Please come up with ten little things that can make a difference in your relationship. To stimulate your creative thinking, I will give you two little things under each of the five C's; reflect on them and then add two (or more) of your own creative strategies.

Communication

    a. Once a day walk up to your mate and share an intimate thought.

    b. When your mate says something, immediately stop what you are doing and really listen.

    c. _____

    d. _____

Caring

    a. Once a day do something thoughtful that shows that you really care.

    b. Always ask how your loved one's day went and give lots of support and encouragement.

    c. _____

    d. _____

Chemistry

    a. Bring home a flower, card, or small surprise gift at least once a month.

    b. Sneak up first thing in the morning, brush your teeth, and put on a little cologne. Then come back to bed for a two-minute chat.

    c. _____

    d. _____

Commitment

    a. Tell your spouse that he or she is the only person you ever want to be married to.

    b. If you ever have a flicker of chemistry for another person, quickly resolve that you will never do anything to fan that fleeting emotion.

    c. _____

    d. _____

Competency

    a. Once a day give yourself a big compliment. Have a smile on your face as you do this self-esteem enhancer.

    b. Always first ask yourself whether your jealous feelings are valid before making an anxious inquiry.

    c. _____

    d. _____

3. Incorporate psychological strategies. There are psychological strategies you can use to improve the five C's in your relationship. Once you understand the dimensions of chemistry, caring, communication, commitment, and competency, you will more easily spot psychological strategies that fall under each of these five key umbrellas.

Even the chapters in the career and mission sections contain psychological strategies that you can use to enhance one of the five C's. For example, (a) learning how to better read your partner's body language will enhance the *communication,* (b) using the understanding response will dramatically improve the *caring,* (c) getting your body in the best shape possible will help preserve the *chemistry,* (d) having a spiritual faith will solidify the *commitment,* and (e) learning how to "punch your own ticket" will help ensure an ongoing *competency.*

The five C's are your directional beams for a happy marriage. Make it your personal commitment to spot them, use them, and celebrate them. This commitment can be a very exciting process because the potential reward of greater intimacy is so exhilarating. Keep this in mind as you examine each of the strategies in this book.

CHAPTER 12

Commitment and Unreasonable Expectations

For some, marital commitment is an absolute: Divorce is an option that will never be considered. To violate this principle may cause more pain than remaining in a horrible marriage. For most, however, marital commitment is not totally absolute. The commitment demands a certain degree of common sense.

But where does a person draw the line? When is commitment an admirable virtue, and when does it become foolish?

Marge has been miserable in her marriage for the past five years. Chemistry is gone, caring is rarely shown, and communication is nonexistent. Only commitment ("hanging in there") remains. Gathering up her courage, she decides to talk to her mother about divorce. After listening for a few minutes, her mother's clipped response is, "Well, exactly what do you want? He provides for you, is not mistreating you, and does not run around. Isn't that enough? What do you expect, anyway?"

It is possible to err in one of two directions when answering the question, "What do I have the right to expect in a marriage?" Many people expect a marriage to be near perfect. They are conditioned from early childhood to have certain expectations. Finding the "right" person automatically means marital *ecstasy;* myths suggesting the *bliss* of marriage are replayed at every wedding ceremony; and even the religious vows are to *always* love, honor, and cherish. You probably have to look no further than your own fantasies to understand this subtle programming.

Does this mean having high expectations is wrong? No! But the key is how people react when they fail to reach all of their expectations. Lovers need the exciting challenge of pursuing their ideals, but they have to be ready to accept less than the perfect marriage.

Other individuals err by not expecting enough in a relationship. There are certain rights and privileges that every person has. In our society men and women have the right to not be physically or emotionally abused, to expect sexual fidelity, to be treated with respect and dignity, and to have the freedom to pursue some individual interests. If a person is denied these fundamental rights, he or she should question the marital relationship. People have the right to walk away from an intolerable marriage.

There is a difference, however, between the individual who refuses to accept an intolerable marriage and one who refuses to accept anything less than an idealistic fantasy of marriage. This is the distinction you will be making as you ask the question, "Are my expectations for my relationship reasonable? Do I have the right to demand changes, or am I simply being spoiled and selfish?"

It is easy to vacillate as you struggle with this question. The factors can be as basic as the welfare of the children, as trivial as a person's physical appearance, as specific as the painful memories of an affair, as global as the quality of love, as practical as matters of finances, and as intimate as the intensity of sexual feelings. One moment you feel you have the right to expect more from your relationship; the next moment you have serious doubts. After all, other people are adjusting to less than what you have. Despite the confusion, however, the expectations issue is crucial, one you will start to answer as you consider two key questions.

1. What are your expectations regarding happiness in a marriage? Do you think an engaged couple would marry if some expert told them, "You will be happy 95 percent of the time and unhappy 5 percent of the time." The answer is usually a resounding yes! But how does this same couple respond when they actually experience unhappiness 5 percent of the time in their marriage? They react as if they should be happy 100 percent of the time and dwell on the 5 percent negative incidents until these experiences assume a disproportionate amount of emphasis within the relationship.

An excellent question to ask yourself as you examine your relationship is, "Do we still have good times together?" Sometimes the quality of the positive times is a better barometer of the relationship than the frequency of the struggling times. The marriage that has 5 percent struggling times and 95 percent neutral times may be in more difficulty than the relationship that has 10 percent struggling times, 70 percent neutral times, and 20 percent good times. Even though the second relationship has twice the ratio of difficult times, there is more hope for this marriage because of the happy times. The good times become the incentive for making the necessary changes.

When I counsel married couples, I often ask them to alternate finishing five incomplete sentences. Each sentence has to be completed several times, and the listener is not allowed to respond unless it is a request for clarification. There can be no defending, justifying, or retaliating. The cardinal rule is simply to listen. The five sentences they alternate saying to each other are:

1. One thing I appreciate (like, admire) in you is _____ .
2. One thing I do not appreciate (dislike, resent) in you is _____ .
3. I try to please you by _____ .
4. I show my displeasure by _____ .
5. As I look at you right now, I see _____ .

Couples probably assume I am focusing mainly on their negative statements when I listen to them. They could not be more wrong. I know they have troubles, or they would not be coming for counseling. I am listening to see if they still are able to express positive feelings to each other. What I want to know is if there are still reasons for remaining together, for committing to the marriage. The lack of good times together may be more significant than the percentage of negative times. Love and hate are not at the opposite ends of the spectrum in an intimate relationship. Love and hate are on the same end; indifference is on the other end. You have to have some positive feelings in order to have intense negative feelings. Indifference (the absence of positives) is the red flag. The lack of positive feelings is a more pessimistic sign for a relationship than a buildup of negative feelings.

How much happiness are you now experiencing in your relationship? What percentage of the time do you have a positive experience? Fill in the appropriate percentages.

_____ % Positive times
_____ % Neutral times
_____ % Negative times
=100 %

Compare this analysis of your relationship with what you want in an intimate relationship. Strive to be honest as you take this introspective look; only an honest assessment will help you clarify the expectation issue. Fill in the percentages that match your expectations for happiness in a marriage.

_____ % Positive times
_____ % Neutral times
_____ % Negative times
=100 %

Now compare what you have (current relationship) with what you want (expectations). Which do you think needs to be changed in order to find your personal happiness?

2. *What are your expectations regarding personal needs in a marriage?* Maslow, a humanistic psychologist, talks about the "hierarchy of needs." His five major classifications of human needs are (a) security, (b) love, (c) a sense of belonging, (d) self-esteem, and (e) self-actualization.

Marriage helps meet these needs. A marriage that does not meet any personal needs is not really a marriage. A commitment to this type of barren relationship is, at best, a rigid holding to legalistic religious principles and, at worst, irrational and sick. Why have a relationship that does not fulfill any basic needs?

Consider each of Maslow's five categories of needs and your expectations for meeting those needs within your marriage. As you look at your expectations, please realize that it is possible to err in either direction. You could be expecting too much from the relationship, or you could be settling for too little.

- ***Security.*** Marriage creates an ongoing relationship and provides a companion who can help take care of you. Security is what you feel as you drive into your garage on a dark, stormy night, knowing you soon will be safely inside your home and have the emotional closeness of another person.

  Some people look to their marital partner for all of their security needs. Those individuals predictably have greater security expectations in their marriages than the individuals who also look to themselves (the inner strength to cope with and survive whatever happens) or other people (friends and family who genuinely care) to form a security base.

- ***Love.*** Everybody desires love. To deny this need is to deny your very essence. You have to look no further than your own experiences to appreciate the emotional high that comes from being genuinely loved and the emotional low that develops when love is lost.

  Some people use marriage as the exclusive source of love (some make a virtue out of this belief) and believe that friends or outside interests take away from this love. When they do this, the spouse becomes totally responsible for the love needs, a potentially dangerous situation (see next chapter).

- ***A sense of belonging.*** Marriage provides a sense of belonging. "Hi, I am Mrs. John Jones, my husband is the . . .," reflects some women's sense of identity through their husbands. This can be positive, but it can also be shaky if the husband is the sole source of belonging. The wise person also uses career, children, church, friends, professional associations, neighbors, and/or hobbies to develop a sense of belonging.

- ***Self-esteem.*** Self-esteem is a sense of personal worth, a liking of oneself. People with positive self-esteem can be their own best friend. When there is a momentary lack of positive feedback from other people, their self-esteem remains high because they can draw from their own battery of positive self-talk.

  Some people rely heavily on their marriage for feelings of self-esteem—the marriage is the base for developing self-worth. The most well-adjusted people, however, also rely on themselves for feelings of self-esteem. They bring their own sense of worth to the relationship.

- ***Self-actualization.*** Self-actualization is maximizing one's potential—a desire to develop one's talents and abilities in a positive and creative fashion. Self-actualization is evident as the artist creates the painting, the businessperson develops an innovative marketing outlet, or the parent skillfully raises a young child to face the complexities of this world.

Security, love, belonging, self-esteem, and self-actualization are vital needs for any healthy individual. These needs have to be met, some through the marriage, some outside the marriage.

Where do you expect to meet these needs? Complete the following charts to clarify this question. (Please note that A + B should equal 100 percent and C + D should equal 100 percent in each row.)

	A Percent of need I would like to have met in the marriage	B Percent of need I would like to have met outside the marriage
Security		
Love		
A sense of belonging		
Self-esteem		
Self-actualization		

This is what you want. Now list what you have in your marriage.

	C Percent of need currently being met in the marriage	D Percent of need currently being met outside the marriage
Security		
Love		
A sense of belonging		
Self-esteem		
Self-actualization		

Carefully compare what you have with what you have been consciously (or subconsciously) wanting—your expectations. You may find the comparisons enlightening.

Your expectations can play a dramatic role in the commitment issue. Unreasonable expectations in your intimate relationship may directly contribute to your unhappiness. Fortunately, expectations are one of the easiest things to alter. Revising one's expectations can often be smoothly accomplished once a person truly accepts the fact that the previous expectations were unrealistic. Accepting the fact that no one relationship will provide 100 percent happiness and no one person will meet all your personal needs creates a climate for positive change.

If your expectations are unreasonable, change them so you can renew your commitment to your marriage. If your expectations are reasonable, you are now ready to ask for relationship changes, ones that a "committed" person actively and forcefully strives to make before he or she considers other alternatives.

CHAPTER 13

Competency

Competency is the most inner-directed of the five C's. Chemistry, caring, communication, and commitment focus on dimensions in your intimate relationship. Competency focuses primarily on qualities within *you*.

The questions surrounding the first four C's usually sound like:

- "To what degree does our marriage currently have these four essential elements?"
- "Which of the four C's is most responsible for the happiness we have in our marriage?"
- "What chemistry, caring, communication, and commitment strategies could we devise to improve our relationship?"

The questions surrounding the fifth C are more personal; they look at each individual rather than the relationship.

- "Does my current level of self-esteem enhance or retard the positive aspects of our marriage?"
- "Do I now possess the ability to be sharing, compassionate, loving, faithful, and sensuous?"
- "Am I able to regulate my moments of jealousy, insecurity, and emotional blues?"

In crumbling marriages, the competency factor raises the issue, "Is the poor marital relationship causing my personal unhappiness, *or* is my personal unhappiness creating the marital difficulty?" This can be a complex and tricky question.

If the marital difficulty is an incompatibility between you and your spouse, a divorce could solve the problem. You could try again in a new relationship after an adequate adjustment period. Many people have been in marriages that involved *relationship* problems; they found that those problems did not resurface in their second marriage.

But what if the difficulty in your marriage is a result of your personal problems? What have you gained by the divorce? The insecurity, jealousy, or feelings of nothingness are not resolved. A new relationship may seem at first to resolve the personal conflicts, but the odds are great that the same problems will reappear as the marriage settles into a normal routine. The personal factors that created conflicts in the first marriage will also affect the second marriage. And it may be worse this time because of other second-marriage complications.

Competency also plays a major role in happy marriages. A person with high personal competency can enhance the emotional peaks in a marriage and level off or avoid the valleys.

Picture a standard car battery. This represents your personal happiness energy source. Now mentally divide this battery in half. One side has a big R, which represents relationships. The other side has a big S, for self.

The relationship portion contains the personal happiness you obtain from a positive relationship. It is recharged by the love, caring, sharing, and fun in your relationship. The self section represents the personal happiness you obtain from yourself. It is energized by your positive self-talk, belief in your worth, positive self-esteem, and being your own best friend.

Competent people are a balance between S and R. They are not totally self-contained. They are not superman or superwoman with a big red S on their chest. If they were, why bother even having a relationship? But they are also not totally dependent on the relationship. If they were, they would be too vulnerable, needy, and insecure when the relationship has a momentary struggle.

To repeat, the competent person is a balance between needing the relationship and being self-contained. When the relationship is going great, the dial can be set fully on the relationship. Most of the energy and personal happiness can come from that half of the battery. It is an easy and fun side. But when the relationship portion of the personal happiness battery is on low energy, the competent person quickly flips the dial to self-containment. This now becomes the source of continuing personal happiness and a powerful problem solver for fixing the relationship side of the battery.

One of my clients, who had done some excellent work on developing self-reliance, pulled out a well-worn card upon which she had copied a saying from a magazine. She showed me the quotation and said, "I knew this quotation had some special meaning for me when I placed it in my purse years ago, but now for the first time I understand the real meaning of it." The card read:

> You cannot be given a life by someone else. Of all the people you will know in a lifetime, you are the only one you will never leave or lose. To the question of life, you are the only answer; to the problems of life, you are the only solution.
>
> Author unknown

Is It "Me" or Is It the Relationship?

There are some marriages in which one of the partners is totally responsible for the strain in the loving relationship. Difficulties erupt because the husband or wife is unable to handle his or her personal emotions. The marital conflicts may have the surface appearance of being a "relationship" problem, but the primary cause stems directly from the individual's personal struggles. The spouse may react to his or her mate's emotional struggles in a less than ideal fashion, but even when the spouse responds with the patience of Job, the compassion of a loving grandmother, the loyalty of a best friend, and the virtue of a saint, the marriage is literally destroyed by the mate's personal problems.

"Is the difficulty I am experiencing in my marriage the result of conflicts within myself, or is it the result of conflicts between the two of us?" This question is one of the most complicated of the marital issues. Many faulty decisions to divorce are made because it was easier to blame the relationship than to admit there was something wrong with "me." Likewise, many marriages that could have a loving ecstasy are sentenced to mediocrity because of personal struggles within one or both of the partners.

How do you distinguish between personal conflicts and relationship conflicts? As the following examples illustrate, it is not always easy.

- Julie is very concerned about her husband's attractive new secretary. Her frequent questions and subtle accusations are creating mounting tension in the marriage. Are Julie's suspicions justified, or do they stem from her personal struggles with jealousy?

- Tom has been emotionally down for several weeks. He is experiencing a deep depression—a real feeling of nothingness. The marriage seems flat, boring, and dull. Is the dull marriage causing his feelings of nothingness, or are the feelings of nothingness (personal depression) making the marriage seem dull?

- John has been unhappy ever since his wife started working. He feels she should stay home and take care of the children, and they have had many serious fights over this issue. Is John really concerned about the children, or is he just feeling insecure because his wife now has more independence and freedom?

The complexities of the question, "Is it me or is it the relationship?" suggest the assistance of a professional therapist. The trained professional could help you sort out the delicate considerations and reduce the potential for self-deception. The therapist does not have *the* answer nor any magic potions to make things better, but he or she could help you obtain insights into what is causing the relationship difficulties. It is hard to develop effective solutions until you have defined the problem.

Throughout my years of therapy and marriage counseling, I have developed a great appreciation for my clients' internal counselor, their inner voice. I still marvel at how accurate and perceptive this inner voice is when it is freely listened to within the safety of a counseling session. It is not the counselor who bestows the insights. The client provides the insights as he or she resists the tendency to shut off the inner voice and carefully listens to this insightful friend. The process is similar to watching a great artist create a beautiful painting.

Your inner voice can speak to you even as you read this book; it can be a wise, valuable counselor. Your inner self-talk alerts you to your role in any marital difficulty; it keeps you aware of your feelings of insecurity, jealousy, and nothingness. Take a moment to reflect on this phenomenon. Recall some of the times that you have listened to your inner voice. Remember how accurate it was.

Your inner voice can become distorted, but you can minimize this distortion if you are aware of some of the reasons why this distortion occurs.

1. A desire to look good in other people's eyes. Most people have been programmed to think it is extremely important to create a favorable impression. "It is absolutely essential to be loved and approved of by virtually everyone in the community," is the clever way Albert Ellis captures our cultural motto. This compelling desire to "look good" creates an inclination to ignore your inner voice as you explain your marital situation to your friends. The comments made to friends and family place a "guilty" verdict on your spouse and an "innocent" verdict on yourself:

"My husband ignores me
—he never shares his
feelings with me,"

    rather than

        "Does my critical
        manner keep him from
        sharing his feelings
        with me?"

"My wife is cold and indifferent—all she does is complain,"

    rather than

        "Do I give her enough
        time? Perhaps I am
        ignoring her."

"I found out that my spouse was having an affair," rather than "Was I partially responsible for him (her) seeking intimacy elsewhere?"

After a while it becomes easier to believe your own statements rather than to listen to your inner voice, especially when you receive such appreciated support from your friends.

2. A tendency to become defensive when attacked. The inner voice is always speaking quietly. It provides analyses, interpretations, and assessments of your contributions to the marital difficulties. This quiet counsel is lost, however, when you are attacked. When confronted, your instinctive response is to defend yourself and protect your vulnerable spots. You vigorously defend yourself even when you know your partner's accusations are accurate. (Perhaps this is when you defend most vigorously.) It seems easier to defend than to agree. You probably have to look no further than your last argument to observe this stifling of your inner voice.

3. A desire to avoid the pain created by the inner voice. When you first start listening to your inner voice, there is a tendency to be too self-blaming and self-depreciating. You find yourself assuming responsibility for all of the marital difficulties as you recall your past personal actions and thoughts. You do not like these feelings, and suddenly you have a strong desire to retreat.

Please do not pull back! There is a logical reason for this initial flooding of negative feelings. Most people have a tendency to avoid the unpleasant; they dam up negative feelings. When you do open up the floodgates, there is the immediate surge of self-depreciating emotions. If you stay with these feelings rather than retreat, however, the initial surge will subside. There will be a natural self-adjustment that places things back in perspective and gives you an accurate picture of the marriage.

The following case illustrates how (a) the desire to look good in other people's eyes, (b) the tendency to become defensive when attacked, and (c) the desire to avoid the pain created by the inner voice all operate to keep a couple from sorting out their personal contributions to their marital difficulties.

In the beginning, Jim and Dora felt extremely lucky to have found each other. They had a special relationship that included chemistry, caring, communication, and commitment. For the first time both felt they were truly in love, and they could not imagine having anything but a happy marriage. Immediately after they married, however, trouble began to surface. The initial problem centered around the amount of time that Jim devoted to his career. Jim thought Saturday was for his career; Dora thought it was for her.

From this innocent beginning there slowly developed an ever-expanding circle of disagreements. By the fourth year of marriage there were several areas of conflict. Dora started feeling rejected and unloved; Jim felt abused and unappreciated. The more Dora became upset, the more Jim withdrew. Jim's withdrawal made Dora feel even more insignificant and devalued. Her expressions of frustration caused Jim to withdraw even further. A destructive snowballing cycle was created.

Both Jim and Dora blamed the other person. Dora said Jim did not show enough love and concern, withdrew rather than discussed their conflicts, and placed everything else ahead of their marriage. Jim felt that Dora never showed any interest in his career, made mountains out of molehills, and was too critical of everything he did.

All outward signs made it appear that Jim and Dora blamed each other for the marital difficulties, but what about their inner voices? What did the wise counsel of their private self-talk say? This inner message did not automatically blame the other person.

Dora knew she struggled with a basic insecurity that had persisted her entire life. She could see the symptoms surfacing once again. Within herself, she realized her fear that Jim preferred his work to her was irrational and unfounded. She knew that many of her verbal attacks were just a release of pent-up emotions, a "protected" way to seek reassurance.

Jim realized that he contributed to the conflict by his tendency to withdraw emotionally. He knew his withdrawal was partially a result of being an adult child of an alcoholic. His unstable relationship with his mother made it very difficult for him to become emotionally vulnerable unless there were vast amounts of loving assurance. Even the slightest criticism started a pull-away reaction.

Both Jim and Dora accurately assessed their personal contributions to the marital conflicts, but they continued to ignore their inner voices in each of three ways discussed earlier.

After friends and relatives became involved, both Jim and Dora wanted to look okay in other people's eyes. Rather than sharing their inner feelings, they mentioned what the other person was doing to make the relationship unfair. Receiving support from friends and relatives made it even easier to feel vindicated and to quiet the inner voice.

Dora tried to keep Jim from withdrawing by forcing communication. Often this was an attacking encounter. Since Jim could not withdraw, his only choice was to retaliate. Many accusations and counteraccusations were made in the heat of the arguments. The time was spent defending against each other's verbal darts, and there was little safe time for listening to the inner voice.

When Jim and Dora did listen to their inner voices, they experienced the initial surge of heavy emotions. Dora felt the full intensity of her basic struggle with insecurity; Jim sensed the gripping fear of being too vulnerable. There was the understandable urge to move away from this position and to avoid the pain. Dora went to a counselor to deal with her pain. Rather than the counselor helping her "stay with these feelings" so she could make the necessary adjustments, the counselor became too supportive. He told her that she should not be so hard on herself. This gave Dora some immediate relief but deprived her of a full examination of her inner voice. Jim was so afraid of his initial reaction to his inner voice that he refused to even go to the counselor.

Fourteen months later Jim and Dora had a long talk. They were able to (a) place the importance of creating a favorable impression in its proper perspective, (b) appreciate the value of a climate which is reasonably free of verbal attacks, and (c) struggle through the agony of feeling 100 percent responsible for the marital difficulty. Listening to their inner voices allowed them to have a candid discussion of their personal contributions to the marital difficulties.

As Jim and Dora had this conversation, there was a resurging of the loving feelings that had originally drawn them together. The beautiful inner voice, once the distortions had been eliminated, gave the answers to the question, "Is it me or the relationship?" The inner voice provided clear solutions to their marital problems.

This sounds like a happy ending for a couple who loved each other very much. Unfortunately, this last conversation between Jim and Dora was a long distance telephone call fourteen months after they separated and eight months after the divorce was final. As they felt the surge of loving feelings, they hung up to avoid further pain. Suddenly, they realized what they had lost by not listening to the inner voice during the marital turmoil.

Perhaps Jim and Dora can still serve a purpose. They can help you realize that you should listen to your inner voice now, not later. Use this powerful resource to take a closer look at any relationship difficulties.

With your wise inner counselor, you will be in a better position to sort out the competency issues. You will improve your ability to distinguish between "me" problems and "relationship" problems and to better determine the true source of three relationship killers: insecurity, jealousy, and nothingness. Once you have this power, you are ready to use your competency to add magic to your marriage.

Insecurity

Insecurity! Learn the full meaning of this word, and your chances of having a happy marriage will improve 100 percent. The successful recognition of one's personal insecurities provides insights matching the beauty of a mountain sunrise; the failure to recognize one's insecurities conceals solutions to marital problems better than the darkness of a moonless night.

Everyone thought Dale and Helen were made for each other. They were committed to each other's happiness and their love was obvious. The first six weeks of the marriage were wonderful. Dale had a special glow as he basked in Helen's love, and friends commented that they had never seen him so happy. Slowly, however, things began to deteriorate as Dale started having doubts. He frequently asked Helen if she loved him.

Despite her spontaneous reassurances, the question would be asked again and again and again.

Soon the "Do you love me?" question was tied into a wide assortment of behaviors. "If you love me, why don't you sit with me when I am watching television? Why did you forget to kiss me when I arrived home (on the rare occasions when Helen did not greet Dale with a kiss)? Why do you work on your projects rather than talk to me?"

Helen attempted to change some of her personal habits, but her husband's list of concerns seemed to get longer and longer. When she did make a change, the next inquiry was, "Why have you changed?" Logical explanations did not suffice, and Helen was becoming more and more frustrated. Dale's demands, questions, and doubts continued, and nothing Helen did seemed to be right. She started dreading even getting a phone call because she could sense Dale's uptightness until she got off the phone and patiently explained who had called and why. Finally, Helen started seeing a therapist. The only problem was that the wrong person was going for therapy.

Dependency is closely related to insecurity. Men are not given permission to show their insecurity through dependency unless it is hidden behind illness or alcoholism. Women, on the other hand, find dependency the most socially acceptable way to express their insecurity. The goal is to find someone who will offer a secure base. Once this person is found, the umbilical cord is inserted, and he is used to provide the necessary protection, safety, and comfort.

This does not mean it is wrong to have a certain degree of dependency. Many marriage counselors describe the ideal marriage as one where there is a mutual interdependence on each other for meeting personal, emotional, and physical needs. Couples who have their personal needs met in the relationship have a special bond. The key, however, is whether the dependency is by choice or out of necessity. Dependency by choice allows a person to revert to a more independent, self-sufficient lifestyle when needed. Dependency out of necessity does not have this option. When one partner is too dependent, the other person may not even feel comfortable getting excited about a career, spending time alone, or talking to someone of the opposite sex.

The dependent person is going to avoid looking like a fool. When the dependent person is struggling with his or her insecurity, he or she is not going to say any of the following statements:

- "You cannot get interested in your job."
- "I want you to always be with me."
- "Never talk to someone of the opposite sex."

Instead, the insecurity is concealed in socially acceptable statements such as:

- "You put your career ahead of me."
- "You never spend any time with me."
- "Remember the time you flirted with Sharon? That is why I am upset when you talk to women."

Unfortunately, the socially acceptable reason only serves to disguise the true reason for the requests. Attempts to alter one's behavior to appease the dependent partner have little benefit because soon there will be another reason manufactured to legitimize the basic feeling of insecurity.

The picture becomes further complicated when an insecure man finds a dependent woman. Now his insecurity is reduced because she "needs him so much," and she feels good because he "takes such good care of her."

Initially, the need systems of the insecure man and the dependent woman may dovetail into a mutually satisfying relationship. The tenuous bond is easily broken, however, when the mutual meeting of needs is disrupted. Often, this disruption can be sparked by a very innocent event such as the birth of a child, a husband's success in his career, a wife going to work, an interesting new hobby, or anything else that gives one of the partners another source for meeting emotional needs. Any change in the insecurity-dependency bond is viewed as a threat. Even counseling, which improves personal security and promotes healthy independence, often initially disrupts rather than improves this type of relationship.

Jealousy

Jealousy knows few boundaries; it can extend to all areas of one's life. Brothers are jealous of each other's accomplishments, a wife is envious of her husband's exciting career, a husband is threatened by the close relationship his wife has with their children, and colleagues are upset by their coworkers' success. In this chapter, however, the discussion on jealousy will be limited to the "green-eyed monster's" concerns about a partner's contact with members of the opposite sex.

You are at a party. An attractive person walks over and begins talking to your spouse. It soon becomes obvious that this person is thoroughly enjoying the conversation with your mate and is finding him or her charming company. As you continue to sneak side-glances, what thoughts race through your mind?

Do you respond with a gripping concern that they might be enjoying each other's company too much? Do you secretly compare yourself unfavorably with this attractive person? Do you try to continue with your own conversation, but find yourself becoming increasingly preoccupied with what is happening with your spouse? Do you struggle with whether you should walk over and join them even though you know they are not doing anything improper? Is there a slight sickening feeling in the pit of your stomach as you feel the sting of jealousy and sense the poison permeating your body? This is jealousy!

Why do people experience jealousy? There are three basic reasons why jealousy may develop in a relationship.

1. The *insecurity* discussed in the last section is often expressed through jealousy. Frequent attempts are made to confirm that one's partner is not interested in someone else. Hundreds of questions are asked accusingly:

    - "Why did you dance with Anne at the party?"
    - "Has George ever shown any special interest in you?"
    - "Was Pat at the conference you attended?"
    - "How do you know he doesn't talk to you simply because he is interested in taking you to bed?"
    - "Is Sharon always this friendly around you?"

        Usually these types of questions are not really asked to detect an illicit involvement; they are merely attempts to reassure the jealous mate. Nevertheless, the accusations take a toll on the relationship. The questions are viewed as attacks on one's character and tend to increase alienation toward the jealous partner. It becomes difficult to maintain a loving attitude when the constant message is, "You are being too flirtatious, not considering my feelings, lacking in good moral judgment, or doing things 'nice' people would not do." The constant probing is nonproductive, regardless of what people have done. If they are not guilty, they will resent the charges; if they are guilty, they will simply become more devious and deceitful.

2. *Projection* means that people see in other people the qualities they have in themselves. For example, a person who is secretly competitive will spot competitiveness in coworkers; the individual who is honest will initially assume someone else is honest; and a person who is disloyal will automatically question his or her friend's loyalty. Until people get sufficient data to the contrary, they often project their beliefs, values, and attitudes onto other people and assume they are the same way.

Your feelings toward members of the opposite sex establish a basis for making assumptions about your spouse. The natural tendency is to assume your partner is having the same feelings and fantasies you are.

If you have a secret desire to "go to bed" with someone,	you have more of a tendency to assume your partner is struggling with the same desire.
If you have an extramarital affair,	you think more about the possibility of your spouse having an affair.
If you enjoy your friends without playing sexual games with them,	

you are more likely to assume your mate is responding in the same way.

A good example of projection is found in a letter written to Ann Landers. The woman asked whether a male friend was correct when he said, "All married men have extramarital affairs." Ann Landers wrote in her column, "No, it is not true that all married men have extramarital affairs, but it probably is true that all married men who say, 'All married men have affairs,' have had affairs themselves."

3. A third basis for jealousy is *reality*. The jealousy is not created by your personal insecurity or projection. In this case it is an accurate assessment of the situation. There is a legitimate reason for feeling jealous because your mate is inappropriately involved with another person. In my opinion, this feeling is really not even jealousy. It is a natural and appropriate emotional response. For example, a husband occasionally being thirty minutes late coming home from work rarely qualifies as a realistic basis for jealousy. His staying out all night, on the other hand, usually does qualify.

Jealousy is very much a part of an intimate relationship. Couples who experience, and then resolve, feelings of jealousy find a special bond being formed. Nothing is so unsettling, or even infuriating, as having a partner who never experiences jealousy. This means there is no vulnerability (Who wants to live with a stone?) or the partner is perfect (Who is comfortable living with a god?). There can be a positive challenge in learning how to successfully handle your struggles with jealousy. Climb this emotional mountain and feel the exhilaration!

Nothingness

Nothingness can be the most deadly of all of the "me" problems. The symptoms of nothingness—depression, flatness, loss of meaning, dullness, and lack of energy—are easily recognized, but the reasons for these negative feelings are difficult to discern. There are telltale signs that provide clues into the "reasons" for the self-defeating struggles with insecurity, smothering tendencies of dependency, or clutching patterns of jealousy. The feelings associated with nothingness are more confusing because they often lack a direct connection to a specific relationship problem. There is no apparent cause for the nothingness, and yet the "blue" emotions are often more incapacitating than the "intense" emotions associated with insecurity, dependency, or jealousy. Attempts to escape the nothingness produce no relief. The individual starts desperately searching for causes for this depressing emotional state.

One leading candidate becomes the marriage. "Perhaps my marriage is the reason I am depressed," is the tentative conclusion. "After all, we have a 'nothing' relationship."

The individual is now faced with a modern-day version of the classical philosophical question, "Which came first—the chicken or the egg?" Did the nothingness (depression) cause the emptiness in the marriage, or did the poor marital relationship cause the personal nothingness?

The best way to attack this question is to examine four possible causes for the feelings of depression:

1. Symptoms of a deeper medical or psychological problem. Diane was very disillusioned with her marriage. She had devoted her life to her husband and children, but now they seemed unappreciative of her efforts. Her husband was deeply involved in his career, and her teenage children were far more interested in their peer groups. Diane felt that she was being taken for granted and being treated like a piece of household furniture. She expressed her feelings to her husband, and he made several changes, but it did not make any difference. Slowly Diane started questioning the quality of her marriage. Surely a "good" marriage would provide more than the dull, depressed feelings she was now experiencing.

Marriage counseling gave no positive results. Likewise, an attempt at a career did not fill the empty void. Diane concluded that divorce was the only solution.

During the middle of the divorce negotiations, Diane went for her annual physical examination. Her physician discovered a biochemical problem and diagnosed Diane as having clinical depression. The psychological symptoms of this medical disorder are sadness, worthlessness, apathy, and little enthusiasm. With proper medication the symptoms disappeared, and suddenly Diane had a new perspective on everything, including her marriage.

A deepening feeling of nothingness (personal depression) needs to be checked out carefully. Sometimes the causes of depression can be complicated and require the services of a specialist. If your depression has any of the following characteristics, you should see a physician to make sure the depression is not a symptom of some major medical or psychological problem:

- Prolonged. You seem to go for days or even weeks without any relief.
- Heavy. The emotional fog has you totally grounded.
- A sense of desperation. You have thoughts of suicide and/or losing yourself in alcohol/drugs.

2. *Repressed emotions.* One popular definition of depression is "anger turned inward"–the anger is bottled up rather than being expressed. Soon a person's emotional energy is spent holding in feelings rather than using the emotional energy to cope with daily stresses and to put a spark into one's life.

Depression is not limited to anger. Emotions can be "bottled up" whenever one:

- Avoids the grief of a death.
- Blocks out the guilt of a misdeed.
- Denies the sadness of a failure.
- Blocks out the pain of a rejection.
- Denies the pangs of jealousy.

It is critical that you realize the possible implications of denying your emotions. Emotions are a vital part of living. Any significant relationship will create occasional feelings of anger, hurt, grief, and pain. If these emotions have available avenues for expression, you will continue to feel alive, maintain a high energy level, and experience continuing personal growth. If these emotions are suppressed, the emotional energy system is stifled. The lessening of emotional expression creates a vacuum that is experienced as nothingness. Eventually, the heaviness of this depression can be more difficult to handle than the feelings that were repressed originally. The empty pit of nothingness becomes larger, deeper, and darker.

How can you shake the feelings of nothingness caused by the blocking of emotions? Perhaps Amy's experience can give you some direction.

Amy went for counseling because she was experiencing a lack of purpose and an emotional flatness in her life. This psychological state was compounded by a painful ulcer condition. Routine inquiries into her marriage quickly revealed a potential problem area. Amy had great difficulty expressing any negative emotions to her husband. She believed that she should always be warm, loving, and accepting in her marriage.

Through counseling, Amy understood what had happened. Amy's mother had carried her emotions on her sleeve and freely expressed her negative feelings. When her mother was a "screaming shrew," Amy was aware, even as a child, that her father was hurt by some of the "hot-tempered" remarks. Amy decided (probably more on the subconscious than the conscious level) that she would never do the same thing in her marriage. She resolved to always keep her negative feelings to herself. The end result was a heavy nothingness that forced her into counseling.

Amy finally began giving herself permission to express her negative emotions. The personal nothingness disappeared, her ulcer healed, and she and her husband started taking constructive steps toward developing a marriage with open communication.

3. Loss of personal worth. Excessive demands can be made on an intimate relationship when there is a loss of personal fulfillment outside the relationship. When the relationship does not offset the loss of self-esteem, there is a compounding of the feelings of nothingness. Soon the relationship is caught up in the web.

James retired from the military after a distinguished twenty-five-year career. Still in the prime of life, he looked forward to being able to do exactly what he wished. The first two months were great, but then the days slowly began to drag. James became bored, lethargic, restless.

Suddenly, his life had no purpose. No one was relying on him for assistance, advice, or direction; no one requested his mature judgment. Inquiries into possible job openings only compounded the feelings. Potential career opportunities were far below his previous accomplishments as an army officer and offered little challenge. James had been stripped of his personal worth through retirement, and it was being replaced by a void.

James turned to his marriage; he expected his wife to fill this newly created vacuum. When the intimate relationship did not "take up the slack," there developed growing dissatisfaction with the marriage; soon it was blamed for the void. "My wife is not as exciting as she used to be," is the observation he recently shared with a close friend.

James blames the trouble on a lack of chemistry, but the real culprit is personal depression. Unless he realizes how his loss of personal worth is affecting his marriage, divorce attorneys may soon be collecting one more legal fee.

Always strive to have a degree of personal worth outside your intimate relationship. Rather than taking from your relationship, it will enhance your relationship.

4. *A poor marriage.* Personal factors unrelated to a marriage may cause a depression that attacks a marriage insidiously and subtly. Sometimes, however, it is the marital relationship that triggers the depression.

Heidi was struggling with feelings of emptiness. She did not, however, automatically blame her marriage to Keith. Instead, she carefully checked out the possibility of the depression being a "me" problem. She determined that the struggle was not the result of a medical or psychological complication. A diagnostic evaluation ruled out medical or deep-seated emotional problems. Nor was it repression of feelings, as Heidi freely expressed her concerns. She experienced much satisfaction in all other areas of her personal life, so a loss of personal worth was ruled out also.

The depression came from the marriage. Keith's basic way of relating to Heidi was through a passive, do-nothing approach. He would express his dissatisfaction by emotionally withdrawing, show his anger by remaining aloof, and respond to requests for more closeness by acting indifferent. In effect, Keith was trying to manipulate Heidi by withholding his love and affection.

Heidi finally did receive relief from the nothingness. After repeated attempts to make changes in the relationship (all of which Keith refused to go along with in his passive, do-nothing way), Heidi filed for divorce. Once the divorce adjustment period was over, Heidi noticed the nothingness had disappeared.

When the marital relationship is the cause of the nothingness, something has to be done about the marriage. Heidi's solution was divorce. Other couples, in similar situations, have said, "We have no choice but to make changes in our marriage—changes that will reduce the nothingness."

Once a person adequately understands the reasons for his or her personal depression, he or she is much closer to knowing what steps to take to reduce this debilitating emotion. The search for this key is not easy, but the potential payoff makes it worthwhile. The other unacceptable alternatives are to simply stay locked into your nothingness or to make an impulsive decision, one based on inadequate data.

How does a person prevent excessive insecurity, jealousy, and nothingness? How does a person create a high level of personal competency and add an adequate S (self) side to the personal happiness battery to compliment the R (relationship) side? One of the most powerful ways to accomplish this is to make sure that you have a positive self-image. This is what gives you the personal power.

Self-esteem plays a major role in any struggle with insecurity, jealousy, or nothingness. The truism, "You cannot be loved by someone else more than you love yourself," captures a fundamental principle within any intimate relationship. If you have a positive self-image, there is the natural assumption that you are prized by your partner, and you believe this until there is strong evidence to the contrary. Any ambiguous situation is automatically given a positive interpretation. Conversely, if you have a negative self-image, your assumption (unless proven to the contrary on a frequent and continuous basis) is that your partner really does not find you desirable. All other people and situations become more of a threat.

Having positive self-esteem does not "just happen." But it is within your power to have this personal competency, a power that is discussed in the next chapter as you learn how to change your M.E.

• CHAPTER 14 •

Competency and the M.E.

Anne and Rebecca both thought that they had solid, happy marriages. They were shocked when their husbands suddenly announced they wanted divorces. No reasons were given by either husband other than the vague, "I do not find our marriage exciting anymore," and "I want more out of life than I'm getting." The marital situations were almost identical, but Anne and Rebecca's reactions to the proposed divorces were in sharp contrast.

Anne responded by verbally attacking her husband.

Rebecca responded by searching for the reasons for the sudden change in her husband's attitude.

Anne was hurt and emotionally closed off her loving feelings.

Rebecca was hurt but continued to risk being emotionally vulnerable.

Anne focused on her husband's moral character and tried to make him feel guilty.

Rebecca focused on what *she* could do to save the marriage.

Both women experienced tremendous personal pain. Rebecca actually felt deeper pain because she remained emotionally vulnerable and continued to reach out to her husband without placing undue demands or pressure on him.

The end results were very different. Anne's marriage ended in divorce. Her reaction to her husband was "justified," but it still contributed significantly to the eventual demise of the marital relationship. Rebecca's marriage improved. It became better than it had been for the past five years despite the emotional upheaval created by the conflict. Her reaction to the situation preserved the marriage rather than adding to the difficulty. What was the difference between Anne and Rebecca? The difference was that Rebecca had a positive M.E. and Anne did not!

A positive M.E. is not limited to the way that people resolve marital difficulties. A positive M.E. affects all aspects of an intimate relationship. A positive M.E. can have a tremendous impact on your marriage.

With a positive M.E., you have a healthy self-reliance, a good balance between dependence and independence.

With a negative M.E., you become overly dependent, and tend to cling and smother.

With a positive M.E., you face difficulties in your relationship.

With a negative M.E., you tend to ignore marital difficulties.

With a positive M.E., you are willing to initiate— to reach out to your mate.

With a negative M.E., you wait for your mate to take the first step.

With a positive M.E., you are less sensitive to criticism.

With a negative M.E., there is a tendency to overpersonalize every criticism.

With a positive M.E., you worry less about the future and feel confident that you can handle whatever happens.

With a negative M.E., you find hundreds of things to worry about and dwell on each one of them.

By this time you probably are thinking, "Okay! Okay! I concede, a positive M.E. is terrific; now please tell me what M.E. stands for." Your M.E. is your "mind's eye." Your mind's eye is your self-image. It is the psychological, emotional, and mental center around which most of your feelings, attitudes, behaviors, and perceptions revolve.

The Mind's Eye

Your mind's eye is a powerful controlling force in your personal life, in your relationships with other people, and in your relationship with your mate. This is why the task of altering your mind's eye becomes one of the most exciting, challenging, and rewarding endeavors that you will ever attempt. Improving your mind's eye is one of the best things that you will ever do for yourself, and for the special person in your life.

Imagine there is a movie screen on the wall in front of you. Flash a mental picture of yourself on this screen. This is your mind's eye. Simply stated, your mind's eye or self-image is a collage of personal perceptions, the mental pictures of yourself that you constantly carry with you.

What is your current mind's eye? Answer the following questions to put these pictures into sharper focus.

1. How do you see yourself physically? How do you feel about your hair, eyes, nose, teeth, face, legs, waist, height,

and general physical build? This is your mind's eye of your physical appearance. Feedback from others influences your perceptions, but you also tend to depreciate, deny, or ignore comments that do not correspond with your own self-perceptions.

2. Do you like your personality? Are you outgoing, reserved, self-confident, easy to talk to, self-centered, interested in other people, moody, warm, and so on? What mental pictures do you have of your personality?

3. How successful are you? How do you feel about your accomplishments in your career, your hobbies, and other endeavors? Are you satisfied with your role as a student, parent, and homemaker?

4. What is your value system? Do you like what you stand for? Is there a congruence between your personal beliefs and the way you act, or do you vaguely realize that you often have to rationalize your behavior? Are you proud of your beliefs about honesty, loyalty, trustworthiness, and integrity?

5. How good a marriage partner are you? Are you willing to both give and receive love? Do you treat your mate the way you would like to be treated?

6. What is your personal security? Do you have the emotional resources to adapt to new situations, cope with rejection, and make adjustments when your life is altered through illness, death, or other tragedies? Do you have the inner strength to handle the emotional turmoil of modern living without being overly dependent on other people?

7. Do you like the way you show genuine caring and concern to your friends? Would you like your friends to be the same type of friend you are?

These mental perceptions combine to form your current mind's eye. When these mental pictures are positive, you have a tendency to respond positively to other people. When these mental pictures are negative, the inevitable result is a more cautious, hesitating response to the significant people in your life, including your special love.

If you have a low self-image, you will tend to magnify your limitations and minimize your personal strengths. One physical flaw, personality shortcoming, talent limitation, or past failure will generalize to lower your entire sense of worth. Having a positive self-image, on the other hand, allows you to override this tendency and keep things in perspective. You celebrate your strengths and accept your limitations. And you trust that your partner can do the same.

If a marriage is truly "bad," it does not make any difference whether a person has a positive M.E. or a negative M.E. The relationship is going to be unpleasant or even destructive. Likewise, if a marriage is "ideal," even a person with a low self-image will probably find happiness. But in the broad gray area between the destructive relationship and the ideal relationship, one's self-image often directly determines what happens in the marriage.

As mentioned in chapter 9, true intimacy only happens when people share their personal thoughts, values, feelings, and attitudes (the real self). If you have a positive self-image, you will find it easier to risk sharing with your mate. The natural fear of sharing your real self is greatly intensified, however, if *you* do not accept your personal qualities. If you do not have a good self-image, your automatic assumption is that the better your partner knows you, the more he or she will see you the same way that you perceive yourself.

Self-Talk and Imagery

Contrary to the assumption made by many people, your mind's eye is not simply a passive reflection of what is happening in your life. Your mind's eye is an *active agent* that controls how you interpret and respond to most interpersonal relationships.

I recall an expression that was the favorite theme of my professor of abnormal psychology: "Always remember," he would intonate, "intellect is a speck on the sea of emotions." Using the basic tenets of Freudian psychoanalysis, we learned that the id is the driving force in our personality, and the fragile ego is always struggling to keep these powerful emotional impulses under control. At times, the ego is partially successful, but usually success is measured in degrees of failure. The message was loud and clear. Emotions are king, and our poor intellect is usually fighting a losing battle.

This same philosophy has drifted into our everyday thinking. Most people feel at the mercy of their emotions. They struggle with stress, anxiety, and depression but feel powerless to do anything about changing these feelings. They hope the emotions will just "go away."

Fortunately, there has been a reversal in this thinking. Some psychologists have begun to challenge this concept. They have said, "Wait just a minute! The reverse may be true! Perhaps it is our thoughts that control our emotions. If we think irrationally and illogically, we will be ineffective, unhappy, and incompetent. If we think in a logical and rational manner, our emotions will follow. We can *choose* to be effective, happy, and competent."

Try the following experiment:

1. Close your eyes and recall a negative, unpleasant event that you have experienced in your life.

2. Notice how you feel as you recall this experience. Do you suddenly feel sad, upset, or unhappy?

3. Now close your eyes again and recall a positive, pleasant event that you have experienced in your life.

4. Notice how you feel now. Make note of these happy, joyful, and pleasant emotions.

5. Go back to the unpleasant event. Dwell on it. Note your emotional state.

6. Now return to the pleasant event. Let your thoughts focus on this experience. Again monitor your emotional feelings.

This activity illustrates the relationship between your thoughts and your emotions. Your thought processes influence your emotional state. If you control your thought processes, you determine your emotional well-being. This is true for previous events in your life, and it also affects your current emotional reaction to other people.

Ready for some simple logic? Negative self-talk is going to lower your mind's eye . . . and positive self-talk is going to raise your M.E.

There is a direct relationship between self-talk, imagery, the subconscious mind, and the mind's eye. This will be explained in more detail later, but one simple way to understand the relationship between self-talk and the mind's eye is to form a picture of an assayer's scales (the kind used to weigh gold and other precious metals). The right arm on the scales is for positive self-talk and the left arm represents negative self-talk. Every time you give yourself a positive comment, you place some weight on the positive arm and your mind's eye becomes slightly more positive. Every time you give yourself a negative comment (self-talk), you place a weight on the negative side of the scales and your mind's eye becomes slightly more negative.

The analogy may appear trite, but the impact is powerful when one realizes this dialogue is not restricted to the conscious mind. Your weights (self-talk) form mental images that are programmed into your powerful subconscious mind. These images are constantly influencing the "truths" stored in your subconscious mind, truths that form the core of your mind's eye. Each piece of "innocent" self-talk has its unique influence on your mind's eye via the subconscious mind.

$P + E = R$. Remember this formula—it can have a major impact on your mind's eye. The wise use of this formula can dramatically change your self-image and enhance your personal competency in your intimate relationship.

> P — stands for Pictures
> E — represents Emotions
> R — equals Reality in the subconscious mind

The powerful principle contained in this formula is that the subconscious mind cannot distinguish between what is vividly imagined and what actually happens in a person's life. The conscious mind makes this distinction, but the subconscious mind does not. *If you vividly imagine something, it has the same impact on the subconscious mind as if it actually happened.*

What a powerful tool this can be! Perhaps this gives additional meaning to the biblical expression, "As a man thinketh in his heart, so is he," or to what Henry Ford said, "Whether you think you can or can't, you are right."

The secret to $P + E = R$ is developing a better awareness of your self-talk. Your apparently innocent moments of self-talk have greater significance than you realize. Your words turn into pictures. The pictures, with the accompanying emotions, flow into the subconscious mind. These imageries soon become *the truth*, and once this reality is locked into the subconscious mind, an energizing drive is established. It activates the powerful subconscious mind, and the new "truths" soon become *the way* of behaving.

Imagery already has a very powerful impact on your life. Unfortunately, you now probably use imagery in a random, unplanned, often negative way. You need to start using this powerful tool in a planned, positive way.

The Power of Self-Talk

Try the following homework assignment for one month to test the effectiveness of positive imagery. At the end of the month, you can be the judge of how well imagery works for you. Remember, however, you will be giving $P + E = R$ a fair test only if you do the imageries for the entire month.

Focus on yourself. Change your mind's eye by using the following three-step approach:

1. Monitor your self-talk during six separate ten-minute time blocks. Use a note card (divided into a negative and positive side) to record the number of self-references. It does not matter whether they are shared with others or merely silently said to yourself. Make a tick mark (lllll) each time you have a positive or negative thought about yourself. After you have completed this activity, total up your marks. If you have more positive marks, congratulate yourself and continue this self-talk pattern. If you have more negative marks (and most people do), you have just discovered one reason why you struggle with a negative self-image.

2. Make a list of positive qualities that you have. Use 3-inch by 5-inch cards to record the following characteristics:

- Two achievements you are proud of.
- Two physical features you like in yourself.
- Two personal talents you appreciate.
- Two qualities that make you a good friend.
- Two ways you are a thoughtful person.
- Two positive parenting qualities.
- Two inner qualities that reflect your best inner essence.
- Two reasons why people like being around you.
- Five ways in which you are a good husband or wife.

Notice how refreshing it is to focus on what you do well rather than limiting yourself to what you do poorly.

3. Look at these cards several times a day. Notice how your internal dialogue improves as you use this structured approach to insure positive self-talk. Now carry the process one step further. As you focus on your positive characteristics, create vivid mental pictures in your mind. See yourself with each quality. These images flow into your subconscious mind as truths. This happens because—and this cannot be emphasized enough—the subconscious mind does not distinguish between vividly imagined material and actual reality. Your conscious mind makes the distinction, but your subconscious mind (a powerful programmer of your mind's eye) treats the vivid imagery with the same authenticity that it gives to actual behavior. This is the powerful effect of self-talk!

Now make up another set of cards for your marriage. Establish 3-inch by 5-inch cards in each of the following areas:

- Recall four times when you were especially close, loving, and intimate.

- Remember three times when you had fun together. Capture these feelings for a moment.

- Recall three incidents when there was a real ego extension, an emotional involvement with your mate (similar to what a parent may feel for a well-performing child).

- Reflect upon a couple of really good sexual encounters together.

- Capture the memories of how you successfully resolved two conflicts and how you felt about being able to solve the difficulties.

- Recall three incidents when there was caring in your relationship, when you really took care of each other's needs.

- Remember two times when you were very giving to your mate; recall the sincere expression of appreciation on his or her face.

At this moment you have to make a *critical* decision. Either you can read on, or you can stop and actually make the cards and create the imageries. If you limit yourself to reading the chapter, the impact will be minimal. If you experience the vivid imageries, you will have *maximized* the value of $P + E = R$.

A French proverb says, "Be careful what you wish for, for it will surely happen." As you glance at your cards several times each day, you will create powerful imageries. Dynamic pictures will consistently flow into your subconscious mind, and your mind's eye will automatically start operating on these new internalized "truths." You will soon have your own proverb that says, "Celebrate what you think about (imagery), because it will soon become a part of your marriage."

A bonus is that a positive M.E. gives you the personal competency to celebrate a relationship of psychological freedom . . . and the beautiful relationships are always ones of freedom.

> I want to love you without clutching,
> appreciate you without judging,
> join you without invading,
> invite you without demanding,
> leave you without guilt,
> criticize you without blaming,
> and help you without insulting.
> If I can have the same from you,
> then we can truly meet and enrich each other.
> Virginia Satir

• CHAPTER 15 •

Summary to the Relationship Section

Some people are blessed. For them, life is an adventure. This is also what I want for you. An exciting adventure as you continue to discover new ways to build

Chemistry,

Caring,

Communication,

Commitment, and

Competency

in your marriage.

The past twelve chapters are just the beginning, the tip of the iceberg. Now pick up the ball and run! Attend the seminars, read the books, watch the TV specials, listen to the radio talk shows, observe the happy marriages, pursue marital counseling, and most important, trust your own instincts as you self-discover how to create greater and greater intimacy. Make it your energizing challenge to celebrate more chemistry, caring, communication, commitment, and competency in your marriage.

This is the true essence of the first magical path!

· PART II ·

CAREER

The Second Magical Path

• CHAPTER 16 •

How Was Your Day?

Your career is probably the most undervalued of the three magical paths. Most people readily accept the importance of having a loving relationship and, at the very least, acknowledge the importance of having a mission for their life. But liking your career? No, that is pushing it too far. You just put up with your career; you use it to give yourself the necessities and pleasures of life; you live with the blue Mondays, the midweek hump, and TGIF. You wait for the day you can "take that job and shove it."

How sad and how damaging a point of view this is! Your career may be *the* critical factor in your quest for personal happiness. A simple look at a typical daily schedule should offer irrefutable proof:

6:30 – 7:30 (one hour) – Get ready for work.
7:30 – 8:00 (one-half hour) – Drive to work.
8:00 – 5:00 (nine hours) – Do your job and have lunch.
5:00 – 5:30 (one-half hour) – Drive home from work.
5:30 – 7:00 (one and one-half hours) – Greet the family, crash, get dinner ready, and eat.
7:00 – 10:00 (three hours) – Clean the house, focus on work-related issues, escape into TV, and spend two minutes in good conversation with your children and spouse.
10:00–11:00 (one hour) – Get ready for bed, watch the news, and grieve the retirement of Johnny Carson one more time.

11:00–11:01 (one minute) – Think about making love but quickly reject the idea. You are too tired physically (10 percent) and too exhausted mentally (90 percent) because your job is an emotional drain rather than an energizer.

Examine this schedule carefully and you will notice that eight hours are spent working, one hour is spent driving while thinking about work (or dreading it), one hour is spent eating with work associates, and up to two more hours are spent getting ready for work, crashing from the work, or doing after-hours work assignments. In other words, twelve hours a day are work related.

Can you even fathom the difference in emotional well-being between the people who "love" their work and the people who endure their work? This is one major reason why liking your career is so important. You spend more time on your career path, good or bad, than the other two psychological paths combined. If you do not find some happiness there, it will put an extra burden on your marriage and/or mission for finding happiness.

Liking What You Do

An interesting question is, "If you suddenly won or inherited a large sum of money, would you still continue in your career?" If your answer is something short of a yes, it could suggest that you truly do not like what you do in your career arena.

On the *Tonight Show* Johnny Carson once asked an alert and animated George Burns, the famous cigar-chomping comedian, then ninety-five years old, "What is your secret to happiness?" Burns answered, "The most important thing is to fall in love with what you are doing."

Burns's comment also triggered a note from a friend of mine who read an early draft of this book. He wrote:

> "I treasure George Burns's comment, and I know there is a significant truth in those words. I know because I have experienced it in my life. I have been fortunate enough to have a love affair with my career. In many respects, it has been my most consistent path for finding personal happiness.

I have known a lot of joy in personal relationships, but there have also been periods in my life when I have experienced deep pain. Likewise, with my sense of mission. At times, I have had a real connection with my soul, and I have experienced the surging waves of joy that these giving experiences can provide. But there have also been times when I have slipped off the mission path and not used this available avenue as well as I could have.

The bread and butter for me has been my career. Naturally, I have moments when my career is bland, stressful, or routine. But this is more than offset by moments when I learn, grow, and create through the challenges of my job. I truly have found a career that gives me immense personal satisfaction. In no way will I ever minimize the importance of this psychological path in my finding happiness."

Shake the old cultural programming that a job is just a means to an end. Instead, make it your ardent goal to have your career become a real source of emotional well-being. Create a job climate that allows you to wake up in the morning looking forward to going to work and to drive home at the end of the day with a sense of fulfillment and personal accomplishment. There are three different ways that you can make this happen.

1. Creatively coping with job stress. To more fully appreciate the relationship between stress and personal happiness, picture a bouncy, energetic, bubbly eighteen-month-old boy. Notice the natural enthusiasm and wide-eyed interest. See his desire to touch, explore, and enjoy. Hear his utterances of delight as he plays with a friendly dog.

Now it is three weeks later, and this same child has the flu. What is your mental picture of this child now? See the listless, apathetic, dragging-around demeanor. Notice the total absence of the enthusiastic energy and joyful squeals. Hear the whiny, complaining little voice. All he does is sleep and mope around.

It is four weeks later. He has completely recovered from the influenza. Now what is his disposition? It is not surprising that all the enthusiasm, energy, and excitement have returned. He is again playfully chasing after his dog.

Job stress can impact in the same way. You have a natural built-in energy system that allows you to interact with life in a high-energy manner. But the flulike qualities of job stress can flatten you emotionally.

It may be a sign of what is happening in the business world that I listed job stress as the first strategy for liking what you do on your job. Maybe the best way to make your career a positive experience is to remove the excessive stress and recapture your natural enthusiasm and energy.

2. *Being well-matched with your career.* Selecting the right career is similar to selecting the right marriage partner. You could be the perfect lover, have a wonderful value system, and possess a superb self-image—and still be miserable if married to the wrong person. The same thing is true for your career selection. You could be the most dedicated, loyal, ambitious, and intelligent employee in the world—and still be miserable if you have a career mismatch.

I have to look no further than myself to appreciate this fact. When I enrolled in college, I declared my major as preengineering. The United States was in the middle of a space race with Russia and needed engineers. This was the hot profession, and everyone said I should choose engineering because I was "so good in math."

Fortunately, I was able to correct this mistake before it was too late. I, quite by accident, discovered psychology. The change meant I graduated a summer school session later than my class, but I found a profession that I love. Every morning I wake up eager to counsel, write, speak, or consult. This would not have been the case had I stayed with engineering. I would have been one unhappy engineer because my interests, personality, and aptitudes clearly do not match that profession. I still shudder when I realize that I could have ended up in a career that was such a personal mismatch.

3. *Positive relationships on the job.* We thrive on close, interpersonal relationships. When we have caring, loving, and sharing connections with other people, we feel joy. When we have strained, competitive, hostile, or phony involvements, we pay an emotional price no matter how hard we try not to let it bother us. The curt comment, the cutting edge of a voice tone, the look that kills even though nothing is said, and the persistent pattern of subtle digs take a psychological toll on the strongest of people.

These emotional responses come into play with your marital partner, with your teenage children, with your parents, and even with your coworkers. Having a camaraderie and a real sense of closeness with people who really care about you can make a tremendous difference on your job. It pays to pay attention to the emotional interactions that happen from eight to five.

Aggressively dealing with the job stress, being well-matched with your career, and developing positive working relationships are the keys to career satisfaction. The next nine chapters will cover these vital factors.

CHAPTER 17

Job Stress

The term "job stress" is freely tossed around, but what does it mean? It is interesting to note the term "marital stress" is rarely used to explain what is wrong in a marriage. The minute a person says he or she is having marital stress, the already anticipated question is, "And exactly *what* is wrong?" Soon there is a lengthy discussion about lack of communication, unfaithfulness, mental abuse, not having enough time together, financial concerns, in-law problems, lack of romantic chemistry, or a myriad of other specific concerns. Any advice is directed toward solving the specific problem rather than alleviating global marital stress.

I do not see an equivalent response when people say they are having job stress. Rather than a careful inquiry into the specific causes of the stress, there is the pet solution quickly offered to reduce the global job stress. Why else would you receive advice such as, "You need a vacation," "Don't worry about it," or "Don't take it home with you"?

I recommend that you take the same approach with job stress that you do with marital stress. First, isolate the reasons why you may be feeling excessive stress on your job. This step is necessary if you want to pursue the critical goal of liking your career and finding personal happiness through the career path.

I find that my clients usually suffer from job stress for one of six reasons. Be my "client" for a few minutes as we consider each of these causes.

1. Job Failure. Like the student who is getting bad grades in school, you do not feel good if you are not doing a good job.

Either you will drop out (quit) or barely pass (go through the motions doing only what is necessary). This feeling of failure is compounded when your teacher (boss) is constantly reminding you of your poor performance through grades (negative job evaluations).

There can be a literal job failure, but often it is a misperception. The feeling of "failure" can occur whenever (a) you feel you do not measure up to *your* perfectionist standards, and this self-feedback pulls you down emotionally, (b) you are doing a good job but have the misfortune of being around other coworkers who are superior performers, or (c) you have a critical boss who takes excellent performance for granted and only comments when something does not go "perfectly." Unfortunately, these experiences will create a sense of failure even though you actually may be doing satisfactory work.

2. *Too much to do.* You may be doing a good job but still feel the stress of "there are not enough hours in the day." This sense of always being behind schedule, never feeling caught up, and having to always rush from task to task takes a tremendous psychological toll. Everything is push . . . push . . . push and rush . . . rush . . . rush. (In fact, I feel the stress just writing down these words!)

Everyone can survive this pressure for a short time (the CPA during tax season, the store clerk during an after-Christmas sale, the owner of a small business during remodeling, a temporarily shorthanded office staff), but if this pattern continues unabated, the pressure can turn into an emotionally draining long-term stress. The difference in psychological states between a person having the time to effectively and efficiently do a job, and the person who always works under "impossible deadlines" is considerable.

3. *Personality conflicts.* If you have a disagreement with your spouse, the predictable advice from your friends is, "I think you should deal with it." The same friends may advise, "Just ignore it," when you have a similar misunderstanding with a coworker.

This bad advice can lead to a tragic mistake. You need to treat the relationships with your fellow employees with a concern similar to what you show your spouse. The reasons are many, but one major reason is that you spend eight to ten hours per day with your coworkers, more "prime time" than you spend with your spouse. This amount of time creates a closeness that affects your emotional well-being, regardless of how much you try to ignore the strains in these relationships.

4. Lack of money. If you are experiencing financial pressures in your personal life, it is natural to blame your job for this frustration. "If they paid me what I deserve, I would not be in this financial bind," is the underlying thought process.

This financial frustration is not technically a job-related stress. It is a personal hassle that spills over to the job. I include lack of money under the job-stress umbrella, however, because so many people persist in making this connection. If you do not have enough money to keep the lifestyle you want, you may feel you are suffering job stress.

Many other personal conflicts can spill over to affect your attitude toward your job. Health problems, marital concerns, parent/child conflicts, or any other personal dissatisfaction can be carried into the workplace. Unless you are aware of what is happening, you may tend to blame your work for the negative emotions. What is felt on the job will be attributed to the job!

5. A mismatch. You have a unique blend of interests, abilities, temperaments, aptitudes, and personality qualities. It is what psychologists call "individual differences." If this pattern comes close to matching the demands of your career, the odds of you finding true fulfillment are greatly increased. Likewise, if your interests, abilities, temperaments, aptitudes, and personality qualities differ markedly from those of people who are successful in a particular career, you are mismatched with that career. The odds of making a positive adjustment are severely diminished.

What kind of matching do *you* have with *your* job? If it is too much of a mismatch, you will always experience low-grade job stress even when you saturate yourself with motivational tapes.

6. Job insecurity. The fear of losing your job can create a gnawing, persistent stress that hangs over your head like an ominous black cloud. The reasons for this fear can vary from a slowdown in the economy, which raises the possibility of job cutbacks to a proposed company merger with the possibility of major personnel changes, and range from a realization that your job performance is substandard to an unfounded anxiety that has no logical basis.

As you can readily surmise, some of these job security fears are job related and others may be more free-floating personal anxieties that spill over to the job. No matter what the basis, however, lack of job security can play a significant role in job stress. To what degree does it affect you?

Okay. Be my client for five more minutes. Look at the six sources of your job stress. Decide what degree is it caused by the following:

	(1 to 10)
Job failure	_____
Too much to do	_____
Personality conflicts	_____
Lack of money/other personal stresses	_____
A mismatch	_____
Job insecurity	_____

To focus your thinking, please write down the number between 1 and 10 (1 is low and 10 is high) that most accurately reflects how much each of these six factors is contributing to your current job stress.

The message is simple. If you are unsuccessful, overworked, embroiled in personality clashes, overrun with a personal struggle, mismatched with your career, and/or have no job security, you will feel job stress. Since work consumes so much of your time, you will also feel *life stress*.

The good news is that you can reduce the job stress through career success, a workable schedule, office harmony, adequate finances, a good career matching, and job security.

Take this giant step toward overall happiness by attacking the job stress in your life. One way to do this is to carefully study the other strategies in this book and apply them specifically to your work situation. A second approach is to shift back to being your own friendly counselor and write some of your own personalized prescriptions. Please answer the following "counseling" questions as you start to develop your own set of strategies for coping with your work-related stress. I have included some hints, but please move beyond them to your *own* innovative ideas that directly address *your* unique work situation.

1. What are three specific things you can do to reduce the feeling of job failure? (Hints: Compete with yourself, that is, maximize your potential rather than comparing yourself with other employees. Take some in-service training to improve your job performance. Override a perfectionist supervisor by relying on yourself for positive feedback.)

   a. _____

   b. _____

   c. _____

2. What are three things you could do to reduce the pressure of having too much to do? (Hints: Do a better job of delegating tasks. Develop a time-management program. Learn how to assertively say, "No", when it is appropriate to do so.)

   a. _____

   b. _____

   c. _____

3. What are three things you could do to alleviate any job-related personality conflicts? (Hints: Directly confront a strained relationship with a colleague rather than passively ignore the problem. Be the first to apologize when there has been a misunderstanding. Be generous with your praising of other workers including your boss.)

   a. _____

   b. _____

   c. _____

4. What are three things you could do to reduce the financial frustrations and other "personal" stresses? (Hints: Develop a better self-awareness of when you are carrying a personal problem to work. Turn a hobby into a fun and financially rewarding part-time second career. Live in the "now," that is, discipline yourself to focus on work hassles at work and personal hassles at home.)

a. _____

b. _____

c. _____

5. What are three things you could do to resolve a possible career mismatch? (Hints: Go for career counseling to explore your interests and abilities. Secretly consult with a headhunter. Exchange job responsibilities with a fellow employee.)

a. _____

b. _____

c. _____

6. What are three things you could do to reduce your job insecurity? (Hints: Acquire additional skills that make you more valuable to employers. Obtain an advanced degree through night school. Tell yourself that no matter what happens, you will handle it and make a good adjustment.)

a. _____

b. _____

c. _____

Make it your courageous goal to expect more happiness from your career by aggressively attacking the sources of your job stress. There probably is no change that will have more impact on your overall happiness. Eight to ten hours a day is a lot of time to spend on anything!

• CHAPTER 18 •

Creatively Coping With Stress

You do not have to read a magazine article, watch a television special, or listen to a speech to find out about stress. You probably have to look no further than yourself to see some of the signs:

- Forgetfulness
- Mental and physical fatigue
- Lack of concentration
- Increased irritability
- Low-grade depression
- Inability to sleep

If you want to aggressively attack debilitating career stress, the first step is to develop an early warning system. You want to be able to detect very quickly when you are starting to experience excessive stress in your professional life. You do not want to wait until you have had a heart attack to realize, "Oops! I have been under too much stress!"

It is important to understand that the early warning signs are very individualized. Your early warning signals can be quite different from the next person's. Your sleep disturbance may create insomnia. Either you cannot fall asleep at night or you fall asleep but then wake up at 4:00 A.M. For another person, twelve hours of sleep a night suddenly does not seem to be enough. Differences also exist with the way you shove the stress into your body. (What the mind conceals, the body reveals.) You might develop migraine headaches while a coworker suffers from an ulcer; your boss may have lower back pain; your secretary, a skin rash.

The psychological reactions are as varied. You may react to stress by becoming irritable and short-tempered, and a friend reacts by withdrawing and becoming more passive. Even sex drives can be affected in varying ways. Too much stress may smother your sexual interest, while too much stress increases your spouse's sex drive.

The key question is, "What are *your* early warning signs?" This awareness is essential for an early intervention. Stop for a minute and reflect on your early warning signs. What are the subtle (or maybe not so subtle) early warning indications that suggest you are experiencing excessive stress? Write down your five most common signals.

1. _____
2. _____
3. _____
4. _____
5. _____

The second step is to decide what to do when you notice some of your early warning symptoms are present. You want to be able to take decisive action; you want to have a game plan. But what do you do? How do you cope with the build-up of stress? Usually you are given three standard pieces of unsolicited advice.

The most common advice is some version of, "Don't worry about it." This is easy for other people to say. After all, they are not standing in your shoes. The predictable impact on you, however, is now you can also worry about the fact that you are worrying about the thing you are not supposed to worry about. Your sarcastic silent thought is, "Thanks a lot!"

A second favorite strategy from friends is their suggestion that you "get away from the stressors." This is the "take a vacation and get away from the problems" approach. So what do you do: Quit your job, divorce your spouse, put your kids up for adoption? Sometimes the "cure" is worse than the disease.

Your friendly pseudodoctor friends may even reach into their medicine cabinet and say, "Take two of these pills in the morning and two at night, and you will feel no stress." Technically they are correct; you start feeling no stress. Of course, you do not feel anything else either as you become a zombie "zonking" through the day.

What is the answer? Is there any way to cope with all the stressors in your life, or must you eventually fall victim to the stress?

Fortunately, there is an answer! Psychological research has indicated that not all people react to the stressors in their lives in the same way. Some people are actually quite stress resistant. They are able to ward off most of the stress that is thrust upon them.

Kobasa and Maddi (Pines 1980) have isolated three psychological qualities that help people become stress resistant. The individuals who possess these three qualities effectively cope with the stress in their careers while the individuals who lack these qualities have far greater struggles with job-related stress.

1. Change. The first quality that separates a stress-resistant person from a less stress-resistant person is attitude toward change. According to the research, the more positive your attitude toward change, the more stress resistant you are. This makes sense because life is synonymous with change. Economic conditions will fluctuate; careers will be altered; your spouse will want changes; you will get older; and perhaps the most sobering realization, eventually everyone you love will leave you, unless you happen to die first. Life is change and change is a part of life. The people who have a positive attitude toward change will always respond more comfortably to the inevitable changes that occur in life.

What is your attitude toward change? Do you like a lot of change in your life? Do you welcome change and even encourage it? If change is not happening, do you make it happen? Or do you prefer sameness? Do you like things to remain constant? Is status quo important in your life?

Your attitude toward change can surface in every area of your life. For example, how do you react when new computer software is being introduced at your place of business? Are you ready to try a new way to process all the business information or is your instinctive thought, "I do not trust this new program; I like the old way of doing things better."

What is *your* general attitude toward change? To be more precise with your answer, select a number between 1 and 10 that best reflects your present attitude (1 is low, 5 is average, and 10 is high). Your attitude toward change is _____.

2. *Involvement.* The second factor that separates a stress-resistant person from one who caves in to stress is involvement. By involvement, I mean the degree of emotional closeness that you experience with other people. Some people like emotional closeness; they want to intimately connect with other people. They like talking, listening, and sharing. They strive for emotional intimacy in their professional lives as well as in their personal lives.

Other people are more aloof and removed. They follow the philosophy that fences make good neighbors, familiarity breeds contempt, and getting too close to fellow workers only complicates the work environment. Some men even hold the characters Dirty Harry (Clint Eastwood) or Rambo (Sylvester Stallone) as their role models for sharing feelings.

Which person do you think is more stress resistant? Is it the person who does not let his or her life get overly complicated by involvement complexities (with the possible exception of one's family), or is it the person who is constantly striving to drop the psychological walls and always moving closer to other people? According to the research, the greater the involvement, the greater the stress resistance.

This answer may initially surprise you, but it should not if you think about it. We are genetically wired to be close to other people. Involvement meets our basic need for this emotional closeness. Granted, there is additional stress in being close to other people (the rejection can hurt more; the feelings are more intense; the concerns are greater), but for most people, it is an energizing stress with overriding positive emotions.

It is emotional alienation that does the psychological damage. Emotional alienation deepens depression, heightens anxiety, and intensifies stress. Involvement, on the other hand, keeps the dialogue cracking and creates a special brand of verbal mental toughness. People use the anchor of close involvement to stay with the dialogue until a misunderstanding is corrected, a misperception clarified, and any ambiguity reduced.

How close do you get to people? Do you drop your psychological facade and reveal your true emotions, or do you always portray your public persona? You have to make this decision whenever you engage in a social exchange with a coworker, secretary, boss, customer, service representative, client, or even the staff person that you rarely see.

What is your current level of involvement with the people in your career arena? Give yourself a number between 1 and 10 (1 is low, 5 is average, and 10 is high). Your involvement number is _____.

3. Control. The third quality that makes a person stress resistant is control. By control, I do not mean the ability to hold your emotions in check. By control, I mean to what degree do you feel that you are in charge of your life?

If you are independently wealthy, have a job skill that is in high demand, have a self-sufficient spouse, and a job where you "call the shots," you will feel more in control. If, on the other hand, you are living from paycheck to paycheck, have a job that is valuable only to your present company, live with a possessive spouse, work for an autocratic boss, and have three children under the age of six, you will feel in less control of your life.

The control issue is also psychological. For example, a colleague walks up and criticizes you. Your emotional reaction will fall into one of two categories. The first is that you will think, he or she said something negative and now I feel bad. Implied in that thought is that *he or she* made you feel bad. The second reaction you could have is that he or she said something negative and you *choose* to get upset over that statement. Implied in this thought is that you could have also chosen not to personalize your colleague's criticism. You have maintained control over your emotional reaction.

To what degree do you feel you have control over your life at the present time? Respond with a number between 1 and 10 (1 is little control, 5 is average control, and 10 is considerable control). Your control number is _____.

The more you feel in control of your life, the more stress resistant you will be.

154 • Finding Personal Happiness

Change, involvement, and control! Make the development of these three qualities a daily affirmation and begin celebrating a new level of stress resistance.

How do you develop these qualities? One powerful thing you can do is to create your own individualized strategies for enhancing the stress-resistant qualities of change, involvement, and control. Always remember that you are in the best position to write the prescriptions for your life.

1. What are three things you could do to have a more positive attitude toward change? (Hints: Gracefully accept that things will not always go as planned and that your most creative challenge will be making the last-minute adjustments. Drive home a different way tonight just to behaviorally declare that you are willing to do things in a different way.)

    a. _____

    b. _____

    c. _____

2. What are three things you could do to have closer involvements with the special people in your life? (Hints: Be there with emotional support when someone is going through a personal crisis. Freely give other people compliments. Take the risk of sharing what is happening in your life.)

    a. _____

    b. _____

    c. _____

3. What are three ways you could have more control over your life? (Hints: Always take responsibility for your feelings whenever you have an emotional response. Take periodic time-outs to relax your emotional system. Develop a sense of humor, and don't take yourself too seriously.)

    a. _____

b. _____

c. _____

Is this exciting? You bet it is! I too have started walking down this path since I read the research on stress resistance.

There are also some powerful stress strategies that you can use to cope with the excessive job stress when it does slip through your psychological armor. Before I introduce these stress strategies, however, let's examine the other two factors in this career section: being well-matched with your career and having positive relationships on the job.

• CHAPTER 19 •

Good Career Matching

The importance of being well-matched with your career is captured in the dilemma that Jim faced. Jim, a handsome thirty-five-year-old man, came to me for counseling because he was unhappy. He said he hated getting up in the morning to go to work, and there was no joy or excitement in what he was doing. An analysis of his situation quickly eliminated four of the standard reasons for this mild depression/job dissatisfaction.

- There were no personal problems from other areas of his life spilling over to affect his attitude toward his job. He was happily married, had many good friends, was financially secure, and experienced a loving relationship with his parents.

- It was not a failure syndrome. Jim already had an accounting degree and an MBA. He was a CPA and doing exceptionally well with a prestigious accounting firm. He was being groomed as an eventual partner in the firm.

- There were no personality conflicts with his colleagues or senior partners. In fact, he described his working relationship with everyone as "excellent."

- He was not clinically depressed. The blue feelings quickly disappeared on the weekends or when he was doing non-career activities. This is noteworthy because a person with a biochemical depression would not be able to have such a quick and predictable shift in emotions.

What was the reason for Jim's unhappiness? The answer was that he did not like the accounting field. Despite his career success, his personality and interest preferences did not match those of the accounting profession.

Jim said he went to college to become a marine biologist. He had worked one summer at an oceanarium, and he found the work fascinating. But everyone told him that there were few high-paying jobs in that field, and he was encouraged to go into accounting or law. He reluctantly followed their advice and predictably ended up with a high-paying and (for him) a less-than-fascinating job.

Jim had a choice. He could give up his lucrative salary and promising career, and start over again. His wife, a professional person, stated she was willing to make this sacrifice if it was what he wanted. Or Jim could stay where he was and try to force himself to like what he was doing. The danger in this option, however, was that he might end up like many men: forty-five years old, father of two children, unhappy, and suffering from a career "midlife crisis" which, he believes, is only solved by a divorce or extramarital affair.

Of course it does not always have to be that dramatic a reaction to a career mismatch. It may merely be a thirty-year prison sentence to a boring job, a mild emotional flatness, or a renewed effort to find more excitement outside the job to compensate for the lack of meaning and purpose within the job.

If you are mismatched in your career, you may want to carefully listen to the haunting lyrics from "The Gambler" sung by Kenny Rogers: "You have to know when to hold them, know when to fold them, know when to walk away, and know when to run." As the old gambler dramatically suggests, a poker player has to constantly decide whether to (a) play the hand he has, (b) throw in his cards and wait for the next deal, (c) walk away from the card game before he loses his shirt, or (d) run because his life is in danger. This is the same type of dilemma that many people face with their career.

My questions do not have the catchy lyrics just as my singing voice does not sound like Kenny Rogers. But the issue is critical in your quest to feel better about your life. These are the important questions. Do you:

- Stay with your career despite the mismatch and endure the predictable square-peg-in-a-round-hole job stress?
- Stay, but make some creative adjustments in your career so it is more compatible with your interests and talents?
- Start making plans to leave your career and find one that is a good match with whom you are?
- Resign today, before the burnout takes an even greater toll, and you start making doctors and therapists rich?

Where are *you* in terms of *your* career? As you answer the following seven questions, keep in mind that if there is a compatible marriage between (a) your career and, (b) your interests, abilities, and personal needs, you will find an extra source of satisfaction. And if there is a mismatch between your career and your interests, abilities, and personal needs, there will be dissatisfaction. The greater the mismatch, the greater the dissatisfaction.

People who like what they do have a tremendous edge in the race to find personal happiness. Imagine two competitors. One starts with fifty hours of her prime time being spent loving what she does, and the other starts with fifty hours hating what she does. How fair is this as they "compete" in finding personal happiness in the rest of their individual lives?

Finding personal happiness is not a race, and it is not competition with others. But if it were, the race between these two individuals would be the mismatch of the century. It would be like giving one runner a 50-meter head start in a 200-meter race.

Resolve to seek job happiness as you respond to the following seven questions. Think creatively, and you will find a rewarding career. Accept status quo, and you will pigeonhole yourself accordingly.

1. Do you prefer working with data, things, or people? An accountant and a computer programmer work with data. A service technician and a landscape architect work with things. A salesperson and a minister have people as their primary focus.

Naturally there is an interplay of data, things, and people in most careers. Every job involves a certain degree of *people* (even if it only means a polite hello to a person walking down the hall), *data* (compiling information for the tax return), and *things* (turning on a copy machine).

But some careers are highly oriented in one direction. A salesperson lives and dies by people; a bookkeeper who dislikes data is going to be one unhappy camper; and an auto mechanic cannot avoid a heavy concentration on things.

Where are you? What is the area that best captures your interests, dovetails with your talents, and piques your enthusiasm? And the obvious second question is: How does your current job measure up in these vital areas?

The people, data, or things component is the most fundamental of the seven key questions that you will be considering in this chapter. Some of the upcoming issues have considerable flexibility in terms of your ability to adjust, but this is often less so with the people, data, or things matching.

Charles is a typical example of what happens when there is too much of a mismatch. Charles and Rita came at Rita's insistence for marriage counseling. Her complaint was that Charles was "impossible to live with." She freely admitted that she still loved him but clearly stated that things were going to have to get better in their relationship. She was tired of his "critical attitude, couch-potato mentality, depressed moods, and indifference toward her."

Some time was spent looking at their marriage but nothing significant was uncovered. They both felt that they still had an underlying romantic love and a deep caring, especially on long weekends or vacations. In fact, it was these good times during long weekends and vacations that motivated Rita to insist on the counseling. She wanted this type of relationship "more than six times a year."

What was the difference on long weekends or vacations? One obvious consideration, which turned out to be the key to their marital problem, was that Charles was psychologically escaping from his job.

Charles quickly became the "boy genius" when he had gone to work for his company. His company was heavily into product research, and Charles flourished in this creative environment. He was instrumental in developing a couple of products that turned out to be very profitable for his company. His reward for innovative research was being promoted to manager of the research department. Now, instead of doing creative research, he was managing the people who were doing the hands-on research. He went from "things" to "people and data."

One year later Charles was stressed, bored, and uninspired. He was tired of meeting budgets, running meetings, fighting company politics, and dealing with all the petty complaints within his department. Through counseling, he became aware of just how unhappy he was with his career shift and how his unhappiness was spilling over into his marriage in subtle ways such as "critical attitudes, couch-potato mentality, depressed moods, and indifference."

To Charles's credit, he took a courageous step. He decided that he could not make the adjustment from "things" to "people and data," and still be happy on his job or in his marriage. He resigned from his managerial position and went back to creative research work. It meant an adjustment in their financial life style, but Rita never complained. She quickly got back her old husband seven days a week: a loving, caring, enthusiastic man.

Take some time and contemplate how you relate to data, things, and people in your life. How well does your career become a good extension of *who you are*? Consider the following three sets of questions as you begin to address this vital issue. Your answers to some of these questions should give a further indication of your personal preference for people, data, or things.

a. Given a choice, would you rather:

- Read a magazine article on people in the news, computer software, or making household repairs?

- Have friends over, develop a new personal bookkeeping system, or build a model airplane?

- Attend a one-day seminar on human psychology, business economics, or introduction to computer repair?

- Be promoted to a position that requires more people management skills, data processing knowledge, or repair expertise?

- Prepare a company talk on improving worker morale, using interoffice memos more efficiently, or making company equipment safer?

b. In your current job, how do you spend your time? Please write down the percentage of time you spend with

People _____ %

Data _____ %

Things _____ %

Compare these percentages to what you would ideally like.

c. In your ideal job, what percentage of the time would you want to spend in each of the three areas?

People _____ %

Data _____ %

Things _____ %

Your thoughtful answers to these questions should help you begin to clarify your current match with your job regarding people, data, and things.

2. *In what ways to you prefer to interact with people on your job?* Even in the "data" and "things" careers, there is a certain amount of interaction with people. In the people-dominant careers, however, it becomes a vital area of focus.

There are four basic ways that you can interact with other people on your job. They are:

- A helping role; possible careers include physician, counselor, or waitress.

- A managing role; possible careers include company CEO, army officer, or supervisor on a production line.

- A persuasive role; possible careers include marketing representative, outside salesperson, or trial attorney.

- An information-sharing role; possible careers include schoolteacher, newspaper columnist, or airline ticket agent.

Even within a particular profession, these people-interaction elements may emerge in different patterns. For example, a trial attorney *persuades* a jury; a legal aid attorney *helps* the indigent; a patent attorney *furnishes* valuable information; and a senior law partner *manages* the less-experienced attorneys.

The same diversity is true with salespeople. A salesperson in a clothing store may be primarily *helping*; a cold-call salesperson is into *persuading* reluctant customers; a pharmaceutical rep *provides* new drug information to interest the physicians; and the sales manager focuses more on *managing* the rest of the sales team.

What are your unique turn-ons and turn-offs? An accurate analysis of your uniqueness will be a major step forward in the essential *people* dimension of your chosen career.

3. To what degree do you like working closely with other coworkers? You may like, and perhaps even emotionally need, other people around you. Even if you prefer working with data or things, you prefer doing it with a coworker. Another possibility is that you prefer doing it alone. You like to have your own psychological work space—and for some it can be a large space. You may even be called a "lone wolf."

One common example is the position of secretary. Some people prefer working in a one-secretary office. They prefer the solitude and simplicity of being the only secretary and would be happy limiting "people contact" to the boss and his or her customers, clients, or patients.

Other secretaries prefer to be part of a larger office. They enjoy the interaction with coworkers, want someone to chat with at the coffee break, and like working on projects with other staff members.

The same lifestyle preference is true for a dentist, accountant, insurance agent, or any other profession. Some prefer being the whole show. They like the concept of the one-man or one-woman office. They do not want to struggle with the normal office politics, competition, jealousies, and conflicts.

Other professionals would feel very isolated in this setting. Putting up with the normal interaction hassles with colleagues would be a small price to pay for the benefits of having other people around to bounce ideas off of, to celebrate with during the successes, and to commiserate with during the setbacks.

Take an introspective look at yourself. Which work setting do you prefer, and how well does your current position match your personal preference?

4. How challenging do you want your career to be? Some people prefer a simple eight-to-five job, one that they can totally walk away from and not worry about until they "punch in" the next day. They want their after-hours focus to be on family, hobbies, church, recreation, or just relaxing. One pitfall with this attitude, however, is that most eight-to-five jobs requiring no after-hours mental energy also end up being the least challenging jobs.

Other people prefer a job that they can really sink their teeth into. They like a job that (a) is a challenge, (b) commands their interest and attention, (c) necessitates the extra energy and effort, and (d) stretches them intellectually.

It logically follows that you should ask yourself two critical questions:
- "How challenging is my current job?"
- "How challenging would I like it to be?"

Always remember that it is possible to err in two directions. You could have too little challenge on your job and experience boredom, indifference, and deterioration of performance; or you could have too much challenge and experience excessive stress, anxiety, or depression. Most people are concerned about the stress of having too much challenge. Surprisingly, the greater danger may be in not having enough challenge.

I will never forget an experience that I had while I was conducting a seminar for the Center for Management Studies at Wichita State University. There were several executives from Boeing, NCR, and other major corporations who shared valuable strategies with the other sixty participants. I was very impressed with the suggestions given by these high-powered executives, but the strategy that impressed me the most was a comment made by the manager of two Kentucky Fried Chicken stores. He said:

"All my employees, no matter what job they have at the store, go through four stages:
- They like their job but they are not good at it.
- They like their job and they are good at it.
- They do not like their job but they are good at it.
- They do not like their job and they are not good at it.

What I try to do is cross-train them and give them a new job as soon as I notice that they have entered the third phase."

This manager wisely recognized that once a person has mastered a job, boredom, indifference, and deterioration of performance are not far behind.

This phenomenon is true for an entry-level position at a fast food restaurant, and it is true for you, whether you are in an entry-level position, a mid-level position, or a high-level professional position. Unless there is continuing room for personal and professional growth, the odds are great that you will experience job boredom and eventually job burnout.

5. *How well does your current position meet your motivational hot buttons?* There are six basic ways that people are motivated on the job: fortune, fame, inner satisfaction, security, an internal work ethic, and emotional bonding. The key is to determine to what extent you are motivated by each of these six motivators.

• *Fortune.* Success is measured by the financial reward, but it is not just what the money can provide. The monetary reward is also a way of keeping score. The money says how good you are! This is why a professional athlete who is making 2.4 million dollars per year suddenly wants 2.8 million dollars. Why? Because another ballplayer has just been given a contract for 2.6 million dollars per year

• *Fame.* Recognition is the key to this motivator. The reward is acknowledgment by one's peers or the general public. The plaques for the walls, the favorable quotes in the newspaper, and the kudos from the boss become energizing turn-ons.

• *Inner satisfaction.* For this person, the reward comes more from within. It is the internal satisfaction of having accomplished something worthwhile that gives the greatest career satisfaction. Solving the problem, closing the deal, or making an outstanding contribution becomes the reward within itself. Even when this person is praised, it is better to say, "You must really be proud of yourself," rather than, "I am really proud of you."

• *Security.* Security is a less energizing motivator, but for some, the best job reward is knowing that there will be enough money for food, shelter, and other essentials for the family on a steady and ongoing basis. The job means the kids can go to college, and there will be a retirement fund for old age.

• *Internal work ethic.* This motivator, sometimes referred to as the Protestant work ethic, usually originates in early childhood programming. The internal message is, "There is virtue in working hard. No matter how menial the task, the right thing to do is to do the best job possible."

• *Emotional bonding.* This person has an immense loyalty and a deep devotion toward helping a highly respected individual or organization. Being a part of the team and contributing to the success of this noble person or cause becomes *the* reward.

Stop for a minute and take an introspective two-question look at yourself. The first question is, "To what degree are you motivated by each of these six job motivators?" Please use a from 1 to 10 scale (1 is low and 10 is high).

Column 1
Personal motivators (1 to 10)

Fortune   _____
Fame   _____
Inner satisfaction _____
Security   _____
Internal work ethic _____
Emotional bonding _____

The second question is, "To what degree does your current job allow you the opportunity to meet each of these six motivators?" Again, use the 1 to 10 scale for your answers.

Column 2
Current job satisfaction (1 to 10)

Fortune   _____
Fame   _____
Inner satisfaction _____
Security   _____
Internal work ethic _____
Emotional bonding _____

If your personal motivators are not met (rewarded and reinforced) on the job, you will experience increased job dissatisfaction. Likewise, if you do have a job that rewards your personal motivators, you have one more positive match in your search for career happiness.

6. *How well does your career match your personal needs?* In addition to the motivational needs, there are also subjective personal needs that can impact how well you like your job. Reflect on the following questions to better understand how your personal needs operate within your job.

- Do you like a high-energy, fast-paced work environment, or do you prefer a more relaxed, laid-back working climate? How well does your current position match this preference?

- Do you like a competitive environment that rewards being the best of the best? Or do you become stressed-out in this type of environment and prefer a cooperative team approach in which everyone is pulling together as one unit? How well does your current work environment match this personal preference?

- Do you like a work environment that is friendly rather than formal, one that has a family feeling, and where co-workers become close social friends? Or do you prefer a more formal working environment, one that is strictly business with little after-hours social life except for the obligatory company parties? How well does your personal preference match what is happening in your company?

- Do you prefer a job with clearly delineated lines of responsibility and a well-defined job description so you know you are in sync with the system? Or do you prefer more flexibility and blossom when you can be creative and in charge of your job responsibilities? You like a boss who says, "You get the job done . . . your way . . . with your game plan . . . just be sure it is on time with a good performance."

As you can surmise, a good match in these subjective, intangible areas can enhance a good career match, while a marked mismatch can increase job dissatisfaction.

7. *Is the problem really a career mismatch?* Before Jim (the case presented earlier in this chapter) decided that his problem was simply a matter of being in the wrong career field (accounting rather than marine biology), he took a look at other possible reasons for his career dissatisfaction. I encourage you to ask yourself a similar question: "Is my career dissatisfaction truly a mismatch with my current career, or is the dissatisfaction actually created by other job-related or personal factors that are occurring in my life?"

As you may recall, I asked a similar question as you were considering the five C's in your marriage. As you were examining the competency factor, I had you pose the question, "Is it *me* or is it the *relationship* that is causing the current marital strains?"

When faced with a serious marital conflict, it is critical to determine whether it is a "me" problem or a "relationship" problem. If it is a marital problem that cannot be fixed, a divorce and remarriage could mean that the serious problems would evaporate. But if it is a "me" problem (depression, insecurity, and jealousy), changing partners probably would solve nothing. It would only be a matter of time before the same problems would surface again and contaminate the second marriage.

The same critical question applies if you are experiencing serious career dissatisfaction. If it is a true career mismatch, changing jobs or modifying your career to form a better emotional and intellectual fit could solve the problem. But if it is a "me" problem (job stress, personality clashes, marital problems, clinical depression, and so on), changing jobs may solve nothing and actually make the situation worse. For example, your new employer may be even less tolerant of your personal struggles.

For sixteen years, Marilyn had been the executive secretary for a prominent attorney. She was one of the highest paid legal secretaries in her city, and her boss was highly complimentary of her excellent work. In her ninth year, she was nominated for and received a prestigious national award that in essence said that she was the best of the best.

Marilyn appreciated all the praise and recognition that she had received, and the first twelve years in her position had been bliss. But the enthusiasm had begun slowly waning over the last four years. In fact, it had eroded to the point that Marilyn decided to go for counseling after reading an article on job burnout in a popular magazine.

Marilyn quickly determined that her job burnout was not the result of excessive job stress (the focus of the article) nor was it the result of personal problems that were spilling over to her career. This was true even though she was having some serious marital problems. Marilyn was experiencing job dissatisfaction because her psychological needs were no longer being met in her current position. She, however, took the time to ask all the right questions, questions similar to the ones discussed in this chapter.

Marilyn decided that (a) she was a "people" person, not a "data" person; (b) one of her real strengths was in "managing" other people; (c) her primary motivator was "inner satisfaction;" (d) she wanted to work for a people-orientated organization; (e) she liked a fast-paced job where she could "call the shots;" and (f) she wanted a job that was a creative challenge.

Marilyn resigned from her secretarial position and took a job with a large professional association. Ten years later, Marilyn became president of the same powerful association. She now has a career that matches her current interests and abilities. Her courageous decision allowed her to make her career a magical path to personal happiness.

I wish the same for you, so please take a careful look at your self-to-career match. It does not always mean leaving your job (Marilyn had a "blissful" match for twelve years as a professional secretary.) but it may require some modifications or adjustments within your current position. It may mean shifting to another department, trading job responsibilities, or even taking a transfer. The first key step, however, is taking the time to carefully look at the match that you currently have.

Once you have a good career match, you will also be free to use goal setting, affirmations, and visualization to stretch for even more career success. These concepts are not included in this section, however, because they are already covered in two other sections of this book. Please review the discussions on goal setting and imagery in the relationship section (chapters 11 and 14) and the mission section (chapters 31 and 32). Simply substitute the word "career" every time you see the word "relationship" or "mission," and you will have a powerful approach for adding to the personal happiness in your career. You will empower your good career match.

• CHAPTER 20 •

Positive Relationships on the Job

The third key factor in liking your career is having positive relationships. As already discussed, the people you interact with in both your private life and your professional life will have a significant impact on your personal happiness. While a strained relationship at work may not extract as heavy a psychological price as a strained marital relationship, the fact remains that the emotional cost can be great.

Put in a more positive way, close interpersonal relationships with work colleagues can add tremendously to your emotional well-being. The differences between (a) the office with warm, caring relationships among the fellow employees, and (b) the office where there is a strained, jealous, and competitive climate can be staggering in terms of the emotional impact on the workers.

Likewise, the attitude created by the boss who emphasizes teamwork, closeness, and generous doses of praising will be in sharp contrast from the attitude created by the boss who treats employees like mere cogs in a wheel. (I recently heard a manager in an accounting firm say, "Professional people do not need praising." How sad!)

The point I want to emphasize and reemphasize is that the personal involvements on your job are critical. If you want to find happiness, you need to pay close attention to your eight-to-five relationships. I learned this truth from John Waters, a very special man.

In 1968 I took a job as Director of Counseling Services for a large metropolitan school district. During my tenure in that position, I had two bosses. One was Mark Davis (not his real name). Mark was one of the most efficient bosses that I had ever had. He had management-by-objectives sheets, complex performance evaluations, planning seminars, and an impressive list of other managerial strategies. He had a computer before computers became the vogue. He was effective and hard working. Under his direction things were organized and structured.

The other boss was John Waters. John was an effective, efficient administrator (although his list of managerial strategies was not as impressive as Mark's), and he was highly regarded. But this is not what made John Waters so special in my eyes.

There was one thing that John Waters did that I will never forget, even though it happened many years ago. On a lazy Sunday afternoon, the doorbell rang unexpectedly. John Waters and his wife were at the front door. They came to deliver a surprise gift for the birth of my son, Todd.

Now I want to ask a question. For which boss did I have no qualms about working overtime or even on the weekend if the job required it? The answer, of course, is that I was willing to make an extra effort for John Waters.

John Waters gave me one thing that I never felt from my other boss. My other boss valued me as a vital employee, an important cog in the wheel. John Waters, however, went one step further. Through that baby gift— and in many other subtle ways— he said, "I value you as an employee *and* I value you as a person." This extra involvement made a significant difference in my attitude toward the job and even in my attitude toward myself. I felt better and my job performance reflected this attitude.

I encourage you to strive for the same level of involvement in your workplace. Upgrade the level of involvement with your customers, coworkers, employees, and bosses. Everyone will feel better, and, as a bonus, it is good business!

So how do you form positive relationships at work? This topic has already been indirectly discussed. The same five C's that add specialness to an intimate involvement can add specialness to relationships within your work area. In fact, the only C that I would eliminate from the workplace is chemistry. The reason for this is obvious: Chemistry is the one C that can both complicate positive relationships on the job and place undue strain on the relationship with your intimate partner at home.

Examine how the four C's can help create an emotional closeness. As you look at the communication, caring, commitment, and competency factors, go back to the relationship section and reread that section with the mind-set, "How could these same principles and strategies apply to my relationships at work?" Specifically, focus on seven emotional-closeness issues that could give you psychological clout as a manager, colleague, boss, or employee.

1. A thoughtful act that shows that you genuinely care pays rich dividends in your marriage and also gives a good return on your job. Wise leaders know that, "People do not care how much you know until they know how much you care."

2. The ten commandments for arguing are not limited to fights with your spouse. They also provide damage control in work-related disagreements, conflicts, and misunderstandings. Effectively resolving conflicts is good for marital relationships and working relationships.

3. The psychological power of praising is not limited to your spouse. Positive feedback creates the same positive response among your coworkers, subordinates, and even your boss. Everyone likes the buzz of a well-placed and well-deserved compliment, and the buzz can linger on, and on, and on.

4. The willingness to confront gently, rather than avoid, developing interpersonal problems helps prevent greater problems in both your home environment *and* your work environment. No one does well under the cloud of unresolved interpersonal conflicts.

5. Using self-talk and imagery to raise your self-esteem works as powerfully in your working world as it does in your personal world. You can only allow others to like you as much as you like yourself.

6. Take the time to *really* listen to someone to send the powerful message, "Your ideas and opinions are important to

me." This is essential at home and at work because people will never feel valued if their words are not valued.

7. The self-awareness that prevents personal jealousies and insecurities from unduly eroding a marital connection can provide the same necessary insights for avoiding petty jealousies and unnecessary competition at work.

The bottom line is this: Emotional closeness at work is based on a genuine caring . . . there are no hidden agendas. You do not establish a friendship because someone has the right business connections or social contacts. Nor is there an ulterior motive to turn the friendship into an extramarital affair or an advantageous business deal. Others will eventually pick up on your true intentions and feel used. More damage will be done than if you had never extended yourself in the first place.

Genuine caring means you are looking for no gain other than the sharing, closeness, and camaraderie. Genuine caring also means that you are willing to make sacrifices for a coworker. You will be available in times of need. You clearly are more than just a "fair weather" friend.

Finally, caring means that you are noncompetitive. You do not resent your coworkers' successes nor are you jealous of their accomplishments. You *genuinely* celebrate the good things that happen to them and their children. Maybe this is the truest test of a real friend. The most trusted friend is not the person who is there to grieve with you when tragedy strikes. This is special and valued. But the truest test is whether the person can genuinely celebrate your successes. This is a person who is truly your friend.

• CHAPTER 21 •

Establishing Positive Relationships

Some of you responded positively to the suggestions given in the last chapter. You like the idea of using the caring, communication, commitment, and competency strategies to increase the degree of personal closeness in your career arena.

Others of you, however, hesitated. This is more personal closeness than you are comfortable with. You prefer more limits or restrictions on the emotional closeness. You would like an emotional glass ceiling on how far you go. If this is where you are, the two strategies given in this chapter are for you. They will increase the emotional closeness, but still keep a cap on the depth that is created by the deeper sharing and deeper caring.

The Power of Praising

I recently had the opportunity to hear a multimillionaire speak to eight hundred businesspeople as he tried to sell them on the advantages of using his company. I was not interested in his company, but before his speech was over, I knew one major reason why this self-made man was so successful. He had perfected a simple but powerful secret.

At least ten times during his hour-long speech, he paused and invited one of his managers up on the stage. He gave a quick thirty-second "brag" on that person and then he went on with his speech. The whole process took only five minutes (ten people, thirty seconds each), not counting the brief walking time.

Can you imagine what happened to those ten people the next day as they went to work for this highly successful leader? What was their attitude toward him after having been praised in front of eight hundred people? What was their sense of self-importance? What was their loyalty to their boss who appreciated them so much?

I would encourage you to follow this millionaire's example. I implore you to override your earlier programming that you should never compliment bosses ("They will think I am a brown-noser."), colleagues ("They will wonder what I am after."), subordinates ("They will respect me less."), or customers ("They will think the compliments are insincere.").

Give yourself permission to praise others. Stop worrying about whether other people may question if your compliments are manipulative, patronizing, or mere flattery. We need to know that it is okay to selectively compliment people on their strengths even though they have other weaknesses. Such compliments do not make us insincere, only discriminating. And we need to stop hesitating just because other people become embarrassed when they receive compliments. Maybe we can encourage them to start accepting rather than "modestly" depreciating all positive feedback.

Recently Susan was having one of those days when she just could not get going. Nothing major was bothering her; it was just a blah Monday. She was going through the motions but not really "with it." As she was trying to wade through her mental fog, she received a phone call from her boss who had been reviewing her marketing recommendations for the company. Her boss was very complimentary about the report, but even more uplifting was his recalling of how her recommendations last year had helped the company land a big account. Suddenly the psychological sun came out. The fog lifted, the blahs evaporated, and her spirits were raised. The rest of the day breezed along. This was the impact of a single positive message.

The strategy of praising is simple and yet powerful. But do not take my word for it. Look at your own life to appreciate the emotional value of praising. Recall three times in your life when a person that you truly valued gave you a genuine, carefully thought-out compliment. What was your reaction? What is your reaction even now as you recall the three experiences? Relive the sense of well-being and remember the afterglow. This is the value of praising.

If you would like to create that type of emotional high in the people you work with, complete the following praising assignment.

1. Take out five 3-inch by 5-inch cards and write one of your colleague's names on the top of each card. Below each name write down three positive qualities for that person.

2. Over the next three weeks, give each person the compliments. Be sure to spread out the compliments over the next three weeks, giving only one compliment each time.

I caution you, however, that your colleagues may not be prepared for your radical change in behavior. The first time you give a compliment, you may detect a subtle nonverbal message which says, "What have you done . . . or want . . . or neglected?" Persist with the compliments, however, and soon the disbelief will fade. Notice how the initial skepticism is replaced with muted signs of pleasure. Watch for the subtle body language that signals this pleasure even when they pretend that it really does not make that much difference.

Ready for a simple formula? If you give other people more compliments, there will be greater emotional closeness. Conversely, if you give other people more criticisms, there will be increased emotional distance. Naturally other factors do impact the working relationships, but one of the most significant factors is the compliments/criticisms ratio.

I encourage you to be keenly aware of the compliments/criticisms ratio in all your relationships. Monitor the ratio of positive to negative comments you give your employees, co-workers, boss, or other ongoing business contacts. Strive to shake the old habit of thinking positive comments but not saying them while you freely give the criticisms (euphemistically called "constructive criticism"). If you sit on your positive comments and say only the negatives, you lose the proper (and accurate) communication ratio that creates positive feelings, better working relationships, and greater emotional closeness.

How about striving for a ratio of giving four positive comments for every negative comment?

The Power of Active Listening

Creatively praising people is one way to improve personal relationships on your job. A second way is to skillfully use active listening to better respond to their verbal and nonverbal communication. Unfortunately, active listening is *the* most underutilized communication strategy. This is sad because the right type of listening can be a very powerful tool for solving problems, changing attitudes, altering behavior, and creating the special emotional closeness that adds magic to your career path.

It is interesting that there are only four basic ways you respond to what a manager, coworker, employee, or customer has said. You usually give (a) an evaluation response, (b) an information response, (c) a clarifying response, or (d) an understanding response. The wise use of these responses can have a profound impact on the ensuing communication and the establishment of positive relationships in the work arena.

1. An evaluation response. An evaluation response reacts to the appropriateness of what another person has said or done. The listener overtly or subtly implies there is a proper way. There is an underlying tone of judgment in the response, an air of rightness or wrongness. You, by your response, evaluate the thoughts, feelings, and behavior of the other person. Typical statements could include the following:

- "Whatever gave you the idea that you could . . . ?"
- "Did you even think what the consequences of your act would be on . . . ?"
- "You should . . ."
- "It is wrong to . . ."

The evaluation response may provide needed direction and guidance. It shows a more "appropriate" way of doing things. The danger, however, is that it creates negative feelings and defensiveness, especially if the other person feels you have not taken the time to understand the situation. Therefore, this response should be used sparingly and only when needed. A steady stream of evaluation remarks may do more harm than good.

2. An information-giving response. An information-giving response supplies facts, opinions, and personal feelings. The assumption is that the other person lacks (or requests) information, and your response is intended to provide this data. The information is given in a nonjudgmental manner (unlike the evaluation response). Sample responses could include these:

- "My advice to you is that you may . . ."
- "The reason I did that was because I . . ."
- "Perhaps you should consider the fact that I . . ."
- "What you may not know is . . ."

The information-giving response provides additional data that others may need. A misuse occurs, however, when the information is given before the problem is clearly defined or the other person's feelings are acknowledged. Too quick an answer may also incorrectly convey the message, "I really don't want to get emotionally involved."

Never underestimate the value of allowing other people to discover the solutions themselves as opposed to your always automatically giving them the answers. The self-discovery approach develops self-reliance and self-sufficiency; the expert-advice approach fosters dependency and passivity.

Although the next two categories of responses are frequently underused, they can dramatically add to the quality of the communication.

3. A clarifying response. A clarifying response is used to gather more information. You do not fully understand what the other person means so you ask questions to receive further clarification. Typical clarifying responses could begin with the following:

- "Tell me more about . . ."
- "What were the reasons why . . . ?"
- "What did you do when . . . ?"
- "How did you feel as . . . ?"

The clarifying response encourages further development of a topic. There is no jumping to conclusions or cookbook answers. The clarifying response conveys interest, helps others understand their situation, and gives you more complete information.

4. The understanding response. An understanding response conveys to others that you understand what they are saying or

feeling. You have crawled into their skin, walked in their shoes, and seen things through their eyes. An understanding response has a characteristic beginning:
- "You feel..."
- "I hear you saying that you..."
- "You seem to believe that..."
- "It worries you that..."

The understanding response develops rapport and encourages others to share more of their thoughts and feelings. It draws people closer together.

The master communicators know that each response pattern is likely to elicit a different reaction in people. Of course, many factors play key roles: the emotions of the speaker, the genuineness of the listener, the current circumstances, and the quality of the relationship between the two people. The response style, however, does have more emotional impact than most people realize.

Here are two suggestions to help you work these responses into your conversations more effectively.

1. Rehearse these four response categories mentally. Review the four response categories two or three times, then reflect on some previous conversations you have had. Replay the conversations in your mind. Which responses did you use? What was the impact? What other responses could you have substituted, and how would these replies have changed the conversations? Examine the way other people have responded to you. Which response categories did they use as you shared your ideas, thoughts, and feelings? What impact did their responses have? What would have been your reaction if they had used one of the other response categories? Dwell on these conversations at your leisure.

This reflection will help you integrate the responses naturally and without the strained feeling that can occur if you consciously think about the categories as you are carrying on an actual conversation. In fact, you may find this reflective-thinking technique a useful tool for smoothly implementing many of the strategies mentioned in this book.

2. Take a closer look at the understanding response. It is easy to ignore the potential value of an understanding response.

The simple acknowledgment of another person's feelings has an emotional value that often outweighs any skillful question, insightful information, or stop-in-the-tracks evaluation. The "I hear you" statement has the amazing power of getting people to share more of their genuine feelings.

The understanding response is powerful because this reply most effectively conveys acceptance. Acceptance means you truly value other people's essence. You may not approve of all of their actions and behaviors, but you accept their personal "being" despite their faults and shortcomings.

Next time another person shares a personal concern try out some understanding responses. You will be amazed at the powerful impact this response can have on the relationship—a positive, dynamic, satisfying, and rewarding impact that will dramatically enhance the emotional closeness.

Another key consideration is to be sure not to restrict your understanding responses to what the other person has said. Instead you respond to their *verbal* communication and to their *nonverbal* communication!

Psychologists have demonstrated that the emotional impact of a message is 7 percent verbal content and 93 percent nonverbal content! If you truly want to understand what people are saying, you need to become more aware of their nonverbal communication. This is the power of body language. It is a tool you can use to become an active listener. This is when listening becomes a creative art.

It is not necessary to give you a short course on how to read nonverbal messages. You are far more perceptive than you realize. You are already picking up people's body language and other nonverbal cues. Appreciate this fact as you reflect on some of your previous relationship experiences. You knew:

- He was angry even though he denied it.
- She was hurt by the joke despite her laughter.
- He liked you but was uncomfortable sharing these emotions.
- She was sad despite the outward smile of happiness.
- He was secretly competitive even though he pretended to be your best friend.

These perceptions are not magical insights; you are merely picking up subtle body language.

A lawyer friend told me an amusing story that shows the transparency of most body language. He shared that he had been asked to do a lengthy television interview on a controversial legal issue. He was understandably nervous, but he did not want to give that impression on the screen; he wanted to come across as a polished and relaxed attorney. He completed the half-hour interview and felt quite good about it. He thought he had successfully created the impression of being very relaxed and comfortable.

Later that day, however, he ran into a professional acquaintance who was a television personality. When she mentioned she had seen the TV show, my trial lawyer friend asked for a critique. He said, "She gave me some positive comments and a couple of useful suggestions. I then made the mistake of inquiring whether I had appeared relaxed during the show. Her answer was priceless, 'Ralph, now that you mention it, I did notice that aspect. You had a rather relaxed, casual position; unfortunately, you were frozen into that position for the entire half hour.'"

Her reading of my friend's body posture had correctly identified his nervous and uptight feeling. Once again, he proved that our body language gives clear messages about our true emotions.

My friend followed up that amusing incident by telling one of his "lawyer" stories. He prefaced the story by saying, "Your body language can kill you."

A famous defense attorney was defending a murder suspect in Texas. The case against the defendant was solid, but the one weak link was the fact that the victim's body had never been found. In his closing argument, the defense attorney jumped on this point. In his best theatrical style, he told the jury, "There is no body; therefore, there is no murder. In fact, the alleged victim is still alive. He has been hiding out for reasons totally unrelated to this case, but he has reluctantly agreed to appear in court to free my innocent client. The 'so-called' murder victim is going to make a dramatic appearance by walking through the back door of this courtroom in exactly thirty seconds." The attorney started counting down "thirty, twenty-nine, twenty-eight, twenty seven"–the tension mounted–"twelve, eleven, ten, nine, eight." All eyes moved to the door at the back of the courtroom—"five, four, three, two, one." The victim did not appear, but the defense attorney screamed, "You looked! This means you have some doubt as to whether the victim is really dead! Therefore, you cannot convict my client!" With that dramatic gesture, he triumphantly sat down. There was a stunned silence.

The jury went out to begin their deliberations. Within a short period of time, they were back in the courtroom.

The judge asked if the jury had reached a decision, and the foreman said they had. "What is your verdict?" asked the judge. The foreman of the jury replied, "On the charge of first degree murder, we find the defendant GUILTY as charged."

The defense attorney jumped up screaming. "How could you find my client guilty? There obviously was doubt or you would not have looked toward the open door!"

The foreman of the jury calmly replied, "It is true that many of us did look—we did have some momentary doubts. During the deliberations, however, two members of our jury noted that the defendant *had not looked!*"

The defendant's nonverbal communication had disrupted the clever ploy. His body language removed the contrived doubt that had been created, and he was convicted on the solid evidence presented.

Start observing the body language in people. There is a rich language in their nonverbal communication. Observe how:

- An employee acts when the boss is approaching.
- A woman or man signals sexual interest.
- An applicant shows discomfort.
- Your secretary clears the desk when he or she is upset.
- An audience responds to a boring speaker.

Practice reading the nonverbal messages. They will tell you many things about other people—things you want to know to help you better communicate.

This is a good time to clarify the two basic purposes in reading nonverbal messages. One is to expose other people, to discover emotions and facts that they are trying to cover up. This is the way the police detective, the employment interviewer, the nosy friend, or the accusatory parent may use body language.

Reading body language will help accomplish this goal, but the "detective" use of body language can create a feeling of being psychologically invaded. During the next encounter with you, he or she is even more defensive and resentful. The relationship is more alienated than ever.

The other way to use body language is to enhance active listening. Human beings have the potential to be tremendously perceptive. You have this potential if you are willing to develop it, and nothing is more flattering to another person than to be really listened to—it is far more satisfying than the most positive of verbal bouquets. This is the gift you give by not limiting yourself to the 7 percent verbal content.

Active listening, when it responds to the total message, becomes a rewarding experience: two human beings in a deep, emotional interaction. As you totally tune in to the other person, you hear what he or she is attempting to share. You have an extrasensory perception, an intuitive sensing. As other people sense your tuning-in, they instinctively make the extra effort to communicate with their voice, eyes, hands, body position, and any other means possible. They want to be heard.

Active listening is just that: *listening*. It is strong on the "understanding" and "clarifying" responses and weak on the "information-giving" and "evaluation" responses. I know because I had a personal experience that forever locked in the importance of doing active listening.

In 1965 my wife (at that time) and I had our first child. Being a first-time father, I did all the traditional things. I passed out cigars even though I have never smoked; I called anyone who could possibly be interested in the news; and I sat bedside with my wife celebrating the joy of that moment. We had a healthy robust son and we were proud parents. I left the hospital at 9:00 P.M., both mother and child were doing fine.

At 5:00 A.M. I was awakened by a telephone call. It was the hospital. The spokesperson said that very serious complications had developed, and she suggested that I come down to the hospital as soon as possible.

When I got there, I was met by a team of doctors. They informed me that bleeding had developed within our son's head and he was critically ill. He was on total life-support systems and had even lost his sucking reflex. They were talking about surgery to open up the head so they could remove some of the blood.

The child lived for eight days and then died. During the blur of those eight days, I distinctly remember four people talking to me:

- The pastor of my church. He was a dynamic minister and one of the leading preachers in the country. I still recall listening to some of his stirring sermons.
- An assistant pastor. I had never really had an in-depth conversation with him before this crisis. It was a large church, and he worked primarily with the youth of the church.
- My best friend. He was probably the best male friend that I have ever had.
- A social worker from the hospital. The first time I met her was when we met at the hospital.

I clearly remember what the four of them did even though it happened thirty-one years ago. The pastor read some Bible verses, said a prayer, and talked about the healing power of God. The assistant pastor, on the other hand, said very little. The scene I do remember, however, is he and his wife sitting bedside listening to my wife and me. One time when I looked up, I saw a tear roll down his cheek.

My best friend gave me a short Norman Vincent Peale pep talk. He talked about people he knew who had faced similar crises, and how, miraculously, everything had turned out okay. He said we should "think positively." The social worker, unlike my friend, said very little. But she listened, really listened, to what I was feeling.

I still remember having negative reactions to two of these individuals and extremely positive reactions to two of them. As you have already surmised, my negative reactions were to the two people I was closest to (the pastor and my best friend), and my positive reactions were to the assistant pastor and the social worker.

Why? The reason is that these two individuals really listened to our pain, grief, and fears. They demonstrated the power of active listening . . . and how too many words, even when they are well intended by well-meaning people, often do more harm than good.

I share this story to remind you that *listening* can be your most powerful communication tool.

(• CHAPTER 22 •)

Stress Strategies

One way to cope with job stress is to fully develop the three stress-resistant factors of change, involvement, and control that were discussed in chapter 18. These powerful qualities help you aggressively deflect the normal career stressors.

But you can go further. You can also have a repertoire of stress strategies available to cope with the excessive stress when the three stress-resistant factors are not enough—stress strategies similar to those Gloria used to survive a difficult crisis in her life.

Gloria was ecstatic when she was offered the position of vice president of sales and service for a large, privately owned company. The president had indicated that she was, by far, the best candidate applying for the job. At that time he said, "Your credentials are outstanding; they forced us to change our normal policy of promoting from within." Gloria knew she was ready for the challenge. She could not wait to get started.

Six months later, Gloria was under tremendous stress. On the surface, everything was great. Sales were up dramatically; service complaints were down 50 percent; expenses had been reduced; and the wealthy absentee owner had called her on four occasions to let her know how pleased he was with her performance. He even told her that she was the person most responsible for the tremendous growth that the company was experiencing.

But underlying this success, problems had developed; problems that were not even Gloria's fault.

The president of the company had become threatened by Gloria's dramatic success and had started taking Gloria out of the management loop. Whenever possible, he communicated with Gloria's assistant rather than Gloria on key decisions. Gloria sensed this change and started wondering, "Is he trying to sabotage me?"

Gloria's assistant was a lifelong friend who Gloria brought to the company with her. Initially, her friend was very appreciative, but he realized that if Gloria was removed, he would have a good chance at the vice president's position. Rather than keeping Gloria informed as to what the president was doing, he was subtly encouraging the president to keep contacting him. Gloria became keenly aware of what was happening when she accidentally overheard a conversation between her assistant and the president.

To compound the situation even more, part of the staff had turned against Gloria. When Gloria applied for her position, there was a key staff person who also applied. This person was not given serious consideration because she was not qualified, but nevertheless she took it as a personal rejection when she was "passed over." There was no open conflict, but there was an undercurrent of petty dissatisfactions and backbiting comments.

So there Gloria sat with an impressive job performance and an owner who was extremely pleased, but with a boss, assistant, and key staff person who were all out to get her.

It was only a matter of time before these constant interpersonal strains started taking their psychological toll. Gloria began sleeping less, worrying more, eating too much, and having an emotional swing between being too anxious and being too depressed. Fortunately, Gloria realized what was happening and took some aggressive action. She devised a plan for combating the job stress. In her creative style, she (a) reduced the stress symptoms by attending a yoga class and joining an athletic club, (b) went for some short-term counseling to fully share her concerns and explore what was happening, and (c) skillfully confronted the situation by asking for a meeting with the owner, president, assistant, and staff person.

What Gloria did was take a multiple approach to combat and overcome the stress and it worked. She reduced her stress and she resolved the problems. I encourage you to have a comparable set of stress strategies in case you ever need to respond to excessive stress in your life.

The interesting thing is that most stress strategies fall into one of five categories. These categories can help you devise a stress game plan that will be best for you. The rest of this chapter will look at these categories and suggest ways for you to develop a game plan similar to Gloria's. The five categories are as follows.

1. Relaxation techniques. Relaxation techniques are primarily designed to reduce the stress symptoms. The goal is to change your body's response (at least on a short-term basis) to the tension, anxiety, frustration, anger, fear, apprehension, and other free-floating psychological and physiological reactions to your career stressors.

One simple yet effective technique in this category is four-by-four breathing. You may even want to try this technique right now. Inhale deeply to the count of four. Then slowly exhale to the count of four. Repeat this four-by-four breathing pattern several times. Each time you slowly inhale, think "deeper"; each time you exhale, think "relax."

You will be amazed at how quickly you feel a sense of relaxation.

2. Aerobic exercise. Jogging, brisk walking, swimming, bicycling, jumping rope, and aerobic dancing are great for reducing stress. These aerobic activities create psychological escape and also give physiological relief. Studies have shown that a sustained physical workout causes actual biochemical changes in the brain. Endorphins, which have a tranquilizing effect on the body, are released.

3. Sharing feelings. Emotionally sharing your feelings with someone is an excellent way to reduce the stress in your life. This strategy is especially effective when there is no holding back as you express your feelings. You totally share your emotions so you can more fully discharge the stress.

This is often done with the assistance of a professional counselor. A close friend may be an adequate substitute, however, if he or she will allow you to fully vent your suppressed emotions rather than being protective. If your friend tries to keep you "from hurting too much," he or she will only deprive you of the opportunity to bring your emotions to the surface, an essential step in releasing the emotions. Your friend's role is simply to be there as a *listening* friend.

As you are expressing your feelings, however, it is important to remember the purpose. The sole purpose is to release the build-up of stress. If you are using it to (a) prove your innocence, (b) smear someone's name, or (c) rally people to your side, you will create rather than reduce stress.

4. Mental toughness. This category of stress-reduction strategies focuses on ways to better mentally process the stressors you have in your life. Having a psychological toughness allows you to (a) not overpersonalize negative events, and (b) pay close attention to the psychological interpretation you give to stressful situations.

It is interesting to observe how different individuals respond to career stressors. For example, I saw many bank executives and savings and loan officers in my private practice during the financial crisis of the 1980's. Many of these individuals saw their financial institutions declared insolvent and taken over by the federal government. Some of them handled this crisis very well; others had tremendous psychological struggles. One distinguishing characteristic that separated these two groups was their mental toughness. The real survivors used mental toughness tricks such as "Punch your own ticket," and "What is my B?" to handle all of the stressors during these difficult times. (See upcoming chapters for more information on these two strategies.)

5. Confrontation. Confrontation means that you do not make the common mistake of coping with career stressors by psychologically running away. Winners do just the opposite. They confront problems rather than passively waiting for the concerns to solve themselves or simply disappear.

Many people become "experts" at avoiding the source of their stress. They will *not* ask why a coworker is upset with them, determine why a customer has stopped doing business with them, or find out why they were not given their annual bonus. Even in their personal lives, they will *not* see their physician to check out a medical concern, find out whether their teenager is really on drugs, or inquire as to why their spouse has shown no sexual interest for the past two months.

Unfortunately, the concerns over the coworker, customer, bonus, or any other stressor continue to grow. This denial or avoidance causes the stress to linger and even compound. It is much better to confront the situation by asking why the coworker is upset, the customer has stopped doing business, or the bonus was not given. There may be a short-term increase in stress, but the end result is usually a decrease in stress because now you have the necessary information to do something about the conditions that created the stress.

Relaxation techniques, aerobic exercise, sharing feelings, mental toughness, and confrontation—these are the powerful strategies for coping with your job stress. These strategies will maximize your chances of liking your career and potentially make it your magical path to personal happiness. Master these strategies by developing *your own* individualized strategies in each of these five categories:

1. Relaxation techniques. Attend seminars on yoga, transcendental meditation, self-hypnosis, and/or biofeedback. All are powerful approaches for relaxing your psychological and physiological being. The secret is to find the one that works best for you.

2. Aerobic exercise. Join an athletic club or fitness center so you have camaraderie and exercise options during your workouts. The camaraderie will inspire you to keep going, and the multiple options for your aerobic workout will maximize your chances of finding a workout routine that fits you. Commit to a regular schedule and you will get in better shape, look better, feel better, and as a bonus, your aerobic workout will become an instant stress reducer.

3. Sharing feelings. Establish a special sharing relationship with a close friend. Make a "counseling" pact that you can always go to each other to share your feelings. For this to work, however, both of you have to be comfortable being primarily a listener rather than an advice giver. As you are making this agreement, you and your friend may wish to review the *sharing* concept of public and real self and the *listening* concepts of empathy, confidentiality, and acceptance as discussed in chapter 9.

4. Mental toughness. Establish the discipline to stop and ask yourself a quick question any time you are experiencing excessive stress: "To what extent is my stress created by outside events, and to what extent is it caused by my 'personal' interpretation of what happened?" As one person wisely said, "Don't sweat the small stuff . . . and most stuff is small stuff."

5. *Confrontation.* Develop more skill in confronting the people who create the stress in your life. Learn the art of approaching them in ways that encourage problem solving rather than increased defensiveness. Often it is a subtle "turn of a word" or a slight nonverbal (body language) message that makes the difference in what happens.

You may prepare for this encounter by first confronting your emotions. One technique is to write a letter to the person who is "causing" your stress. In the letter, express all of your anger, hurt, and resentment. Blast him or her if you feel like it. But here is the catch: after you have finished the letter, put it in a drawer and have a good night's sleep. Reread the letter in the morning and then tear it up. This technique gives you an emotional discharge, but it does not create new conflicts (that is, a response to your letter).

Once the emotions are discharged (relaxation, aerobics, sharing, and mental toughness may also help in this area), you can confront the person who upset you in a more measured way, and the odds of resolving the stressful conflict are greatly increased.

Another strategy that you may find useful in confronting the source of your stress (whether it is another person, an event, or an internal conflict) is to ask the three magical questions discussed in chapter 37. These three powerful questions are excellent tools for fully understanding the true issues surrounding your job stress.

Relaxation techniques, aerobic exercise, sharing feelings, mental toughness, and confrontation are the foundations for developing your stress strategies.

Now let's narrow the focus and discuss three specific strategies for coping with career stress. The next three chapters will give you my favorite three career stress strategies that I use on a daily basis.

• CHAPTER 23 •

Self-Talk and Job Stress

In chapter 14 I discussed how self-talk can have a major impact on the competency factor in your marriage. But self-talk clearly is not limited to the way you function in an intimate relationship.

Self-talk, as the term implies, refers to the quiet inner conversations that you have with yourself many times a day. Unfortunately, you may not even realize what is happening unless you pay special attention. This lack of awareness does not alter the fact that your self-talk has a tremendous impact on the way you cope with the stressors in your career.

How do you talk to yourself? Would you say that most of your self-talk is positive or negative? Take an informal four-question quiz to better answer this question. Check whether the "a" response or the "b" response comes closer to your typical self-talk.

1. Your boss asks you to give a fifteen-minute presentation at the board of director's meeting. What is your first thought?
    _____ a. "This is great! What a wonderful opportunity to show how well our department is doing."
    _____ b. "Oh, no! How can I ever give a talk? I probably will make a fool of myself!"

2. You have always received compliments about your hair, smile, and eyes. You have to modestly admit that you like

these physical qualities. On the other hand, you wish you were ten pounds lighter and your nose was slightly shorter. As you meet a key business contact for the first time, what is your self-talk about your appearance?

   _____ a. "I hope they notice my hair, eyes, and smile."

   _____ b. "Are they turned off by my weight and nose?"

3. You make a mistake, not a major mistake, but one that causes some minor inconvenience for other people. What is your self-talk that evening? Do you:

   _____ a. Say one hundred times, "How could I have been so stupid?"

   _____ b. Balance the self-incrimination by thinking, "I made a mistake that time, but most of the time I do it right."

4. You pause for a minute in your busy day and look into your psychological mirror. As you take this fleeting self-examination, what is your most frequent self-talk about the many aspects of your job performance?

   _____ a. I like the way I _____ (and you hear yourself finishing the sentence with a *positive* self-reference).

   _____ b. I hate the way I _____ (and you hear yourself finishing the sentence with a self-depreciating comment).

As these four examples suggest, your mind races along each day having many thoughts about your talents, values, accomplishments, appearance, relationships, past behaviors, and daily experiences. This happens so naturally that you may go through these verbal gyrations without a second thought.

Although this self-talk appears innocent, it is not. Your self-talk has a dramatic impact on your life. The impact can be damaging, but it can also be a dynamic force in helping you cope with your career and personal stressors.

Your self-talk often turns visual and becomes a powerful programmer of your subconscious mind. But even when your self-talk does not unleash the awesome power of your subconscious mind, it can have a tremendous impact on your psychological well-being. Just as the steady pounding of the waves reshapes the oceanfront rocks, your self-talk delivered in a persistent manner can dramatically change your stress level.

Aggressively control your self-talk by monitoring how you talk to yourself. Start hearing the quiet little self-references that have previously slipped by unnoticed. Always remember that every time you have a negative thought, you add to your stress level. Each additional negative thought adds even more stress—too much negative self-talk and the stress level can reach crisis proportions. Each positive thought, on the other hand, contributes to a decrease in your stress level; each additional positive self-reference lowers it even more. Whether your stress is raised or lowered is determined, in part, by your ratio of positive and negative self-talk messages.

Take any situation where you do not live up to your expectations or perform as well as you would have liked. Maybe you even goofed. This naturally increases your personal stress. What do you do? Your self-talk probably sounds something like this:

- "How stupid of me."
- "There I go again."
- "This is just like me, a failure."
- "I knew I couldn't do it!"
- "You should be embarrassed, you klutzy fool!"

You not only have an unsatisfactory performance to increase your stress level, but you compound the damage by giving yourself continuing and recurring negative self-talk after the performance. What you should say instead is:

- "This is not like me!"
- "Next time, I will do better!"

With this positive internal conversation, your self-talk reduces, rather than magnifies, the impact of the negative performance.

The same rules of self-talk apply when you perform in a way that lives up to your expectations. This job performance temporarily reduces your stress level. But how do you respond to this successful performance? Too often, people react by saying such things as:

- "Oh, it was just luck."
- "I could never do that again."
- "Other people should get all the credit."

This modest, self-effacing talk may be appealing to other people, but think of the impact of this self-talk on your stress level. It lessens the value of your performance, and your self-talk is actually preventing you from having positive feelings. Instead, what you should say to yourself is:

- "That's just like me!"
- "This is the way I will perform in the future!"

In addition to your personal self-talk, it is important to become more sensitive to the emotional impact of the messages you receive from others. GIGO (garbage in, garbage out) is an expression that computer enthusiasts often use. GIGO suggests that if you place bad information into the computer, the only thing you will receive in return is bad results, no matter how sophisticated the computer.

The same process is true for you. If you continually receive negative messages from others, the end result will be more stress on your job. I am not saying that I am opposed to negative messages or that you can never profit from criticism. What I am saying is that even the best criticism will increase your stress level at the same time that it is modifying your behavior. If this is true, surely you want to limit the amount of criticism you receive and make sure it is truly valid, useful criticism.

Perhaps a golfing analogy illustrates the effects of too much criticism. Several years ago I decided to start playing golf. After a few times on the course, I decided to take an informal lesson from a friend who was an excellent golfer but an inexperienced teacher. My friend, Jack was most "helpful." Every time I took a swing, he offered another golfing tip:

- "Keep your left arm straight."
- "Bend your knees more."
- "Hold your head still on your backswing."
- "Lead your swing with your hips."
- "Keep your right elbow in."
- "Keep your eye on the ball."

- "Keep your head down."
- "Bring your club back slowly."

And the list went on.

Then my friend concluded, "I now want you to put all these suggestions together and really hit the ball." I swung and completely missed the ball! My score on the next round of golf was seven strokes higher.

Out of desperation, I went to the pro who was considered the best golf teacher in the Kansas City area. The pro started my lesson by simply asking me to hit some golf balls. After watching me for twenty minutes, the pro said, "Bob, I want you to rotate your hips this way," and he showed me what he meant. He made the same correction five other times until I had it grooved.

Before he made a second suggestion, the golf lesson was over. At first I felt "ripped off." I had paid him a big fee and he had only given me one tip. What about my head, hands, feet, shoulders, legs, and seat? I did not say anything, but the next time I went golfing, I noticed that I was hitting the ball longer, straighter, and my score was the best ever. Suddenly, I realized what had happened. The pro had picked out the one aspect of my game that needed the most fundamental change. The pro trusted my kinetic sensing and natural athletic ability to make some of the other changes. He did not feel that it was necessary to call all of the minor errors to my attention and "tie me up further."

I later shared my observation with the pro. He laughed and said, "Let me share a secret with you. Many of my golf lessons are the result of all the how-to books on golf. As people start playing better, they rush out and buy another book. They try to make too many mental corrections, and they get all confused. My lesson helps get them back in touch with their natural swing."

This is the effect of most criticism. It has a tendency to inhibit, retard, tie up, and increase stress levels rather than provide positive changes in behavior.

Even the most useful criticism probably temporarily increases your stress level. Therefore, any criticism should be evaluated by the following question: "Is this criticism valuable enough to justify the temporary increase in my personal stress level?" If it is valuable enough, then additional steps should be taken to ensure that other input is forthcoming to keep the stress level manageable.

Often you can make the same changes in behavior without going through a highly negative process. For example, assume that you just gave a presentation to all the mid-level managers in your organization. Since this is the first time you have given this presentation, you may want some feedback in order to revise it before you present it to the board of directors. How should you phrase the request for feedback? Many would probably ask, "What do you think I should change or revise in this talk?" So each of your colleagues would offer his or her requested constructive criticism. You probably would receive confusing and contradictory comments:

- "You did not use enough illustrations."
- "I felt you placed too much emphasis on marketing strategies."
- "There was not enough group participation."
- "You did not cover company strategies adequately."
- "You did not lecture enough."
- "There should have been a longer question and answer period."
- "I disagree with your analysis of . . ."

And the list grows as each individual gives a personal reaction to the thing he or she liked the least.

In the meantime what happens to you? Like the golfer, you are overloaded with constructive criticisms. By the time your colleagues are through, you are confused, discouraged, and probably thinking, "I may never give a talk again." You drag your battered psyche out of the meeting.

Instead, the way you could phrase your request for critiquing is, "Would each of you tell me the thing you liked best about the talk?" The feedback would then sound like the following:

- "Your focus on . . . was very useful."
- "Your enthusiasm made it easy to maintain interest."
- "The group participation was a nice change of pace."
- "I liked the way the topic of . . . was covered."
- "The lecture portion was especially effective."

This approach validates what you did well. As a result, your enthusiasm is high and you cannot wait to repeat the talk. Later, as you think about your talk, you realize that no one made a positive comment about one specific item, so you make a mental note to change that part or perhaps completely drop it. This allows you more time for the aspects that really went well. You still have your information for revision, but not at the expense of a stress battering. You have avoided unnecessary psychological garbage and your self-esteem soars.

Start becoming more aware of the impact of self-talk. Be especially sensitive to the way you talk to yourself and to the feedback you get from others. Because of the workings of the subconscious mind, these two types of messages have far more impact on you than you may realize.

Unfortunately, you will receive criticism. It is an integral part of the business world. You cannot avoid it—it is not even good business to do so—but you can bolster your self-talk by learning how to "punch your good-feelings ticket." Once you have mastered this self-talk strategy, you will have a powerful way to process customer complaints, negative evaluations, and all other forms of criticism.

The Art of Handling Criticism

Picture the following scenario to better appreciate the delicate art involved in handling negative feedback. Someone walks up to you and gives you a stinging criticism (or at least it feels like a "stinging" criticism). Your immediate reaction is to defend yourself, and this is exactly what you do. But what is your message to the other person? It is, "You are wrong!"

The person who delivered the original criticism does not want to appear wrong, so he or she automatically offers evidence to support the criticism. In essence, he or she is criticizing you a second time.

You naturally defend yourself a second time. Now your implied message is, "Not only are you wrong, but you can't hear either!" The other person, by now more emotionally heated, responds by giving you a third round of criticism accompanied by a more personal attack on your personality. You defend yourself for the third time and . . . well, you get the picture. With each defensive statement, you set yourself up for another round of criticism. Unfortunately, it is not merely another round of criticism. It is an escalating round of criticism . . . like putting gasoline on a fire.

A better way to handle criticism is to use the empty-bucket approach. Whenever people criticize you, immediately form a mental image of them holding an old wooden bucket half full of water. The water represents their negative feelings, and your first goal is to empty this bucket. At this critical stage, you never defend yourself or pull away. Instead, you encourage the emptying of the bucket by having them explain more fully what their complaints are. Responses like, "Tell me more . . . I can understand why you are upset . . . I am so glad you came to me . . . I see . . . And then what did you feel?" will keep them going until their bucket is empty. And you can always tell when the bucket has emptied because their body posture will relax and their voice tone will soften.

Then, and only then, do you explain your position . . . because only then will they be receptive to your explanation. Always remember, first you empty their bucket. It is the essential first step if you want to keep your customers. The trick is doing this without being psychologically battered by the negative feedback. This is where you regulate self-talk via "learning how to punch your good-feelings ticket."

Thirty-eight years ago, the following incident introduced me to the importance of punching my own good-feelings ticket. I still look back upon it with amusement, although I am not sure it was as amusing at that time.

I was twenty-one years old, a senior at the University of Minnesota, a psychology major, and "in love" with my female lab partner. (I still have very pleasant memories of white rats running through mazes in "darkened" laboratories.) I went home for the Christmas holidays, but I had to see my "true love" at least once during that vacation period.

I was not going to drive a hundred miles in forty-degrees-below-zero northern Minnesota winter weather just to turn around and come home. So I arrived back home at 3:00 A.M. as, I assumed, an emancipated twenty-one year old adult.

My mother met me at the door: I recall the scene as if it were yesterday. She had on a blue, quilted bathrobe, her waist-length hair was down, and the all too-familiar big black Bible was nestled between her upraised hands. (It is amazing how big a Bible looks at 3:00 A.M.!)

What did she say to me before I could even step out of the arctic cold? She did not say, "Are you hurt? Is everything okay?" Likewise, she did not say, "You should have telephoned so I would not have worried." Despite the Bible, she did not say, "Good little boys do not stay out with girls until three o'clock in the morning."

Instead, in her very serious religious tones, she said, "WHAT WILL THE NEIGHBORS THINK?"

I was programmed at an early age to be very concerned about what other people thought about me. Their opinions were critical to my happiness. But I cannot blame my mother for all of this; it seems to be a natural part of our culture. This is readily observable any time we watch young teenagers. They become obsessed over what their friends think about them. Any fad has to be blindly followed, any mannerism routinely imitated, and any new figure of speech quickly repeated. It is essential to be just like the rest to be accepted.

By the time a person reaches adulthood, the flaws in this "What will the neighbors think?" programming have become apparent. You probably have to look no further than your own personal life to understand what I am trying to say. Events have happened in your life that have turned earlier, positive feedback into a mixed bag of both positive and negative messages:

- The wonderful stage of "young love" has become a marriage with all the normal conflicts, frustrations, and hassles.
- The company that so heavily recruited you is now more focused on your performance quotas and less-than-perfect job evaluations.
- Your loving, compliant, six-year-old daughter has grown into an "independent" teenager.
- Your image in your community has been tarnished by a number of normal mistakes, misfortunes, and miscalculations in your personal and/or professional life.

You now realize how dangerous it is to rely solely on others for your good feelings about yourself. You are forced to make a transition from allowing others to punch your good-feelings ticket to punching your *own* good-feelings ticket!

The Good-Feelings Ticket

Picture a 3-inch by 5-inch ticket with a string attached hanging around your neck. This is your imaginary good-feelings ticket, and your goal is to get it punched so you feel good. To appreciate this picture, remember when you walked into the school cafeteria as a young child and asked the cafeteria worker for a carton of cold chocolate milk. She would reach down and punch your milk ticket, and then you would receive your "reward."

You turn to your boss to have him or her punch your emotional ticket, but he or she hesitates because it means you might ask for a raise. Next you seek out some of your customers, but all they do is complain about the one thing that went wrong while ignoring the ninety-nine things that went well.

Slightly battered and bruised, you turn to your personal life to get your good-feelings ticket punched. You reach out to your spouse, but he or she stopped punching your ticket the minute you said, "I do!" Finally, in desperation, you turn to your appreciative, adolescent children, but they do not even know what a ticket puncher is!

The only way to consistently feel good, as you probably have already surmised, is to learn how to punch your own ticket. There are two ways to do this. One way is to develop a habit of consistently giving yourself positive self-talk. (This has already been discussed.) The second way is to learn how to filter the feedback you receive from others.

Picture the ticket around your neck once again. Only this time, mentally place a filter in front of the ticket that assesses the compliments and criticisms you receive.

If someone gives you a compliment, your new filtering system immediately asks, "Do I really deserve that compliment?" If you do, you smile and say, "Thank you." But (and here is the critical aspect) *you* are the one who reaches down and punches your good-feelings ticket.

If you do not deserve the compliment (it is overstated or mere flattery), you use the same filtering system. You are polite—

you smile and say thank you—but here is the secret strategy: You do not punch your good-feelings ticket.

If you start faithfully practicing this with compliments, you will have an automatic, learned response when you receive a criticism. You will not let other people punch your good-feelings ticket in a negative way. Instead, you first run it through your filter.

This mental processing is necessary because you do not deserve 80 percent of the criticisms you receive. Do not be surprised by this statistic. People criticize because you deserve it, and they criticize you because they are jealous, competitive, depressed, scapegoating, insecure, suffering from low self-esteem, or blindly following a model they observed as a child.

Your filtering system can start processing the negatives the same way it handles the positives. You should always first ask, "Do I deserve that criticism?" If your answer is no, you reject the criticism, and you do not punch your emotional ticket. The criticism is sloughed off like water off a duck's back. If your answer is yes (one time in five), you integrate the criticism and make constructive changes. For this mental processing to work, however, you will have to faithfully practice the ticket-punching technique on the easy part, that is, the compliments.

I consistently find that individuals who learn to punch their own ticket have a renewed surge of personal power, emotional well-being, and self-confidence, while the individuals who passively allow others to punch their emotional ticket eventually lose the power of self-reliance and experience a gradual increase in personal and job-related stress.

Punch your *own* ticket and take control of *your* emotional life!

• CHAPTER 24 •

The Endorphin Fix

Reader's Digest had an article on how to beat the emotional blues. The authors appropriately mentioned that two of the most used (and successful) strategies were (a) prescription drugs, and (b) "talking out" therapy. They then added that there were other strategies, more in the category of self-help, that were also successful in combating these temporary states.

Which of the following self-help strategies do you think the authors thought were the most effective for overcoming the emotional blues triggered by job stress?

1. *Music.* Turn on some music that matches your blue mood. After you emotionally connect with the music, start changing the music to be more upbeat, light, and positive. The music will give you an emotional boost.

2. *Positive thinking.* You are a product of your emotional thoughts. Force yourself to think more positively, and your emotions will follow.

3. *Naps.* During sleep you will dream, and your dreams will give you a psychological release from your built-up stresses and tensions. Some psychologists call this dream escape.

4. *Diet.* There is a greater connection between the food you eat and your emotional state than you may realize. The wrong foods can pull down your emotional mood and the right foods can help lift your mood.

Which do you think the authors rated most effective of the self-help strategies? The answer is designed to pique your interest. The answer is . . . none of the above! The strategy the authors rated highest of the self-help strategies was the endorphin fix! The authors did not use the term "endorphin fix," but what they were describing was that effect.

Without exception, every person I have met who uses the endorphin fix swears by it. They report that it relaxes, mellows, and tranquilizes, yet simultaneously energizes, motivates, and stimulates. Now that is my kind of fix! It sounds like a wonderful way to stay "up."

The endorphin fix is both simple and difficult—simple because it is automatic, it happens naturally; difficult because the steps necessary to create this spontaneous process involve discipline.

The endorphin fix, as many of you already know, is the emotional high that follows a vigorous aerobic workout. And the fix is not only psychological. We now know that an aerobic workout creates biochemical changes in the brain. Endorphins are released that create the tranquilizing and energizing effects described previously.

Few people question the benefits of physical exercise. Some are already committed to a regular exercise program of running, power walking, swimming, aerobic dancing, or biking. Many are not working out, but have an exercise bike gathering dust in the garage, a paid but unused membership in a health club, and a bundle of good intentions that "one of these days I am going to start."

The key factor in implementing the endorphin fix strategy is not trying to sell you on the benefits of a regular thirty-minute aerobic workout. You already know that it can have a dramatic impact on the level of your job stress. Instead, the key is to determine why some people are willing to go through the exertion, pain, and fatigue of a vigorous workout, while others are not able to overcome this imposing obstacle even though the rewards are fantastic.

What are the factors that separate the "junkies" from the people who never get "hooked" on this powerful (and positive) drug? Is it because they have a greater stress level? A more addictive type personality? A better self-image? A sick desire to punish themselves? All of these may apply in some cases, but the key factor is the psychological plan that the devotees use with their exercise program.

Maintaining a regular workout schedule is challenging. Accomplishing this admirable task requires discipline, denial, and pain. (Whoever said thirty minutes on the exercise cycle was pure fun?) For some, even the thought of doing a workout brings up mental pictures of agony. It is easy to start focusing on the discomfort, fatigue, and exhaustion when you are working out rather than thinking about how good you are going to feel when your endorphins kick in (after fifteen to twenty minutes).

There is a question of whether the positives do outweigh the negatives, and desire and motivation may falter. After all, you can tell yourself "no pain, no gain" only so many times.

Usually there has to be the extra incentive, push, or motivation to keep with the program. This is where, once again, your own creative talents can enter the picture. You can create your own motivational program for releasing the powerful endorphins.

Psychologists frequently argue about the most effective way to make changes in your life. Each of the five most popular learning theories has a group of "true believers" fueling the debates that have gone on for years. The five ways (all are mentioned elsewhere in the book) these experts use to create positive changes are as follows:

1. The information method. The assumption behind this approach is that you lack adequate knowledge. Once you have been provided with this knowledge via lectures and written material, you will reason "this is a better way so I will make the change."

2. Cognitive dissonance. The theory underlying cognitive dissonance is that the best way to make a change is to "just do it." Once you do a new behavior for a sufficient period of time, your belief system will shift. You will actually start liking what you are doing, and the new behavior is established.

3. Reinforcement theory. This theory, originally made popular by B.F. Skinner, postulates that a rewarded behavior will continue and grow in strength; and a behavior that is not rewarded will be extinguished.

4. Imagery. This psychocybernetics concept suggests that what you vividly imagine goes into your subconscious mind with the same impact as if you had actually done the behavior. Once it is firmly planted through a planned series of visualizations, it will automatically start showing up in new behaviors.

5. *Modeling.* Modeling was popularized by A.L. Bandura. His theory demonstrated how the behavior we observe in others (parents, bosses, peers, teachers, and heroes) has a far greater impact on our future behavior than we would ever imagine. This is why the behavior of our parents is often replayed in our own lives.

Trying to decide which is the most effective learning theory is an interesting academic exercise. But the true winners step beyond these intellectual considerations. They reason that all have merit, so why choose? They try all five simultaneously.

Try this approach with your workout program. Use the multiple-learning approach to create a challenging but achievable change in the way you maintain your physical well-being. Take a creative inward look as you develop personalized strategies for each of the five learning theories:

1. *The information method.* What are two good books or articles that you could read on this subject? Browse the self-help section of a book store, ask your "physically-fit" friends, or better yet, ask a physical fitness expert. Pick up this educational material and put it on the top of your "to read" stack.

2. *Cognitive dissonance.* Make yourself a promise. You will faithfully do a workout for three weeks (twenty-one days). No matter what the excuse is, you will stick it out for that limited period of time. Do this and you will create a cognitive dissonance, that is, a behavior that says "I am working out," and a belief that says "I do not like working out." Within the twenty-one-day period, the dissonance is resolved by the belief shifting to "since I am working out so faithfully, I must actually like it." And soon you, like other physical fitness devotees, will actually like it!

My exercise plan for the next twenty-one days is_____
_____.

3. *Reinforcement.* Establish a reward that you will give yourself when you complete the twenty-one-day program. It could be a new outfit, a vacation, or anything else that gives you great pleasure. This is your deserved reward for a job well done!

My reward is _____.

4. Imagery. Get a vivid mental picture of what you are going to look like after you have been on your physical fitness program for a period of time. See the svelte body, the slimmer waistline, the improved muscle tone, the athletic look as you stroll down the mall, and all the other signs of a well-honed physical machine. See these pictures especially during your workout. These intense pleasures will offset the "pain" of the vigorous workout.

My mental picture is _____.

5. Modeling. Surround yourself with friends who exercise on a regular basis. Listen to their chatter about fitness, notice what their bodies look like, and even watch them do a workout. Let them be a modeling inspiration for you. Write down two names and give them a call, right now! (If you do not have any friends in this category, drive over to a health club and watch an aerobics class. Never underestimate the impact of modeling for making eventual changes in your life.)

Simultaneously use these five learning theories and watch what happens to your fitness program and your ability to use your endorphins to control your career stress. A bonus: Once you have developed this five-learning-theory approach for getting in shape, you will have coincidentally mastered a powerful approach for making any change in your life—a change that can alter your marriage, career, or mission path.

• CHAPTER 25 •

What Is My B?

Would you like to take 25 percent of the stress out of your life? Would you like to dramatically reduce your frustration, anger, disappointment, hurt, tension, and heightened concern? If you would, pause for a minute and ask yourself, "What is my B?" With this simple question, you will acquire a powerful stress strategy.

Albert Ellis of Rational Emotive Therapy fame developed what he called the A-B-C formula. *A* stands for the *activating event*, or the assumed cause, that triggers the stress reaction. It may be a chewing out by the boss, a failing grade in school, a loss of prestige in the community, having to do four hours of work within the next two hours, or a driver cutting in front of you on a city street. *C* is the *consequences* of the activating event. It is the frustration, anger, disappointment, hurt, tension, or heightened concern referred to earlier.

The logical assumption by most people is that the activating event (the A) causes the consequences (the C). But according to Albert Ellis, this is not entirely true. He maintains there is an intervening variable (the B) that is a major contributor to how a person reacts. Often it is not the activating event that causes the consequences but rather the *B* or *belief system* about the event. In other words, it is the *interpretation* of the event, not the event *per se*, that creates the negative emotions. It is the "awfulizing" and "catastrophizing" of the event that create the majority of the stress reaction.

For example, you are driving down the street and run into some road construction. The two lanes of traffic are being funneled into one. Being a good citizen of your city, you get into the back of the long line. You have already waited through two traffic lights and just before you get to the orange pylons, you glance into your left rearview mirror. In the lane that is being blocked off, there is a car speeding along. The driver is passing cars until he pulls up next to yours. Then the right turn signal light goes on, and he starts muscling his way into the traffic line just in front of you. What is your reaction? You have to make a split-second decision: "Which is more important, principle or my left front fender?" You have fantasies of driving a tank and running over him.

Why are you so upset? You assume it is the activating event, that is, his pulling in front of you. But Albert Ellis would say, "No, it is your B!" And what is your interpretation of this event? Was your B that it only slowed you down two seconds and it's not worth getting upset about? Or was your B that this was not fair; the creep took advantage of you?

Once you fully understand the A-B-C concept, you have tremendous new power. As you start taking responsibility for your emotional reactions, you will automatically feel in control of them. If you, on the other hand, assign the responsibility for your emotions to other people, you will assume that you have little control over your emotional feelings.

A good example of this loss of control is when you hear that a coworker has made a cutting remark about you behind your back, and you become upset. Your unquestioned assumption is that his or her remark is what created your emotional response. Do this and you are always at the emotional mercy of their comments. People can "wipe you out" any time they choose.

It is much better for you to assume responsibility for your emotions. You can choose how you want to interpret your coworker's remark. Among your alternatives are these:

- Pity ("It is just a reflection of his insecurity.")
- Understanding ("She is basically a competitive person.")
- Skepticism ("The report is probably exaggerated.")

- Rejection ("I do not automatically assume other people's perceptions of me are accurate. After all, it is just that—a perception.")
- Forgiveness ("I know she is going through a tough time.")
- Questioning ("Why did this third person choose to give me this negative information?")

What a dynamic way to live! Start developing this "What is my B?" self-reliance. Start it today! Every time you have an emotional reaction, add a silent "and I take responsibility for that feeling." If you do this, you will be amazed at how quickly you start gaining control of your emotional responses and take a giant leap toward controlling the stress in your job.

What is my B? To increase your awareness of how your B operates in your life, take the following introspective look. First, write down an event that has created excessive stress in your life.

The activating event was _____

_____

_____

_____

Next, record the consequences, that is, the emotional reaction that you had.

My reaction to the event was _____

_____

_____

_____

Now the interesting question is to what degree was your reaction the direct result of the event, and to what degree was it magnified by a negative interpretation of the event or minimized by a positive interpretation?

To better understand this processing, write down two sets of B's. In the first column, write down a set of interpretations that you had (or could have had) that would magnify the impact of the event and intensify the stressful reaction. In the second column, write down a set of positive B's that would keep the event in proper perspective and minimize the emotional reaction.

Negative B's	Positive B's
1. _____	1. _____
2. _____	2. _____
3. _____	3. _____
4. _____	4. _____

Which set of B's comes closer to matching the self-talk interpretations you had? Perhaps you now better understand why you had the emotional response you had.

To further illustrate how this process works, study the following example:

The activating event. The company I work for is going through a major reorganization. The rumor is that several positions in my division are going to be eliminated.

My reaction. I have become very anxious, concerned, and apprehensive. I have lost my confidence in making tough decisions that could impact on the company, and I feel somewhat paranoid whenever I receive a call from one of the top executives.

Is it the actual event (the rumor) that dictates the stress or is it the pattern of self-talk?

Negative B's	Positive B's
1. "I just know that my position is one that is going to be eliminated."	1. "I have done an excellent job and I am sure they recognize that."
2. "I will never be able to find a job as good as this one."	2. "I have good job skills and I could find another position if I had to."

3. "This probably means that my children will not be able to go to college. Their lives are ruined."	3. "A brave man dies but once, a coward a thousand times. I will worry about losing the job only when it happens. In the meantime, I will continue to do my excellent work."

A person does not need a Ph.D. in psychology to figure out the emotional consequences of either set of B's during the next year of company instability and rumor.

"What is my B?" Always ask yourself that question whenever excessive stress invades your emotional system! Remember, no one can make you feel a certain way; you are in control of your feelings. Or as Eleanor Roosevelt so eloquently stated, "No one can make you feel inferior without your consent."

CHAPTER 26

Summary to the Career Section

Some people have a career that is a positive, exciting, self-actualizing pursuit that gives them great satisfaction and personal happiness. They wake up in the morning eager and excited. They like what they do!

You can have a similar walk down this magical path if you (a) aggressively take the necessary steps to keep the career stressors under control, (b) have a career that matches your unique talents, interests, needs, and temperament, and (c) have close, satisfying relationships at work with people who know the difference between competition and camaraderie . . . alienation and affection . . . tension and trust.

Make it your personal goal to "do whatever it takes" to obtain a stress-managed lifestyle, a great career match, and emotionally close relationships in your pursuit of an "I like what I do" career.

This is the true essence of the second magical path.

PART III

MISSION

The Third Magical Path

CHAPTER 27

Mission

Mission has been placed last in this book, but it definitely is not least. In fact, I personally believe that a sense of mission potentially is the most compelling way to find personal happiness.

A mission allows the deepest expression of your soul. It adds the extra dimension to your life. A mission reaches parts of your inner self that not even a wonderful relationship or smashing career achievement can touch. There is a depth to this soul expression that is replaced by no other experience.

In September 1957 I was an Army recruit stationed at Fort Leonard Wood, Missouri. Basic training was as bad as they said it would be. (Actually it was not that bad, but a soldier was expected to complain constantly.) The first "freedom" was a weekend pass at the end of the fifth week if a recruit "survived" the Saturday morning inspection.

We were lined up, and the tough, battle-scarred, "true grit" drill instructor (he made John Wayne look like a sissy) was going to inspect the troops. The suspense was heavy; a weekend pass was very special after all privileges had been taken away for five weeks.

Standing there, I was having fantasies of what I would do with my free weekend. My plan was to catch the bus and go to Columbia, Missouri. I already had my ticket. I imagined meeting a "Susie" (a Stephen's College coed) or a "Cathy" (a Christian College coed) and having a fantastic weekend. Jack, my closest Army buddy, was having even richer fantasies. His new bride, whom he had not seen in five weeks, was waiting outside the gate. She had traveled 350 miles hoping he would get a weekend pass and they could be together.

As we were standing in formation, Jack suddenly exclaimed, "Oh, no!" I whispered, "What's wrong?" He moaned, "I forgot my canteen!" Everybody knew what would happen. This eagle-eyed drill instructor would notice the missing canteen, give Jack the "dying soldier in the Sahara Desert" lecture, and Jack would be assigned KP for the weekend!

Suddenly I had a moral dilemma. Do I spend the weekend relaxing in Columbia pursuing "Susies," or do I spend it peeling potatoes? Just before the DI reached our row, I grabbed my canteen and slipped it to Jack. The DI noticed my missing canteen, gave *me* the chewing out, and I ended up with the weekend KP!

Why did I give my canteen to Jack? This caring act was a tapping into my best inner core to reach out to someone who needed help. And Jack was not the one who gained the most from the experience. The sense of euphoria and well-being I had that weekend while peeling potatoes far exceeded any fun I would have had in Columbia.

I do not share this personal story to tell you what a wonderful, altruistic person I am. The truth is that recalling this incident has been rather self-indicting. I cannot remember enough experiences like this in my lifetime.

This story highlights the emotional benefits that can occur when you reach out to someone else. Unlike the high that occurs after a physical workout, this high lingers. Even now, thirty-nine years later, I have a wonderful glow as I recall the canteen episode.

In *Psychology Today* (October 1988), Allen Luks talks about the psychological benefits obtained from helping others. He called it the "helper's high." He reported that people who help others in a personal way (hands-on as opposed to just giving money) experienced the following:

- A "high" similar to what occurs after vigorous exercise.
- Relief from stress-related disorders such as headaches.
- A surge of later positive memories as they recall a helping experience.

- A wonderful glow.

I know this is true because I have felt the emotions. The unfortunate fact is that I have not been a helper often enough. But I have a powerful strategy at my disposal whenever I choose to use it.

Maybe you do also! But it can move far beyond an occasional helper's high. This same principle can be upgraded to a mission, a concept you will better understand after you examine what a true mission is in the next chapter.

• CHAPTER 28 •

What Is a Mission?

Karl finally discovered the four qualities that best define what a true mission is, but only after he struggled on all three of the magical paths.

Karl and Vicki started dating while attending an evangelical Christian college. During their senior year, before the graduates scattered to all parts of the country, there was a subtle encouragement to find one's spouse. The thinly disguised message was, "You will never have a better opportunity to find someone of your faith to marry." Traditionally, the chapel bell was rung every time someone became engaged and by the spring semester of their senior year, the cheerful ringing began sounding like a somber tolling for the still unengaged.

Karl later admitted he knew there were some critical elements missing in his relationship with Vicki, but he yielded to her pressure. Three weeks before graduation, he gave her an engagement ring. The chapel bell was rung once again, and six months later they were married.

Their marriage was supposed to be a "marriage made in heaven," but it never turned out that way. They had a "Christian commitment," but the special "in love" feeling never developed for Karl. This lack of romantic closeness was compounded by Vicki's habit of constantly putting Karl down with verbal barbs, sarcastic comments, and humorous digs. It was the way her mother, a nagging perfectionist, reacted to other people, and Vicki had obviously perfected this communication style. She frequently referred to Karl, even in public, as Klutzy Karl.

Despite the obvious marital problems, however, Karl made a reasonable adjustment. He gave Christian caring to Vicki, showered love on their two sons, and used his career to find an added degree of personal happiness.

Karl had an outstanding college record, and he was heavily recruited by several companies when he graduated. He finally decided to go to work for a small but innovative and rapidly growing company. He started out as a salesperson and his combination of talent, drive, and integrity made him the top salesperson within three years. Being the best inspired him to do even better, so it was not surprising that he was eventually promoted to a management position.

Being a manager was even more exciting for Karl. He liked encouraging other salespeople to become peak performers; he relished the challenge of staying one step ahead of his company's competitors; and he enjoyed making critical decisions that were responsible for much of his company's rapid expansion and dynamic success. When his company was bought out by a Fortune 500 company, Karl was pleased. His initial thought was, "Now I can compete in the big leagues." He looked forward to the new challenge, but quickly found out that he was no longer going to be a superstar.

The new company had its own way of doing things and its own people for doing it. Karl's role was to follow the procedures established at the national level. Suddenly, Karl was no longer developing innovative marketing strategies, making creative responses to counteract a competitor, or devising new ways to motivate the sales force. The challenge of the job had been stripped away and the emotional blues were not far behind.

Karl concluded that the best solution for his mild depression was not to make a major career change at this time. Changing jobs or transferring to the corporate headquarters where the key decisions were made meant uprooting his kids at a critical juncture in their schooling and moving away from his ill mother. Karl also concluded that making changes in his marriage was not the answer. He reasoned that he had made a "comfortable" adjustment, and raising the issue of the missing romantic chemistry or lowering the protective wall that successfully deflected his wife's verbal darts would only make things worse. It could even rekindle an earlier desire to leave the marriage.

Karl decided to look in another direction for his personal happiness. He remembered what he had been taught about Christian service in college, so he began volunteering his time to two different charitable organizations. Six months later, Karl felt proud of his efforts, but there was a mild disappointment. These activities had not helped him capture the feeling he had been seeking.

Counseling helped clarify the problem. Karl's perception of helping was doing a series of "good deeds." Once he realized that pursuing a mission is more complex, he began taking positive steps down the third magical path.

People who have a compelling mission that consumes their lives in the most positive way always seem to have a mission with four qualities. And some—unlike Karl—do not wait for adversity to seek out this mission path. Their walk is equally satisfying (Or is it more so?) when it is an extension of a happy marriage or a self-actualizing career.

1. The mission has vision. To be fully energized, a person's mission must have a visionary thrust. A quotation I referred to earlier, "Seldom do you exceed your expectations; even if the opportunity arises, you generally fail to capitalize on it," captures the need for having a dynamic mission picture.

Later in this section, we will examine the benefits of defining inspiring mission goals and learn how imagery can be used to program these goals deep into your subconscious mind. At that time you will be asked to establish some compelling mission goals and fully energize them via imagery.

A mission, a true sense of mission, however, moves beyond a noble goal statement powered by visionary imagery. In order to capture the full essence of an uplifting mission, you need the other three qualities.

2. The mission is unselfish. A mission is different from a set of goals or a life pursuit. A life pursuit to become a millionaire or the goal to win an Olympic gold medal gives direction to one's life. It energizes the psychological forces, but the gain is primarily selfish. The main focus is on the reward, accomplishment, or fame that is personally derived from the outstanding feat.

A mission does not focus on personal rewards. Instead, the focus is on what others will gain. The energy is directed toward making other people's lives secure, comfortable, and happy.

There are little signs that suggest the motivation is unselfish. The gifts are anonymous (Even the warm thank yous from appreciative recipients are carefully avoided.), there is a deliberate attempt to avoid any publicity (There is no big splash in the society section of the newspaper unless the goal is to focus attention on a cause.), and the inner thoughts are on the benefits to others, not on how it is "good business" to give.

There is no need to define unselfishness because you already know the difference between being selfish and unselfish. I have done both types of giving in my lifetime, and I can feel the difference between the two sets of emotions. Perhaps you can do the same thing.

3. *The mission is spiritual.* The Greeks have three different words for the word "love." *Eros* is the romantic love, *philo* is the brotherly love, and *agape* is the God like love for others. The people with the deepest sense of commitment often have an *agape* dimension to their mission. When asked why they serve and give the way they do, they frequently refer to their faith or their deep love for less fortunate people. Their mission is merely an expression of a compelling force created by a sense of what is truly important in life.

> At the close of life the question will be not, how much have you got, but how much have you given; not how much you have won, but how much you have done; not how much you have saved, but how much you have sacrificed; how much have you loved and served, not how much were you honored.
> Nathan C. Schaeffer

I do not want to leave the impression that a spiritual faith is essential to have a true sense of mission. But for many, perhaps even most people, this dimension is very much a part of their missionary zeal.

4. *The mission is congruent.* For a mission to be truly a mission, the outward behaviors and the inner motivation have to be in sync. It is possible to espouse noble goals, make a genuine attempt to be unselfish, have a religious faith, and still miss the mark when it comes to having a deep sense of mission.

The goals need to move beyond the ideals espoused by others; the unselfishness must encompass more than an admirable social responsibility; and the spiritual dimension must transcend merely an obedient following of religious "shoulds" established by church leaders.

The mission drive has to come from the inside out. There has to be a congruence between your inner desires and what you do. The mission goals are ones that *you* want; the unselfishness is fueled by a sincere caring for other people; and the spiritual dimension comes from a love that dwells deep within your soul. This is a lofty mountain to climb. Many of you may be asking, "Is this even possible?"

Yes it is possible! I believe this because I spend hours each day getting to know people as they truly are. Many of my clients often lack visionary goals, are totally selfish, and show little spiritual joy. But many of these same clients have moments when they create visionary goals, are completely unselfish, and express an *agape*-type love toward others. These superb qualities surface from within their inner being.

This happens so frequently that I have to believe the odds are great the same thing is true for you, especially since you have taken the time to read this far into the mission section. Reflect on yourself for a minute. Yes, you have moments when you lack direction, are completely selfish, and have little spiritual connection. But you also have moments when you create visionary goals, possess a quality of giving that captures your unselfish attitude, and feel a deep connection with a spiritual force.

Treasure these moments. It is this portion of your inner being that adds the sustaining energy to your mission and provides a special meaning to your life. It allows you a means of transcending your brief walk on planet Earth.

• CHAPTER 29 •

Mission and the Midlife Transitions

At his twenty-fifth high school class reunion, Robert could not say enough good things about his wife, Suzette. He told his classmates that he had never been happier in their marriage, and it was obvious by the way he treated her. He was attentive, loving, and went out of his way to introduce her to all his friends.

Robert and Suzette were especially excited about their children. In a modest way, they shared that their daughter was captain of her high school tennis team and was recently announced as a National Merit semifinalist. Their son, one of two sophomores to make the starting lineup on the varsity football team, had received four A's and one B on his last report card. Robert and Suzette had to conceal their pride as they talked about their children's impressive accomplishments.

Robert and Suzette were just as successful in their careers. Robert was one of the youngest senior vice presidents his company had ever had. The company rumor was that Robert might leapfrog over a couple of older senior vice presidents and become the next CEO. He clearly was on a career fast track.

Suzette stayed home with the children for several years but had gone back to teaching five years ago. Last year she received the Outstanding Teacher Award in her school, but her real excitement was having just been accepted to law school. She was ready to launch a new career at age forty-three.

Ten years later Robert and Suzette did not even attend his thirty-fifth high school class reunion. They were too embarrassed to go. Instead, they were sitting in my office.

Robert left his company and had been floundering in his career ever since. He had been fired from two jobs in the past five years. He may have had a drinking problem, and he confided that he was having an affair with his secretary.

Suzette had put on thirty pounds and appeared to be mildly depressed. Her law school plans did not work out, and she was back in education as a "burned-out" teacher. She was also totally discouraged over the lack of emotional and sexual intimacy in their marriage. She had already consulted with a divorce attorney, and counseling was a last-ditch attempt to stop the emotional erosion in their marriage.

What happened? Why did two happy, achieving individuals stumble between the ages of forty-three and fifty-three? The reasons are complex, but the bottom line is that both failed to successfully negotiate some normal midlife transitions.

Many people struggle with midlife transitions that stand in the way of their finding personal happiness. For some, this midlife transition is so traumatic that it is often labeled a midlife crisis or the midlife crazies.

What is the midlife crisis? First, let's emphasize what it is not. It is not a newly discovered medical disease; it is not a set of psychiatric symptoms of a neurotic person; and it is not an indication of underlying psychological inadequacy. The so-called midlife crisis is merely a heightened reaction of anyone who is struggling with a midlife transition.

Once a person understands the significance of midlife transitions, it is easy to appreciate why this is often a difficult period in one's life. What is interesting is that some individuals make these transitions in a positive, enthusiastic, almost inspiring manner while others fall into a struggling, apprehensive, even depressed mode.

Why do some people sail through this middle-aged period while others find their psychological boat capsizing? Interestingly, I often see the third magical path make a dramatic difference.

But I am getting ahead of myself. Before we consider how the three magical paths—and especially the mission path—can guide you through the troubled waters of midlife, I would like you to examine the eight main reasons why my clients (and most people) struggle with these midlife transitions in the first place. As you examine these reasons, you can more readily see why the midlife transitions can be so difficult and why the mission path can be so important at this critical juncture in your life.

1. Self-fulfilling prophecy. Observe the rituals at the fortieth birthday parties. Listen to the "humorous" messages that are sent in 101 clever ways. The gifts and cards all refer to the loss of youth, vitality, and virility. The "you have just had the big one" message is supposed to be laughed off, but what is the message that slams into the subconscious mind? It must be awful since some people start dreading their fortieth birthday at their thirty-fifth birthday party.

Listen to the jokes in the men's locker room. The "Why look? I bet you couldn't even get it up!" replaces "Do you think you can score?" The humorous but deadly message is, "You are now over the hill sexually." And the implied message is, "If you are over the hill sexually, you *are* over the hill!"

2. Career plateau. Many career paths are similar to a pyramid—a lot of room at the bottom but little at the top. Within a corporation, only one of the seven vice presidents can move up to be president and only one of the eight department managers will be the next vice president. About midlife, many people realize their opportunities for additional career advancement have stopped. The upward surge has ended. It may be they have "risen to their level of incompetence" (the famous Peter Principle), or it can simply be there are no available slots at the next level in the corporate pyramid.

This can be a very depressing realization. Forty-five seems too young to accept there will be no more spectacular promotions and no more impressive salary increases. It is difficult to move from the career fast track to spending the next twenty years locked into one's current position or even struggling to hang on to what one already has.

3. Empty nest. Many parents put tremendous emotional energy into raising their children. Some make it their full-time career. Then, when the children leave home, suddenly there is a big void in the parents' lives. This emotional void creates an emptiness, a nothingness, a loss of purpose. Unless this understandable void is quickly filled with something else, the howling winds of midlife can hit with full fury. The devastation caused by this storm can be even more widespread when the children resist the parents' renewed efforts to hold on. ("Why are they so unappreciative after all I did for them?")

4. *Signs of aging.* There are many telltale signs that you are aging. The muscles ache longer after a physical workout; you notice how old your classmates look at the high school reunion; your interest is piqued whenever you hear a discussion about cosmetic surgery; and you feel violated when someone asks your age.

Other signs are less obvious. The excitement of the upcoming vacation is tempered by the concern, "What happens if I get ill on the trip?" When you have a birthday, you notice that you no longer reflect on how many years you have lived. Instead, you find yourself doing a subtle projection. The silent question is, "How many years do I have left?" As Pat Rodgers, a San Antonio–based radio talk show host, has quipped, "I have started planting bigger trees at my house. I want to make sure that I live long enough to see the shade."

5. *Fear of dying.* If aging is stressful, what about the prospect of dying? In midlife, death becomes a reality. No longer do the optimism and sense of immortality that you had as a teenager protect you from the realization that someday you will die.

You find yourself now going to as many funerals as weddings; you may have recently faced your first health scare; friends *your age* have been stricken with life-threatening diseases; your parents, now in the late stages of their lives, may soon die (or already have); and you find your eyes reading the obituary columns or you quickly divert your glance when you turn to *that* page.

For the first time you have to face your own mortality. No longer can you avoid questions such as, "How do I face death? What happens to me when I die?" What once were philosophical questions, now become practical ones.

6. *The biological clock.* Several of my female clients are concerned about having children. They are in their thirties and single or unhappily married or concerned about their financial status. They are not ready to have a baby, but they also realize they do not have many years left. Their biological clocks are ticking.

This stress can be compounded when a woman reaches forty. At this time it is medically risky to have a child. What happens psychologically when this option is lost?

For some women, the pressure of not having more children is a relief; for others, it is no big deal. For some women, however, this is a stressful adjustment. There can be a feeling of loss of worth, sometimes even compounded by the thought, "I cannot have more children, but my husband could if he found a 'younger' woman." (And this fear can extend beyond the ability to conceive. Women often hear a different message regarding aging and attractiveness. Older men are praised for their career success, and older women are told that they have "aged nicely.")

7. *Loss of sexual adequacy.* If the biological clock is a concern for some women, then the fear of losing sexual adequacy is a crisis for some men.

Masculinity and sexuality are closely tied together for most men. Many young boys are indoctrinated with the cultural programming that size, adequacy, and sexual success are important; this is what makes a man a man. When these aspects are questioned, there is trouble. Many happy marriages abruptly take a negative turn for no reason other than the husband was unwilling to confront his sexual concerns. It seemed easier to assume that there was something wrong with the marriage than to examine why he was unable to sustain an erection. The next step was either to try it with another woman or to visit a divorce attorney.

8. *Too few goals.* The enthusiasm of youth helps create many professional, personal, and family desires, and there is an eager pursuit of these goals. Then around middle age, one of two things happens. Either the goals are reached or there is an acceptance that some of the earlier aspirations are unobtainable. Suddenly there are no goals to pursue, no stars to reach for, no mountains to climb.

When there are no new goals, the earlier "charge" is replaced with a current "complacency." The excitement for life is lost in a series of rituals. The patterns become too consistent, the habits too familiar, and even lovemaking faithfully follows the same predictable steps. Soon everything has too much sameness. The marriage becomes dull, the career boring, and anything new, different, and adventurous is a mere memory from the past.

Self-fulfilling prophecy, career plateaus, the empty nest, signs of aging, fear of dying, the biological clock, concerns about sexual adequacy, and not enough goals—these are all reasons why the midlife adjustment can be difficult. So what does a person do to prevent these potentially destructive aspects of midlife? Once again I would like to point you in the direction of the three magical paths, especially the third path that can play a vital role in your search for happiness.

The truth is that some marriages do go flat and some careers do plateau. One solution is to recreate the marital magic or re-energize the career. This was discussed in the first two sections. A third alternative is to look toward the mission path at this critical juncture in your life. This is what many resourceful people do.

• CHAPTER 30 •

Selecting a Mission

Barbara was ecstatic when she retired at age fifty-two. As she looked back on her thirty years in public education, she said, "For the most part, it was a very satisfying career, but the last few years were rough. The ever-increasing problems with teenage gangs, parent apathy, student disrespect, weapons on campus, and lack of public support for education finally got to me. Thank God, I could retire after thirty years. I don't think I could have made it to age sixty-five. I was already in the advanced stages of teacher burnout."

Five months later, Barbara realized that full retirement was not the answer either. ("The summer was wonderful, but by the end of October, I was restless and bored.") Her husband was still consumed with his career, the children were away at college, and the demands of being a conscientious English teacher had prevented her from developing any compelling hobbies.

After talking to the pastor of her church, Barbara decided that a part-time mission was the answer. Following the advice of her friends, she decided to use her expertise with adolescents to do volunteer work with struggling teenagers and their parents at the local Girl's Club. Unfortunately, this mission did not turn out to be a positive experience. Instead of enjoying a helper's high, Barbara began feeling the same burnout she had felt in the classroom. The problem was that Barbara forgot to do one essential thing as she stepped on the mission path.

We will come back to Barbara's mistake shortly, but first consider how Stacy made a similar mistake. Stacy was devastated when her teenage son was killed in an automobile accident. She had never known such pain in her life. In fact, there was a period of time when she was not sure she would ever recover from this tragic loss.

Fortunately, she took two steps that allowed her to find her way back. First, she went for some grief counseling. ("The counselor made a big difference. He made me face my pain rather than allowing me to run away from it.") Second, she joined a support group for parents who had lost children. ("The group really gave me the support and encouragement that I needed. I don't know how I would have made it without them.")

Slowly, Stacy began to realize that she needed to fill the void that had been created by the loss of her son. Her marriage was not the answer. Her perception was that her marriage was not bad, but it was not good either. She said, "We are just two different people. The 'in love' feeling faded years ago, but there is enough caring and respect to hang in there." Her career offered a similar dilemma. It was not a totally negative experience, but it was a "routine administrative position that lacked any real challenge or opportunity for advancement."

Stacy decided, after reading a book on community service, that the best way for her to fill the void was to help other people. She briefly considered working with other parents who had lost children, but quickly decided that would be too painful. It would only be a constant reminder of her own painful loss. Instead, she decided, after reading an article on the "Graying of America," to direct her mission energies into the ever-growing problems of senior citizens.

Nine months later, Stacy was totally dissatisfied with her mission. It clearly had not filled the void in her life, nor had it given her the emotional high that she had hoped for.

Why? The problem is that Stacy, like Barbara, forgot to take one essential step before she began her journey down her mission path.

Both Stacy and Barbara were wise in looking to the mission path for their happiness. It was the best solution for both of them. The problem was that it cannot be just any mission path.

Once Barbara realized that her burnout extended to *any* work with teenagers, she started considering other options. After a careful introspective look, she realized the population that really captured her concerns was senior citizens. She shifted her mission endeavor to that group, and six months later she reported that she was extremely happy. She now had her helper's high, and she really looked forward to working with "these wonderful people."

Stacy realized that her mind, heart, and soul really reached out to the many families who had experienced a loss similar to hers. Once she was able to risk reconfronting her personal loss, she realized this was her mission calling.

Stacy quickly found that her exquisite joy came in helping others recover from their tragic losses. A well-deserved bonus was this mission pursuit also helped Stacy best cope with the ongoing pain over her own loss. Helping others became the best way to help herself.

The solution for both Barbara and Stacy was not just having a mission. It was having the *right* mission!

Selecting a mission should be done as carefully as you select a spouse or career. Actually, this is an overstatement because it is much easier to change your mission than it is to change your spouse or career. But I make this strong statement to capture your attention. I want you to take the time to carefully select a mission path that captures the best parts of *your unique soul.*

Many people select a mission path that is (a) primarily determined by the persuasive pleadings of other people, or (b) a quick emotional response to the immediate needs of some worthy cause. There is nothing wrong in these charitable acts, but this method of choosing a mission path lessens the chances of your mission becoming the ongoing, rewarding experience that makes it one of the three magical paths for personal happiness. For this to happen, there needs to be a more thoughtful selection process.

Before you select a personal mission, I would encourage you to ask yourself seven questions that will drastically increase the odds of your mission becoming an inspiring challenge rather than a perfunctory obligation and will shift the mission pursuit from a moral "ought to" to a compelling "want to."

1. Who would you like to help? The word that I want to emphasize in this question is *you.* If you merely respond to the people who you perceive as needing your help the most, you may soon find that your mission drive functions like a Roman candle, that is, it burns intensely for a brief time but then it fizzles out. For your mission to be sustaining rather than temporary, you need to pay the most attention to what *you* need.

For example, losing a parent or grandparent may draw you to working with older people in nursing homes. A struggle you overcame as a teenager may give you a special identification with struggling teenagers. The fact that you never had children may draw you to a project that is concerned about the welfare of young children.

Perhaps this is why the most effective volunteers in the highly successful Alcoholics Anonymous (AA) programs are people who have experienced alcohol abuse. They have been there, and this very personal, emotional experience provides the special commitment as they help people who are still struggling with alcoholism issues.

Consider some of the following populations. Which ones hold an intrinsic interest for you?

- Single parent families
- Severely ill children
- AIDS patients
- College students needing financial assistance
- Elderly people
- Members of a minority group
- Out-of-work individuals
- Pregnant teenagers
- People going through a loss

Look into your soul, your emotional needs, and your life experiences. Which groups of people hold a special place in your heart? It is essential to take this introspective look if you want your mission to become a magical path to happiness.

2. *Do you have a cause that commands your attention and creates passion within you?* Once again, as with the population that you reach out to, this energy may come from your life experiences rather than a reasoned determination that says, "This would be good for my community, state, or nation." In other words, determining how this cause is valuable to others is important so it is not a misguided effort. Just as important for keeping your mission sustaining, however, is making sure that it taps into a cause that is intrinsically important to you.

Some common causes that create this passion are listed as follows:

- Environmental concerns
- Abuse, poverty, and other child-welfare issues
- Reawakening the spiritual life in people
- Improving public education
- Women's rights issues
- Reforming city government
- Antipornography (or any other community ill) campaigns
- Pro-life or pro-choice issues
- Discrimination issues (and you can name the group)

What are the issues that create a stirring within *you*? This is the birthplace of a compelling mission. When you combine your favorite cause with your favorite population, you have the makings of a consuming mission that creates a magical path toward your personal happiness. And the nice plus is that it is also good for other people. Everyone becomes a winner!

3. *In what way would you like to help?* There are different delivery systems for your compelling mission. The trick is to find the approach that is best for *you*. You need an approach that best matches your needs, interests, and talents. Some of the most common delivery systems are listed here:

- *Hands-on*. You have direct contact with the people you want to help. You personally do the counseling, coaching, teaching, or advising in a one-to-one or one-to-group approach. This provides the most personal touch, one that could be extremely important for you even when it is not the most efficient approach.
- *Managerial*. You prefer managing or coordinating rather than the hands-on approach. For example, rather than spending two hours serving soup at the Salvation Army (hands-on), you spend the same two hours recruiting other people to help serve the soup. As a result, your two hours of effort could mean twenty volunteers each spend two

hours serving soup. There is less of a personal touch but a satisfaction that you accomplished more.
- *Behind the scenes.* You prefer the role of a support person. For example, rather than delivering the Christmas gifts (hand-ons) or coordinating the holiday Toys-for-Tots project (managerial), you have your greatest satisfaction repairing the toys, helping purchase the toys with the donated money, or sorting the toys according to the various families' needs. Your mission needs are best met as a behind-the-scenes worker.
- *Fund-raising.* You are a salesperson at heart and you reason that you might as well use this talent in your mission endeavors. No one has to convince you of the critical need for additional funds for your mission project, and your greatest challenge is convincing the business community and the general public that your project is special. When they do direct part of their charitable budget in your direction, you experience the helper's high.

As you can see, there are different strokes for different folks. The key is finding the avenue that is best for you, the one that maximizes your personal happiness as you bring happiness to others through your unique mission endeavor.

4. How much time do you have? Two hours per week fully energized and totally focused on your mission project will be better for you than six hours per week when you are frazzled and fragmented, thinking about other things that you need to be doing. The more limited time will allow a satisfying walk down your mission path while the overextended time will add to your stress. Be realistic. Given all your other responsibilities, how much time do you now have for your mission pursuit?

There are two factors you may want to consider as you schedule in your time. The first is to include your family in your mission activity. If you do this, you will simultaneously have quality family togetherness and be devoting time to your mission. As a bonus, it will provide a wonderful model for your children. They will have personal exposure to a third magical path for finding personal happiness in their own adult lives as well as developing an in-depth social consciousness for the needs of their community.

The second consideration is that now you may have only a limited amount of time because of your other commitments. But what happens when these responsibilities lessen (children leave home, you retire from your career, and so forth)? If you already have a compelling mission, you can merely expand the time you devote to this magical path. Without a compelling mission, you dramatically increase the odds of slipping into an emotional depression when major relationship or career transitions occur. This issue will be considered in greater depth in chapter 33 when we look at retirement and the mission path.

5. *What are the little intangible factors?* In addition to the group served, cause expressed, method used, and time expended, there are three other factors that you may want to consider as you refine your mission pursuit.

- Would you like to use an established talent? Or would you rather develop a new talent to add sparkle and variety to your mission effort? For example, you could (a) overcome your minor fear of speaking by becoming a speaker for a charitable organization, (b) do hands-on manual labor as a change of pace from your desk job, or (c) develop your listening skills by taking training as a volunteer counselor on a crisis hot-line. Developing a new talent could give your mission effort a unique self-actualizing challenge.

- Would you prefer to be part of a large group such as United Way, American Heart Association, or Salvation Army where everything is already organized and you can hit the track (mission path) running? Or would you have more challenge and satisfaction by actually developing the mission plan as you work with your book study group, Sunday school class, or neighborhood organization?

- Would you like to be a specialist or a generalist? You may prefer carefully selecting one pet mission project, and spending your lifetime having impact in that area. You could actually become a recognized expert, or at least an identified leader, in a worthy cause. On the other hand, you may choose to work in a number of areas to add more variety to your mission pursuit. You could even find this variety adds an extra stimulation to your efforts.

In all three of these areas (talents, group size, number of projects), any choice is okay. The trick is deciding which avenues best propel your mission enthusiasm.

6. *What are the community needs?* In earlier questions, I emphasized how important it is to tap into your personal needs in order to ensure that your mission is the most sustaining and rewarding. The question of community needs is designed to ensure a proper balance. You want to make sure your mission effort is serving a legitimate need or else it is just a wasted effort, rarely a compelling reason for sustaining a mission pursuit.

For example, if your special area of interest is already being addressed by an active, vital, on-target group, you probably do not need to form a splinter group to address that community concern. You do not want your mission project dividing the available charitable resources, setting up unnecessary competition, or duplicating others' efforts. Either join the ongoing group or shift to a mission area that is of interest to you but is not being adequately addressed at this time.

What are your community's needs? The best way to answer this question is to ask. Ask your city officials, community spokespersons, social agency heads, and religious leaders. They will tell you how well the needs of the following groups are being met in your community:

- Latchkey children
- The homeless
- The unemployed
- Battered women
- Abandoned animals
- Single-parent families
- Juvenile delinquents
- Abused children
- Inner-city residents
- Elderly adults
- Underachieving students
- Any other deserving groups of people

Your challenge is to match your personal needs with a community need.

7. Are you doing what God wants you to do? This question may surprise some of you, but many people's mission is highly motivated (or even inspired) by their personal relationship with God. Their mission is an extension of a religious faith that says "do good things for others." Some even maintain that a mission is essential to preserve their faith. (". . . Faith without deeds is dead." James 2:26.)

If your connection with God is an integral part of your mission pursuit, you will definitely want to add the, "What does God want me to do?" question to your personal and community considerations. If you have a deep religious faith, this could actually be *the* fundamental question for creating the most inspiring, energizing type of mission.

I will come back to the faith and mission issue in chapter 34, but first I would like you to begin a formal goal-setting process for your mission. As you establish goals for your mission in the next chapter, please be sure that your mission considers (a) what population you want to help, (b) the cause that commands your attention, (c) the method for helping, (d) the amount of time that you have, (e) how the little intangible factors enter in, and (f) the needs of your community. If you are also including a religious faith in your mission formula, please add (g) the direction God wants you to pursue.

(• CHAPTER 31 •)

Setting Mission Goals

Recall when you were twenty-two years old. Remember your goals. Even if they were not formalized, you still had mental pictures of the following:
- What kind of home you would have.
- How successful you would become in your career.
- Who you would marry.
- How much money you would make.
- How many children you wanted.

You no longer have the same goals. Some of them have been discarded because you realize you will not reach them, and others have been pushed aside by more immediate concerns. This, however, is not what usually causes the midlife slump discussed in chapter 29. This midlife slump occurs as you reach many of your goals, and you expect that the ecstasy of these accomplishments will carry you through the rest of your life. Instead, there is a letdown.

This letdown should not be surprising because it is the pursuit of the goal, not the reaching of the goal, that provides most of the sustaining enthusiasm and excitement. Your emotional system is not most energized when you walk across the stage at graduation, receive the promotion at work, complete the mission project at your church or synagogue, survey a well-manicured lawn at your home, or open the gifts on Christmas Day. There may be a brief surge of intense pleasure, but it is quickly replaced by a feeling of "Is this all there is?"

The real life-sustaining energy comes from pursuing (as opposed to reaching) the goals. It comes when you are studying the college courses, striving for career excellence, doing the church/synagogue project, planting the trees in your yard, and preparing for Christmas Day that you feel most alive. Granted, there is extra effort and maybe even stress involved in these pursuits, but even these mildly negative emotions keep the juices flowing. You feel energized and directed. You are excited as you anticipate accomplishing the goals and delight in the challenges that are presented. When it is all done, it is over! Now there is the brief glow followed by complacency, the depressing complacency of having no energizing goals.

What is the best way to break out of this complacency? The answer is obvious: Establish a new set of goals that will start the whole process over again. If you set new goals—and use the dynamic concept of imagery—you will trigger an avalanche of energizing processes to ensure your personal happiness.

The goal-setting strategies work in all areas of one's life, and most people do set goals for their relationship and career paths. These same individuals, however, frequently neglect to even consider this dynamic goal-setting and imagery process for a mission pursuit. This is why I elected to place the primary goal-setting focus in this section of the book. The goal-setting and imagery strategies, of course, apply as well to the marital and career paths.

Are you ready to set some new mission goals for your life? As you contemplate this question, consider five guidelines for making your goals more dynamic.

1. Make your goals specific. When establishing your goals, a specific statement such as, "I am going to block every Tuesday from 7:00 to 9:00 P.M. and every Saturday from 3:00 to 5:00 P.M. to work on my mission project," will create behavior changes quicker than a general comment such as, "I want to spend more time on my mission project." An action statement such as, "Starting today, I am going to investigate, join, and become active in a community service club" will bring results while a passive, "I would like to do more in my community" will be quietly forgotten in the crush of your daily responsibilities.

A concrete goal captures your attention; a vague goal is easily pushed aside "until later," so always make your goals specific.

2. Make your goals positive. Always state your goals in positive rather than negative terms. Establish a goal to have healthy lungs rather than to give up smoking, or to have a slimmer body rather than to give up chocolate candy bars. Positive goals are inspiring; the reward is built into the goal statement. Negative goals are "bummers" because there is the constant reminder of the pleasure that you are having to give up.

Within the mission area, you should focus on the wonderful things you will be doing not on the sacrifices you will be making to complete your mission project.

3. Make your goals challenging. For a goal to be realistic, it needs only to be honestly imaginable. You do not have to know how to get there! This is the most important of the goal-setting guidelines. If you limit yourself to goals you already know how to reach, you are severely restricting your potential. It is okay, in fact, recommended, that you set goals even when you do not have the foggiest notion how to accomplish them! After the goals are set is when you start noticing ways to reach your ambitious mission goals.

4. Make your goals energizing. I recommend that you do not establish goals that force you to compete with others. This competition, often stressful and draining, creates all sorts of hidden agendas. Rarely is there the well-defined competition of athletics in the "real" world. Instead, this unspoken competition creates a climate of, "How can I beat other people while pretending I am not in competition with them?" Sometimes even churches and charitable organizations get caught in this emotional trap.

It is much better to compete with yourself. Your goal is to fully develop *your* talents and maximize *your* potential. This competition (with yourself) is energizing and inspiring.

5. Make your goals flexible. For some strange reason, many people have the mind-set that once a goal is established, it is automatically set in stone. A person either reaches *the* goal (and succeeds) or does not reach the goal (and fails). Please change this mind-set and make your goals more fluid.

If a mission goal turns out to be too high, lower it. You do not fail because "failure" is merely a signal that a correction is needed. If the goal is too low (as is more often the case), you raise it. You strive to maximize your potential rather than settle for mediocrity. As mentioned earlier in this chapter, the greatest psychological joy comes during the pursuit of your goals not when you reach your goals. Becoming is better than being.

Pause for a moment in your reading and contemplate what mission goals you would like to have for your life. (And yes, you can slip in a few relationship and career goals if you wish.) Take off your judge's robes and let yourself go. Take out a sheet of paper and write down five goals. Ink it and think it!

Five Goals for My Life

1. _____
2. _____
3. _____
4. _____
5. _____

Congratulations! You have just taken a big step toward reenergizing your life.

Setting goals is exciting and energizing! Setting goals makes things happen! Setting goals is the impetus for change!

But the best part is still to happen as you will discover when you read about imagery in the next chapter.

CHAPTER 32

The Power of Imagery

If you were to ask me what my favorite psychological strategy is, I would say, without hesitation, that it is imagery. If you were to ask what I think the world's most powerful psychological strategy is, my answer would be the same: imagery. So it is not surprising that I recommend imagery as an effective method for fully energizing your mission goals. You were introduced to the imagery concept in earlier chapters. Let's review and expand on this concept.

Imagery is power! It is the $500,000 secret of winners. It was imagery that helped Kurt Gibson hit the dramatic home run in the 1988 World Series, Martina Navratilova capture her ninth Wimbledon tennis title in 1990, and the Dallas Cowboys win the 1993, 1994, and 1996 Super Bowls.

Imagery is not limited to world-class athletes. Imagery is the powerful tool that Winston Churchill used to raise the morale of the English people during World War II, Dr. Martin Luther King adopted it in his struggle against an entrenched social injustice ("I have a dream"), and Dr. Carl Simonson has used it to cause remission in cancer patients.

Imagery is the tool that has inspired many of the great scientists, artists, and inventors. It also is the technique that thousands of "average" people have used to maximize their ability to overcome a public-speaking phobia, make their first million dollars, recover from a horrible tragedy, and achieve far beyond their earlier expectations. Imagery is a constant companion of peak performers, the soul mate of creative thinkers, and the best friend of your desire to establish a dynamic mission path.

Why is imagery so powerful? Imagery is powerful because it is the tool that allows you to harness the raw energy of your subconscious mind. To better appreciate the subconscious mind, picture a majestic iceberg floating in the north Atlantic Ocean. As you hold this picture, you may recall from your fourth grade geography class that only 10 percent of the iceberg lies above the ocean surface and 90 percent lies below!

This is about the same ratio between your conscious and subconscious minds. Ten percent is above the surface, the conscious portion of which you have awareness and control. Like the iceberg, however, 90 percent of your brain lies beneath the surface of consciousness. This is the portion over which you have much less awareness and control, but this lack of awareness in no way lessens the impact your subconscious mind has on your behaviors, thoughts, emotions, and reactions.

The message is simple. If you want to maximize your abilities, talents, and psychological goals, you must use your subconscious mind as aggressively as you use your conscious mind.

As mentioned earlier, the imagery formula is $P + E = R$. Remember this formula. Repeat it until it locks into your memory bank as firmly as the alphabet. See the formula. Hear it. Feel it. $P + E = R$. $P + E = R$. $P + E = R$.

Originating from psychocybernetics, this dynamic concept contends that whatever you "Picture with Emotions" enters your subconscious mind as "Reality." Your conscious mind easily distinguishes between reality and vividly imagined material. If you did not make this distinction, you would soon be labeled as schizophrenic or psychotic. But your subconscious mind, the 90 percent that lies beneath the surface of your awareness, does not make this critical distinction. If you vividly imagine something, it goes into your subconscious mind with the same impact as if it actually happened. And once these imagined "realities" are locked in, they start affecting your behavior and emotions.

Winners use this quirk of the subconscious mind to their advantage. They see themselves (mental pictures) with great feeling (emotions) achieving their goals (reality). Then the magic happens. For some "unexplained" reason (because it is subconscious), there are more A's in school, smashing career successes, energized relationships, dramatic improvements in performance, and impressive gains in any other area that your heart desires. This is the power of the subconscious mind released through a program of well-planned imageries.

Trust this concept; accept it on faith. To a certain extent you *have* to trust because the process is, by definition, subconscious (below your level of awareness). It is not unlike what you do when you use your personal computer. You are not aware of what happens inside your PC, but you trust that the right data will bring the correct results. And past experience has proven this to be true. Your subconscious mind will deliver the same good results if you properly program it via imageries.

Look back at the mission goals you established in the last chapter. Although I am sure they are excellent goals, there probably is one major thing wrong with them. As they are now written, they are mainly designed for your conscious mind, the 10 percent of the iceberg that lies above the surface. Now put these goal statements into a language that best ensures they will be absorbed by your subconscious mind. Turn each of your goal statements into a dynamic affirmation via a simple four-step process.

1. Picture yourself having *already* accomplished each goal. See yourself having just completed a very worthwhile mission project. This step is critical because the subconscious mind is extremely powerful but rather stupid. Not only can it not distinguish between vividly imagined material and reality, but it also only processes in *present* time, unlike the conscious mind which can think in future time. In other words, rather than seeing what you will do someday, see yourself as having already done it.

2. Experience the emotions that you would have at the moment of accomplishment. See the appreciative smiles, sense your inner pride, capture the ecstasy of the helper's high. This step adds the appropriate emotions to the imagery.

3. Using these mental pictures with the accompanying emotions, rewrite each of your mission goal statements. Vividly

describe what you have just accomplished! One suggestion is that you record these affirmations on 3-inch by 5-inch cards.

4. Once you have finished the affirmations, start reading... rereading... seeing... and feeling yourself having already reached each of these affirmations. Do this several times a day. This now becomes your new reality in your subconscious mind (P + E = R).

The rest is automatic. The mission affirmations will reprogram your subconscious mind and gradually work their way into your everyday behavior. You will find personal happiness through your dynamic mission path.

If you faithfully do the imageries, the changes will surpass your highest expectations. This is the raw power of the subconscious mind.

CHAPTER 33

Retirement and the Mission Path

I have two mental pictures of what I am going to do on my eighty-fifth birthday. First, I am going to complete my daily forty-five minute aerobic workout, and then later in the day I am going to give a one-hour speech to 150 sixty-five-year-old "youngsters." I am going to teach them how to enjoy retirement.

This speech will be somewhat hypocritical because retirement is a concept I cannot accept. I personally will never retire. I do not want to suffer the Bear Bryant syndrome (a serious medical illness that occurs within eighteen months after retirement), nor do I want to go through the morose mood that I see many retirees experience.

I have watched several of my clients retire. I have seen their depression, sense of worthlessness, lack of sustaining purpose, and unfair demands on their marriages to fill the newly created void. I have concluded that it is not good for people to retire. It is much better to think either in terms of a consuming mission program or a part-time mission/part-time career package.

To pull off this ambitious game plan, you need to start planning for this transition now. You do not want to wait until age sixty-five! Now is the time to develop new skills and pursue additional training on a leisurely and positive basis. Now is the time to establish a plan of action. Now is the time to get your expanded mission path ready to be launched at the appropriate time.

Retirement could be one of the most exciting times in your pursuit of personal happiness. For the first time in your life (unless you are one of the lucky ones who already "loves" what you are doing), you can choose an endeavor that you *want* to do. You could pursue a mission path that you always wanted to follow but previously could not afford to do.

Norman Vincent Peale has asked the classic question, "Has the greatest event in your life already happened?" At retirement, you may be able to position yourself to give a resounding "no" to that question, either through an energizing personal mission or an exciting second career. And you may actually be able to combine both attractive alternatives.

As mentioned earlier, I have seen many clients struggle with retirement. Other clients, however, have done an excellent job making this transition. There are three reasons for this.

1. They do not rely on hobbies to totally fill the void created as they leave their primary career. Consider the example of John. John loved two things (other than his wife and children of course). His passions were hunting and fishing; he lived for the opportunities to do either. He eagerly looked forward to his sixty-fifth birthday when he would be free to spend as much time as he wanted on his two consuming hobbies.

Once he had unlimited time, however, he found that hunting and fishing were not as enjoyable as they once had been. They did not give him the same emotional "high" that he had experienced before he retired from his job.

What he failed to realize was that a large part of the high came from the fact that hunting and fishing had been the best ways he had used to escape. Getting away from the pressures of his stressful job had created the peaceful high. Once he had nothing to escape from, the hobbies lost part of their emotional impact. Hunting and fishing had allowed him to temporarily run away from the job stress, but they did not help him run away from the "now there is no purpose for my life" depression that replaced the earlier stress. Only after he developed a comprehensive mission package, one that added a renewed purpose to his life, did he find that the joy of hunting and fishing returned.

2. The people who "retire" successfully make sure their mission and/or new career paths keep them as busy (or nearly as busy) as their old full-time job. When you are working ten hours

a day, one of your fondest mental pictures is having more time for hobbies, shopping, working out, or just plain relaxing. But the answer is not to suddenly have *ten* additional hours per day to pursue the activities that need *two* additional hours per day. Stretching these activities out to ten hours will only add to a sense of boredom. And this nothingness will soon be visited by its twin, "the emotional blues."

One definition of psychological depression is anger turned inward. Another interesting definition of depression is "lack of movement." If you are taking ten hours to do two hours of activities, you are more vulnerable to the "lack of movement" depression.

How much free time would you like to have at the time of your retirement? As you contemplate this question, please remember that workaholics are unhappy doing nothing. If you felt the need to keep yourself very busy before retirement, you probably will need to stay busy after "retirement." In your present "overworked" state, you may think that having less to do would be wonderful but, trust me, one month of inactivity is all you will need to drive yourself (and everyone around you) crazy.

3. The people who make the best transition do not make inordinate demands on their spouse to fill the void created by the loss of their career. Often I see the following pattern in my clients. For the first month after leaving the primary career, the retiree is in "hog heaven." He or she can sleep in, putter around, make some overdue repairs on the house, and complete all the nuts and bolts projects that have been on hold for years.

But suddenly there is nothing to do! At this precise moment, many look to their spouse and the unspoken request is "make me happy." If they have had a good marriage, the extra time together may be cause for celebration. But for every marriage that celebrates this extra time together, there are two marriages that take a step backward.

Their marriages have become complacent. They are more comfortable when they are busy with their personal routines, and they have an understanding that says, "I know that we do not meet many of each other's emotional needs, but we still want to stay together." Sudden demands that their marriage change, after settling for a compromised relationship for the past thirty-five years, may not be the recommended course of action for someone age sixty-five to seventy. The additional time, rather than creating closeness, only means "getting in each other's hair." If they are not careful, soon the marital relationship, rather than the recent retirement, will be blamed for the newly created emotional blues.

As you consider your lifestyle beyond age sixty-five, you may want to ask yourself the following question: "Would my spouse and I *really* want to spend more time together or are we better off with 'business' as usual?" Your last two vacations without friends or children should easily help you answer that question. And if you say, "But we never take a vacation just for the two of us," you may have just clearly answered your question.

I am really committed to what I am saying, but I suspect that I cannot ask all of you to buy into my full-time mission or part-time mission/part-time career philosophy. Therefore, I am including some strategies for the readers who will fully "retire" (or limit themselves to a more modest mission package). In my counseling with clients, I have found that:

- The people who retire well stay active. With an enthusiastic zeal, they continue to seek a full life while the people who do not retire well slow down, do less, and take three times as long to complete even the simple tasks.
- The people who retire well think young. They have a mental attitude of sixty-five going on fifty, while the individuals who struggle with retirement are sixty-five going on eighty.
- The people who retire well keep learning. They are constantly discovering new things. The eighty-year-old mother of one of my friends is a good example. In the past six years, she has traveled around the world without ever leaving Texas thanks to the excellent travel books that are available through the public libraries. The people who shun learning about new things are sentenced to living in the past and struggling with mental atrophy.
- The people who retire well enjoy the stimulation of new acquaintances (including the energy of younger people) while the people who remain stagnant limit themselves to old friends. When their friends die or move, they have no one.

- The people who retire well make peace with their eventual death. They live each day to its fullest and worry about dying only when it happens. Others spend each day anxiously waiting for the heart attack or diagnosis of cancer. They develop a retirement mentality in which they become obsessed with death.

If you choose this retirement package, great! And I would encourage you to use the goal-setting and imagery concepts to maximize this five-part strategy. For the rest of you, however, I want to go back to the concept of a mission/second career transition and eliminate the dirty ten-letter word beginning with an R. Now is the time to do the planning that ensures a smooth transition when you reach sixty-five or seventy.

Paint two mental pictures. One is you with an energizing, exciting, and stimulating mission path at age sixty-seven. The other is with a simple retirement at age sixty-seven. Which picture do you like the best? If the answer is a mission, remember that this transition does not start when you are sixty-seven or when you are a depressed sixty-six or a crashing sixty-five. It starts today! Now is the time to eliminate the R word and substitute the phrase "a sense of mission, the third magical path."

• CHAPTER 34 •

The Spiritual Force

In chapter 28, I alluded to the spiritual dimension of a mission. I suggested that a spiritual faith could be one of four vital factors in your obtaining the deepest, most compelling sense of mission. In this chapter I would like to broaden the issue of spiritual faith because I frequently see how this factor plays a major role with my clients.

As I introduce the spiritual dimension to your mission pursuit, I realize that this particular focus may be a turn-off for some of you. If you see most religious people as "uptight," believe God is only a myth, or find yourself secretly cheering on Madelyn Murray O'Hair as she fights against any public expression of religion, you may want to simply skip this chapter.

Most of you will respond positively, however, because people have always looked beyond themselves for answers. Throughout history philosophers have searched for the meaning, the truth, the answers to the whys, the reason for being. The Greeks looked to the heavens and defined their gods. The Indians had the Great Warrior in the sky. Modern-day people talk about a universal subconscious connection between people.

Is it ignorance that creates these illusions—or a natural outlet for the superstitious nature of people—or a way of feeling protected from the unknown? Interestingly, even as ignorance is replaced by scientific knowledge, superstition is pushed toward the ridiculous, and psychological mental toughness helps control the uncertainty of the unknown, the interest in transcending oneself remains high.

Maybe St. Augustine was right when he said, "And the heart of man is restless until it finds its rest in Thee." Perhaps when people find this inner peace, it is easier to find their happiness path, be it in a good marriage, a satisfying career, or a compelling mission.

While preparing to explain how a spiritual faith can add to the mission path, I have struggled with a dilemma. How broad or narrow should I make *my* concept of God? Is it okay to use the term "Christ" or "Jesus," or should I only use "God" to better include the members of the Jewish faith? Or perhaps I should broaden my concept even more by referring to God as a "Supreme Being." I finally decided that making my concept of God too broad would be a disservice to everyone.

If I were listening to a Moslem, a Hindu, or a member of the Jewish faith, I would not want them to "water down" their comments about their faith to be sure to encompass my religious beliefs. I respect their religious beliefs, and I would prefer that they freely express their convictions and trust me to be able to make any necessary modifications. I am making the same assumption with you. Therefore, when I discuss God I will refer to Him in a way with which I am familiar. This will make my statement more crisp, even for the readers who have a different belief system.

Are you still with me? Are you ready to make the abrupt transition in this chapter? Are you ready to see the possible role that faith plays in your walk down the magical paths?

Does a religious faith help one find personal happiness? For some people, one could have serious doubts.

- Legalistic Larry has ten thousand religious rules and spends most of his time analyzing whether he and his family are abiding by each and every rule. He is saddled with the arduous task of making sure that each rule is followed to the "letter of the law."
- Guilt-ridden Grace believes she should be perfect and any sin, no matter how insignificant, creates deep remorse. She is still troubled over relatively minor sins that she committed years ago. Rather than her faith providing a freeing forgiveness, it merely compounds her depressing guilt.

- Hypocritical Harry espouses one set of values on Sunday morning and lives a very different lifestyle the rest of the week. He is known as a person who says one thing but does another. This attitude costs him dearly. He has lost the respect of his colleagues (a hypocrite is loathed more than a sinner) and has had to suffer the emotional consequences of lying to himself.
- Judgmental Jane is constantly critical of others because they do not live the same pure life that she does. In her tight-lipped, set-jaw, look-down-the-nose-at-others manner, she is always noticing when others do something "wrong." But she is not happy despite the comfort of her holier-than-thou attitude.

Should religion be blamed for these attitudes? I think not! In my opinion, it is merely a distortion by people who are using religion to mask their insecurities, elevate their weak self-esteem, release their hostility, or control their shaky impulses. If they did not have religion to hide behind, they would quickly find another acceptable way to legitimize their emotional struggles.

The truth of the matter is that a healthy spiritual faith has just the opposite effect. Throughout my twenty-five years of practice, I have seen many incidents where a spiritual faith has had a very positive impact on people's lives. In fact, I have seen the pervasive nature of a deep faith reach out and give more than a compelling sense of mission. It actually touches all the major areas covered in this book.

Perhaps we should look at ways that a spiritual faith can impact in some of these areas.

1. Caring. Caring in a marriage does not just happen because one is in love. There are millions of people who are in love, but they are selfish. Caring is a quality that comes from within. It is a quality that usually develops from one of three sources. One source is one's parents. Some are blessed with caring parents who teach their children the importance of caring. The parents are powerful models for their children, models that children absorb and carry into their own marriages.

The second source is one's spouse. Many enter a marriage with deficiencies in caring but connect with someone who is caring. While some may perpetually take advantage of this caring attitude and use it, others are won over by the specialness of their mate's caring. Slowly, but surely, they develop the same caring philosophy.

The third source is God. God epitomizes the ultimate in caring. *Agape*, a Greek word for totally unselfish love, is synonymous with God. *Agape* is the love that allowed God to sacrifice His own Son for the welfare of others. When a person connects with God, this caring love can become a central part of his or her personal life.

People who have this connection incorporate certain guidelines for living that are communicated through principles such as the Golden Rule, "Love your neighbor as yourself," the Ten Commandments, "By their works you shall know them," and the Good Samaritan. All of these principles have, as a base, the welfare of others, and as they "sink in," a person develops a more caring lifestyle.

They also have a role model for living because Jesus was the perfect *model* of caring. Jesus cared for the handicapped, the sinner, the rich ruler, the blind, his disciples, the prostitutes, little children, the tax collector, and even the hypocritical Pharisees. As a believer studies the life of Christ, the model of caring rubs off. It becomes a model that His followers strive to duplicate.

When a person becomes more caring, guess who becomes one of the biggest winners? You guessed it—one's marital mate. The second C becomes very important in their marriage.

2. *Commitment*. A deep religious conviction helps a couple take a different mind-set toward their marriage. They know that they made a vow to God, one committed to the permanency of their marriage.

This commitment does not guarantee bliss and happiness. Problems do not automatically disappear. But there is a resolve, an active decision to always think in terms of, "How can we improve our marriage?" The question, "Should I leave my marriage?" is only used as a last resort, not the flashing question every time there is a marital conflict. With this strong commitment comes the courage to risk change. With no commitment the tendency is to hold on to the scared attitude, "I had better not rock the boat; he or she may leave." And all the inadequate behaviors continue until the boat sinks!

The impact of commitment is well illustrated by the examples of the Bensons and the Martins. In the past Bill and Carol Benson and Tom and Diane Martin have used almost identical phrases to describe their marriages.

- "The excitement has waned somewhat. I wish we could recapture some of the sexual turn-on." (chemistry)
- "You are being selfish. Why do you always consider what you want and take me for granted?" (caring)
- "You do not share your feelings the way you used to." (communication)

These are legitimate concerns, but neither marriage is in deep trouble. Remaining married still appears to be the best alternative for both couples, and it is what they want. The two couples are different, however, in one major way. The Bensons have, as a result of a recent religious retreat, made a full commitment to remain in the marriage. The Martins, on the other hand, are still taking the attitude, "You are going to have to make changes before I fully commit." Contrast what is happening with the two couples' first three Cs as a result of their differences in commitment.

Chemistry

The Bensons have started working at putting more romance into their marriage. They have developed a clever plan of sending the kids to the grandparents every Saturday afternoon. There are more candlelight dinners, more surprise gifts, more special nights out, and more weekend trips.

The Martins are still hassling the romance. They blame each other for the problems, they fantasize about other relationships, and each refuses to take the first step in trying to bring back the chemistry.

Caring

The Bensons have started realizing how much they need each other. They will be together long after parents are dead and children are gone. "I had better learn to treat this best friend in a special way" is their recent motto.

The Martins care for each other, but this concern is floundering in third place, well behind the caring they show for their children and respective parents. "Why should I give more than I am getting?" is their current attitude.

Communication

Bill and Carol Benson now realize that simple acceptance, not constant requests for change, is what encourages the deepest level of sharing in a relationship that is "in for the long haul."

Tom and Diane Martin still pursue the no-win course of demanding changes in each other before they are willing to risk sharing their feelings.

A spiritual faith is not essential to have a renewed commitment to a marriage, but all of the couples I have worked with who have used their faith as an aid report that it does make a major difference.

3. *Forgiveness.* A deep spiritual faith can be a significant force in helping people overcome one of the most traumatic of the marital crises: the extramarital affair. Nothing is more gut-wrenching than discovering one's spouse is having an affair. There is a flood of emotions (pain, anger, hurt, and confusion), a sick feeling in the pit of one's stomach, and a sense of helplessness. The emotions fluctuate between the despair of personal inadequacy and a rage toward one's spouse and between a feeling of "What did I do wrong?" and "How could you do a thing like that?" The world is shattered; it seems the pieces will never be able to be picked up again.

What does a person do with all of the intense emotions? What are the alternatives? The instinctive reaction is, "Get out! I never want to see you again!" In our Judeo-Christian value system, the extramarital affair is usually considered the most serious marital transgression. In some circles, it is the *only* justifiable grounds for divorce. One adulterous act, no matter how casual the sexual encounter, is worse than twenty years of emotional, mental, and even physical abuse. It is Truth with a capital T! But a deep faith can offer another alternative.

An affair does not automatically have to be the end of a marital relationship. Many couples—despite the intense hurt, loss of trust, and violation of the intimate code of fidelity—have used the affair as an indicator that their relationship was in trouble. They realized that they could no longer ignore their marital difficulties and pretend that they did not exist. In many cases the end result has been a more solid, caring, and loving relationship than they ever had before. And during this crisis, many have used their spiritual faith as an aid in forgiving their mate.

Sex is very intimate. Perhaps this is why it is so difficult to forgive and forget. And this is why people struggling to give a total emotional forgiveness need God. Many people have told me that they could not forgive their spouse's extramarital affair. They could not, that is, until they finally used outside assistance. Only as they applied the following passage were they able to climb the mountain of true forgiveness and recreate emotional closeness in their marriage:

> For if you forgive men when they sin against you, your heavenly Father will also forgive you. But if you do not forgive men their sins, your Father will not forgive your sins.
>
> (Matt. 6:14-15)

4. *Positive relationships on the job.* One of the key factors in the business world is to have the (a) respect, (b) trust, and (c) loyalty of your employees, colleagues, bosses, and clients. Individuals who command this respect, trust, and loyalty soon join the prestigious circle of career winners. Stephen R. Covey in his best seller, *The Seven Habits of Highly Effective People*, persuasively makes this point.

For many, a spiritual faith becomes a major player in their ability to create these three key factors. The model presented by Jesus (and other religious leaders), the Golden Rule I referred to earlier ("Do unto others as you would have them do unto you."), and the drive to please God all contribute in an impressive way to their overall demeanor. Their word is more binding than the most carefully drawn contract; their sense of fair play becomes an inspiration to others; and their genuine caring creates that intangible emotional bonding.

As mentioned earlier, some people's religion becomes a turn-off. Fortunately, for every Legalistic Larry, Guilt-Ridden Grace, Hypocritical Harry, or Judgmental Jane, there are many others who become a Respected Robert, Trustworthy Theresa, Principled Paul, or Inspirational Ina.

You have seen this. Perhaps you have even been lucky enough to have this type of boss, coworker, or employee. And you may even remember how positively you responded to this person and how they gained your respect, trust and loyalty.

You could walk this same positive path. A spiritual faith can make *you* a winner in the business world as well as in your personal life.

5. *Coping with stress.* One of the great existential struggles for many people is dealing with the sobering fact that their body will age and eventually end its existence. In other words, someday they will die. Some confront this reality very well, but others resort to elaborate psychological escapes or the midlife "crazies" in order to avoid the issue. In a frantic attempt to hold on to life, they abruptly alter their lifestyle (buying the red sports car), escape into a frenzy of activities (or even worse into drugs, alcohol, and depression), impulsively make a career change, or leave an established relationship for a new "exciting" one.

Underlying these impulsive acts are the following realizations:

- "I am getting older."
- "Life is passing me by."
- "I'm not going to live forever."
- "Some day I will die."

No longer does the enthusiasm and optimism of youth mask this undeniable fact. The good news is that a deep faith can help us conquer this fear. The fear fades because death no longer means the end of our existence.

Can people conquer the fear of death without a spiritual faith? Yes they can! They can reduce most of the stress, fear, and anxiety through a mental courage that accepts death as a natural end result of life. Many, however, lack this mental courage. They avoid this sobering reality by repressing their thoughts about death. Unfortunately, repressed material has a tendency to resurface in disguised ways. Soon it is expressed through physical ailments ("What the mind conceals, the body reveals."), frantic avoidance ("Eat, drink, and be merry for tomorrow you may die."), or an eroding depression ("What's the use? The best years are behind me.").

A faith in God gives a second alternative to mental courage. With this belief, there is no continuous concern about dying. For many, the realization that death is not the end, but merely a transition to an even happier state of being, has a calming effect. It turns stifling stress into creative energy, incapacitating fear into uplifting assurance, and immobilizing anxiety into peaceful serenity. Life is lived with an expectation of even more.

> No eye has seen,
> No ear has heard,
> No mind has conceived,
> What God has prepared for
> those who love Him. (1 Corinthians 2:9)

6. Overcoming tragedy. A spiritual faith can help you dig especially deep when you have to overcome tragedy in your life.

I have seen many tragedies: A businesswoman is struck with a debilitating illness that leaves her confined to her home; a popular TV weatherman falls off a second story balcony and has a critical head injury; an executive's career is ruined by a financial scandal in which he is falsely accused.

I could expand on any of these stories and tug on your heartstrings, but you already know about tragedy. Unless you are one of the lucky few, you have already experienced tragedy in your life. You have had to cope with a death of a child, a major financial reversal, a life-altering illness, a serious automobile accident, a divorce or death of a spouse, the stumbling failure of an adult child, or the deteriorating health of a parent.

I have had the opportunity to observe firsthand how many individuals cope with these personal crises. Some people have recovered from these tragedies in ways that are nothing short of inspirational. Like the proverbial phoenix bird, they have risen from the ashes, picked up the pieces, and gone on with their lives in remarkable ways. Many have ended up with a greater compassion for others, a deeper appreciation of life, and a better understanding of what is really important.

Others never recover. They dwell on what could have been, hang on to their bitterness, or simply give up on life. They sentence themselves to a dark, gloomy, morose psychological prison. They believe that their life could never be the same, and thus life is just endured until the end.

What is the difference between these two groups? Of course many things become components of a successful equation. Factors such as loving relationships, ability to look at the big picture, and good mental health all enter the picture, but two specific factors also make a big difference. The people who have these two qualities seem to survive tragedies quite well, and the people who do not have a balance of these two almost contradictory factors struggle more with life's tragedies.

- *They never give up.* There is an optimistic belief that the odds can be beaten. They never give up the belief that things will get better, that they will overcome, that they will get through it.

- *They gracefully accept what is.* People who make the best psychological adjustment to tragedy have a serene acceptance of the inevitable. Rather than holding on to what could have been, there is a celebration of what still is. They have the mental courage to make the best of what is left.

Balance is the key. The balance between these two factors maximizes a person's psychological adjustment during times of tragedy. If the scale gets too loaded in either direction, the odds of recovery are less, as illustrated by the following example:

A young woman with a promising career is in a serious automobile accident. She is told that she only has a 30 percent chance of ever walking again. She suffers through agonizing pain doing everything possible to force her legs to respond. At the same time, there is the serene acceptance that she will live a full and productive life even if she never walks again. The key is to maintain this balance. If she has only *persistence*, she may give up psychologically if she does not make a total recovery. If she has only *acceptance*, she will not adequately push herself physically during the therapy phase.

Keeping the balance . . . persistence and acceptance . . . keeping the balance . . . courage and serenity . . . keeping the balance . . . a never-give-up attitude and a graceful acceptance of what is . . . keeping the balance. This is the secret in overcoming tragedy.

And for many, their spiritual faith is the key factor in keeping this delicate balance . . . a delicate balance that adds compelling depth to their ability to cope.

Some deeply religious individuals believe that God will shield them from all harm, tragedy, and unwanted change, and many of their prayers are requests for God to do just that. I have mixed feelings about this theology because I see too many incidents where it does "rain on both the just and the unjust" and where "bad things do happen to good people."

God may not always shield a person from tragedy, but I do clearly see how a belief in God helps people endure and overcome the natural tragedies that do happen. A spiritual faith helps people cope more effectively with some of the true tragedies of life such as an untimely death, a catastrophic illness, or a life-altering accident. In some rather spectacular ways, a well-defined faith helps people recover from these tragedies, pick up the pieces, and go on with their lives. Their faith gives them a special edge that others lack, and they often attribute this strength to their connection with God. It is this connection that preserves the balance between a never-give-up attitude and a graceful acceptance of what is.

7. Enriching one's mission. Most of us struggle with "selfishness." This very human attitude surfaces in many of our relationships. We have a need for a reward; we have to see what we are gaining by our efforts. With friends, we anticipate how they will be returning the favors, but what if they do not? With business associates, we obtain more career opportunities, but what if they cannot give us anything? With a spouse, we receive more love and affection, but what happens when the love is not being returned? When we do not obtain a "return," resentment can develop. Soon we are holding back from the people who do not reward our efforts.

But what about the person we all admire, the person who seems to give with no thought of a "return"? You have met someone like this. You have also been impressed.

What makes this person so special? So generous? So giving? What are the secrets that cause this person to march to a different drummer? These unique people usually have a very positive self-image. They feel good about themselves and they want to share this joy with others. They have reached the pinnacle of a positive self-image and they want to pull other people up with them. They know that in giving, they lose nothing.

Quite candidly, there are some people who only need this factor. They do not need a religious faith to transcend their selfishness. They have had a peak psychological experience and they respond accordingly. Most of us, however (at least I speak for myself), have not reached this stage of self-actualization. To give fully, we need an extra aid and this is where an intimacy with God enters the picture.

Our payoff transcends what our friends, spouse, or business associates can give. The payoff comes directly from God. This reward does not eliminate the "selfish" tendency but turns it from a negative to a positive. It is the act of pleasing God that gives us our good feelings. This payoff keeps us sharing, caring, and giving—a behavioral expression of our intimate relationship with God.

John was a banker who had worked at First National Bank for the past fifteen years. He found the work exciting, challenging, and rewarding. On the eve of his fifty-second birthday, he was anticipating the expected promotion to senior vice president.

Then came the crushing blow; he was passed over. When he asked why he did not get the promotion, he was told that the bank was pleased with his performance, but he lacked the "scope, vision, education, and banking background" to assume this new position. Suddenly, John realized a painful truth. He had reached his glass ceiling within the bank. He could comfortably continue in his present position and the bank was pleased with his performance, but the door was closed to any promotions.

John turned to his children. He started giving them all of his energy and tried to meet all of his needs through them. The predictable happened. The children started feeling the pressure to be successful for their father. He wanted to be number one in their lives, but they were more interested in being involved with their friends. Suddenly there was too much closeness, too much desire for togetherness.

The same thing happened when John reached out to his wife. John had supported her independence, her schooling, and her career. Now he was threatened. He wanted her to always be around, to limit her involvement to him. John forgot that no one person can meet all of another person's needs, and this pressure began placing a strain on the marriage.

Fortunately, John realized what was happening and he pulled back. But what did he do? Did he lose himself in alcohol, engage in a depressive self-pity, find another woman, develop a meaningless hobby, or passively accept his new station in life? Any of these things could have happened and they often do. John, however, had three outlets for his creative energy: career success, interpersonal relationships, and a behavioral expression of his faith. His faith gave him a third purpose.

John threw himself into community service. He found purpose through giving to others, a direct expression of his faith in God. Over the next five years, he organized three athletic leagues for teenagers, started a community counseling service for families with financial difficulties, led an aggressive fund-raising project that enabled his church to build a new sanctuary, chaired two highly successful United Way campaigns, and was elected president of a community-minded service club.

Recently, John received a plaque from a prestigious service organization. His plaque lauded his tremendous contributions to the renewed community pride and to the spirit of "helping" that exists within the city.

John had a purpose, a purpose energized from his faith, a purpose that added another dimension to his life and helped him regain his personal happiness. His spiritual faith helped him walk down the third magical path . . . a compelling life's mission.

• CHAPTER 35 •

Summary to the Mission Section

An intimate relationship excites the heart, a career stimulates the mind, and a mission energizes the soul. Wise people know that a mission with vision, unselfishness, spirituality, and congruence can be a very powerful and compelling way to find a sustaining personal happiness. They never underestimate the potential of the mission path.

A bonus is that the mission path is often the route that has the most flexibility. People can be immobilized in a marriage ("It takes two to tango.") and/or trapped in a career ("I can't afford to change.") but shifting to a new mission is easy.

A mission can quickly help override a mediocre marriage, uninspiring career, or midlife transition. Even better, a mission can create unique sources of inner joy and personal fulfillment. It truly does become a helper's high . . . a true emotional ecstasy.

This is the true essence of the third magical path.

• PART IV •

OVERCOMING OBSTACLES

• CHAPTER 36 •

Another Introspective Look

Looking at your marriage, career, or mission obstacles may not be easy. Reading this section of this book is similar to going to a therapist or counselor. Any positive change will require a careful look at yourself and your situation. Mentally prepare for this introspective examination by putting yourself in the following scene.

ROBERT E. LINDBERG, Ph.D.
Psychologist

You are sitting in my waiting room. This is your first session and you are very nervous. Your anxiety overrides your feeble attempt to assume a relaxed and calm manner. The pain and confusion in your marriage have motivated you to make this appointment, but now you wonder, "What am I doing here?" Your urge is to get up and walk out. You glance at your watch. It is 1:50 P.M. Ten minutes to go.

Thoughts race through your mind as you sit there with sweaty palms, rapid heartbeat, and strained breathing:

• *What will I find out about myself?* "I keep telling myself that most of our marriage difficulties are my partner's fault, but is that really true? Will the 'shrink' tell me I am really the one who is at fault? After all, there are many things I could have done differently. Perhaps the therapist will even discover some personality quirks and difficulties I am not aware of."

• *Do we really have a problem?* "What is wrong with me? Why can't I be happy in my marriage when many of my friends have it much worse? Why am I turned off to my partner by such insignificant little things? One of my friends says I just want too much, that I am a romantic idealist. Perhaps she is right."

- *How can I justify what I have done?* "Will I have to talk to the counselor about my affair? What is he going to say? I keep telling myself the only reason I was unfaithful was that I was so unhappy in my marriage. But is that really true? Perhaps I am just a person of low morals. Maybe I won't have to mention the affair during the counseling sessions. I hope he doesn't ask."
- *I am really scared.* "What will happen to me if I get a divorce? Could I ever make it financially? I can't support myself and my children on what I make now. And what will happen to my children? I have heard how devastating a divorce is for children."
- *Surely my marriage is not in this much trouble.* "Why did I come? Is it too late to get up and walk out? It probably is, but I am just going to come this one time. Why should I dwell on my problems anyway? It will just make things worse. Perhaps time will take care of everything. After all, some things are best left alone."

You glance at your watch again. It is 2:00 P.M. It is time for your appointment. It sounds as if the door is about to open. Your breath stops.

It is now several weeks later. Again, you are sitting in the waiting room. Even though you have not discussed it with your therapist, you sense this is the last session you will be having with him. You almost laugh as you think about the anxiety you felt before the first session. This change does not mean, however, that the sessions have been fun. Many times you have wanted to stop the counseling, but now you realize how valuable the process has been. As you wait, you remember some of the difficult questions you have finally been able to answer.

- "Can I change my feelings toward my partner?"
- "Is my unhappiness sufficient justification for demanding changes in our relationship?"
- "Do I have sexual problems or is it a lack of chemistry in our marriage?"

- "Are there some things I could do to change the communication pattern in our relationship?"
- "Am I just being selfish? Do I have the right to expect my partner to spend more quality time with me?"

You marvel at your ability to have found answers to these difficult questions. Your counselor deserves some credit, but there is the inner satisfaction that most of the insight came as a result of your personal commitment to take a careful look at your intimate relationship.

It is 2:00 P.M., time for your appointment. When the door opens, you triumphantly walk in for your last session.

Are you ready to experience such a feeling of confidence, of triumph? You can! The door is open—just walk through the pages of this section. You will experience both the agony and ecstasy of committing to an introspective look.

CHAPTER 37

The Three Magical Questions

What do you do if you cannot find a loving relationship path, a rewarding career path, or a compelling mission path? How do you then find the personal happiness that you earnestly seek and desire?

The answer is obvious. You renew your effort to get back on one of these three essential, exciting, and energizing paths. In this section, I will suggest three powerful ways to make this happen. They are:

1. Having the courage to confront the existing problems via the three magical questions.

2. Going for some carefully chosen, competent counseling.

3. Valuing the importance of persistence to overcome earlier failures.

This chapter will take an in-depth look at using the three magical questions to solve some of your current struggles, chapter 38 will discuss going for professional help, and chapter 39 will highlight the enduring value of persistence, persistence, and persistence.

In counseling, I often remind my clients to look at the total picture while making important decisions. I try to point out that decisions made impulsively or based on partial data are usually regretted. Only as they consider all aspects of their situation do they increase their odds of making the best decisions. This takes time because it frequently is necessary to examine certain key aspects of a decision more than once. Each time a slightly different perspective or understanding may emerge.

It would be wise to apply the same principles in reading this book. Study the sections that are of greatest concern to you and reread individual chapters several times. Each reading may trigger new insights into some of your feelings and behaviors. Carefully reflect on what you have read and apply it to your uniquely individual situation.

The time comes, however, when the analysis has to turn to decision making, and this is where the three magical questions come in to play. They help you make the tough decisions.

The three magical questions for your three magical paths are:

1. What is the problem?

2. What are your alternatives?

3. What are the consequences of each alternative?

Study these questions. Understand the full emotional impact of the three magical questions by doing the following introspective exercises.

What is the Problem?

"What is the problem?" is the most critical of the three questions. Most people are close to a solution once the problem has been clearly defined. One industrial consultant was asked why the Japanese compete so successfully with the Americans despite their limited natural resources. The wise answer was, "When Americans have an industrial problem, they spend fifteen percent of their time defining the problem and eight-five percent working on finding the solution. The Japanese reverse these percentages. They spend eight-five percent of their time carefully defining the problem, and fifteen percent finalizing the solution."

Always remember that if you create answers to pseudo problems, you will obtain pseudo solutions. And if you develop answers to real problems, you will maximize your ability to create authentic solutions to your marriage, career, or mission struggles.

How do you face the problem? The answer is simple. You reduce the ambiguity—the uncertainty—by gathering information. You resolve to go for the truth. You seek the answer even when you walk under the shadow of fear that the truth may be negative. The immediate result may appear more painful, but the end result is usually an honest, straightforward solution to the problem. Even when the problem cannot be totally resolved, the direct confrontation places the situation back in perspective and establishes the foundation for developing better coping techniques.

Carol, a physician's wife, hated her husband's hectic schedule. It was a source of constant irritation. She felt medicine was his only interest, and she subtly kept asking him to prove that she came first.

- "If you really loved me, you would let someone else take your emergency calls this evening."
- "You show more concern for your patients than you do for me."
- "If you really cared about me, you would stop teaching part-time at the medical school, and you would reduce the size of your practice."

These testing statements reflected Carol's hidden concern: "Does he really prefer his career to me? Does he find more fulfillment in his professional life?" Not knowing added to her unhappiness and was the major cause of her minor depression.

Then there was a major confrontation where Carol totally forced the issue. During this discussion, Carol's husband finally admitted, "Yes! My career does come first!" He tried to explain that he deeply loved her and the children, but agreed that his career as a physician was extremely important . . . the *most* important thing.

At first, Carol was deeply hurt (the hurt was more intense than the ambiguity), but she made a quick recovery. The message was clear; she *knew* where she stood. It was not everything she wanted, but there was no more doubt or uncertainty. She started realizing that she was going to have to meet some of her personal needs in other ways. With the removal of the ambiguity came the freedom to become more fulfilled in her own personal life. She enrolled in college and started taking concrete steps toward having her own career. Her increased self-reliance created a change in the relationship with her husband. It became a relationship with fewer demands and less time together, but one that developed into a loving, sharing relationship between two independent people.

Take a *careful* look at a problem or concern that you have. Feel free to select any area: conflict on the job, personal stress, marital strain, lack of a mission purpose, and so on. Write out the problem as you see it.

_____

_____

Stop for a minute. Is this really the problem or just a surface expression of an underlying problem? Reflect on this for a couple of minutes and then redefine the problem.

_____

_____

Good job! But does the problem need even further defining? Always remember, "There ain't no use running if you are on the wrong path." Are there some other factors that enter the picture? What about fear of the unknown, insecurity, lack of assertiveness, concern as to how others would react, or other emotions that are a part of the "real" problem?

Reflect on this and then restate the problem one more time.

_____

_____

Are you to the bedrock? Have you fully defined the problem? As you can see, you could walk through this process several more times.

What Are the Alternatives?

The second step is to list all possible alternatives to the problem. This is when you use your best creative energies to come up with all possible alternatives. At this stage, all alternatives, good and bad, are viable. Wait until the third step to assess the wisdom of each option.

Be sure that status quo (keeping things the same) is one of the listed alternatives. Status quo freely chosen as the best option is accepted better than status quo accepted by default (making no decision).

Ask for suggestions from other people only after you have exhausted your own ideas. An alternative that you come up with has more chance of being accepted than the identical suggestion from someone else.

Angela went for counseling because she was becoming increasingly concerned about the emotional erosion in her marriage. During her short-term counseling, one of her homework assignments was to use the three magical questions to obtain a better understanding as to what the real problem was and what she could do to recapture the specialness with her husband.

She asked herself all the right questions as she mentally reviewed the five C's. Is there still a *chemistry* that creates romantic attraction, triggers a desire for close sexual contact, and adds a special sparkle to the relationship? Is there still a *caring* that fosters genuine concern, creates a mind-set of acceptance rather than nonacceptance, and provides the comfort of being best friends? Is there still a *communication* that encourages the sharing of the real self, sends positive rather than critical messages, and stimulates emotional intimacy? Is there still a *commitment* that accepts reasonable expectations, encourages a desire to make the marriage work, and seeks an emotional bonding? Is there still a *competency* that controls unwarranted jealousy, creates adequate self-sufficiency, and celebrates positive self-esteem?

Angela concluded, after completing the "What is the problem?" question, that their main problem was a chemistry problem that was created because they had become too busy, distracted, stressed, and careless. What were Angela's alternatives given the chemistry problem that she had isolated? You will notice that she listed *all options*, not just the positive ones.

1. Accept what is and not make sex such a big deal.

2. Make a promise to myself to do one romantic thing (a flower, card, little note, and so on) each week.

3. Continue in counseling with a renewed resolve to put romance back in the marriage.

4. Faithfully use romantic images to fill the unconscious mind with sexual desire.

5. Contact a lawyer. I cannot live in a marriage that does not have an ongoing sexual romance.

6. Block out times—with the same degree of discipline that I do for job responsibilities—that are reserved for the two of us to be together romantically.

7. Pull away from the relationship emotionally until my husband realizes that something is missing, and he decides that he had better pay more attention to the sexual romance.

8. Remember to do more nonsexual touching, that is, do not only touch when I am wanting to be sexually close.

9. Have an extramarital affair so I can meet my sexual needs without having to leave a marriage that is good in all other ways.

10. Strive to be more open and sharing of my true feelings and emotions. ("Sex without intimacy is exciting, sex with intimacy is ecstasy.")

11. Issue an ultimatum. Tell my husband that he has to give more time to the relationship, especially the romantic part, before even more damage is done.

12. Be more spontaneous and vulnerable in lovemaking. Add the variety that keeps sparkle and newness in the romantic encounters.

13. Decide to wait until a specific later time to work on the chemistry issue (for example, children have left home, career has stabilized, and schooling is completed).

14. Work on self-esteem so I minimize my concerns when the sexual chemistry is not a part of our relationship.

15. Join a health club/fitness center to ensure that my body is always in the best shape possible.

16. Religiously block out one weekend per month that is just for the two of us. After all, our marriage is worth this special commitment.

I encourage you to do the same *in-depth* process with the specific problem that you isolated as a result of your "What is the problem?" probe. List *all possible options* that you can come up with.

Once again, I want to remind you that you are simply doing brainstorming during this "What are the alternatives?" listing. You will wait for the third magical question to decide the merits of each of the specific alternatives.

Take out a sheet of paper and list all the possible alternatives that you have to your specific marriage, career, or mission problem.

There is one observation that I probably should make at this stage of the three magical questions process. This relates to the fact that you may feel that you do not have a sufficient number of alternatives. If this is so, I would encourage you to consider three things.

1. Go back and define what the problem is more carefully. Take some time to do introspective, reflective thinking. Read a couple of good books on the subject to expand your horizon on possible options. Do not limit your alternatives to the way you have done things in the past. Release your creative mind to find new and different ways to attack the problem.

2. Ask friends for *alternatives*. (Note the emphasis on alternatives.) Do not allow them to jump to stage three where they start giving you advice, that is, the consequences of each alternative. Encourage them to slow down and brainstorm with you. Monitor their jumping ahead to consequences just as I have been encouraging you to monitor and discipline yourself.

3. Go for counseling, not just to find *the* solution but to consider all possible options to your specific problem. A wise professional counselor may provide options that you never even considered. And yes, monitor even the professional

counselor if he or she jumps to solutions before your options have been carefully explored.

What Are the Consequences of Each Alternative?

The third magical question, "What are the consequences of each alternative?" is where you carefully analyze each of your possible options. You project to the best of your ability what would happen if you elected that alternative. Once *all* possible alternatives are listed, there is automatically more of a commitment to a course of action. The fantasy of waiting for a magical solution is reduced.

There is also a realization, especially for the most difficult decisions, that there are no ideal solutions. All the alternatives have some negative elements. This understanding makes it easier to aggressively choose an option with some negative consequences rather than continuing to wring one's hands while waiting for the nonexistent 100 percent positive solution.

Once again you need to realize that it is more powerful to "tease" the consequences of each alternative out of yourself rather than simply asking others for the information. Consequences that you consider are readily accepted; consequences that others suggest may be initially resisted.

For illustrative purposes, take another look at the inadequate romance in Angela's marriage. Listed below are the consequences that Angela came up with for each of her sixteen alternatives.

1. Accept what is. "No, this is not an option. For me, sex and romance are too important."

2. Do one romantic thing each week. "I will start doing that this week . . . and encourage my husband to do the same."

3. Continue in counseling. "Yes, I have already committed to do this."

4. Use romantic images. "I like this option. I am going to use my subconscious mind to fuel sexual desires and I am going to create imageries for my husband to use also."

5. Contact a lawyer. "No, this is premature. In fact, this is not even an option at this time. I would stay in the marriage rather than leave if this was the only problem."

6. Block out specific times. "Yes and there has to be a discipline to this. It is not just done when everything else is finished."

7. Pull away emotionally. "That is not going to work. I am afraid that approach would only compound the sexual distance that we already have."

8. Do more nonsexual touching. "I love it! And maybe I need to do a better job of telling my husband how important this is."

9. Have an extramarital affair. "No, this alternative may be acceptable for some people. I would leave my marriage first."

10. Be more open and sharing. "This may really be the key, at least for me. We simply need more time to ourselves, even away from the children, for this open sharing."

11. Issue an ultimatum. "I am first going to try the positive loving approach. But if that doesn't work, I will issue some type of demand."

12. Be more spontaneous in lovemaking. "We both need to put fun back in our sexual relationship. We need a vacation-type sexual mentality during our normal lives."

13. Postpone the romance issue until later. "No, life is for living now! We need to confront the issue before it leads to more serious problems such as an extramarital affair."

14. Work on self-esteem. "Always a plus, but I do not think self-esteem is the issue here. I deserve a good sexual relationship."

15. Join a health club. "I am already a member, but I could lose a few pounds. Maybe I will increase the number of days I work out."

16. Block out weekends. "I am going to insist on this and block them out for the next four months. I am going to give our sexual chemistry and marriage the importance that they deserve."

Angela's case illustrates how you can move closer to a solution or at least a set of strategic steps by carefully analyzing the consequences of each of your alternatives.

Do the same for each of the alternatives that you developed for your relationship, career, or mission problem. Project to the best of your ability what the consequences are for each of your alternatives.

As you complete this process, you will discover why I call these steps the three *magical* questions. As you can now sense, you have new directions for getting back on a magical path.

The magic usually happens after the decision. This is when you are free to use your personal energy to start a plan of action. This is when you are able to shake the immobilizing shackles of merely worrying about the problems or passively waiting for the ideal solution. This is when good things begin happening.

Take whatever time you need to make the decisions regarding the concerns in your marriage . . . or your career . . . or your mission . . . or any personal concern. Just remember that most of the positive changes in your life will happen after you have (a) defined the problem, (b) looked at all the options, and (c) selected the best course of action.

I have found that 80 percent of the time this approach solves the problem. In the other 20 percent it may be necessary to gather more information or seek outside help to (a) better define and understand the problem, (b) come up with more creative alternatives, and/or (c) better understand the consequences of your alternatives.

CHAPTER 38

Finding a Competent Counselor

I want to dispel the myth that only people with major psychological problems go for psychotherapy or counseling. Nothing could be further from the truth. Therapy can be used to maximize personal potential as readily as it can be used to resolve personal pathology. It often is the psychologically healthy people facing situational problems (marriage, career, or mission concerns) who profit most from psychotherapy or counseling. They have the tools for making quick and dramatic changes, and they do just that! Counseling is highly recommended if you find yourself still struggling after working through the three magical questions.

Counseling can help you in at least three different ways:

1. Counseling eliminates the possibility of a deeper psychological problem. Sometime one's personal unhappiness has nothing to do with not being on one of the three magical paths. The symptoms of unhappiness may be the same as those of an unfulfilled person, but they are really indications of a deeper emotional or medical problem. Proper diagnosis can help you spot and change these conditions.

2. Counseling helps you face the truth. Our instinctive tendency is to try to avoid the unpleasant and shy away from the situations that create negative emotions. Unfortunately, this natural tendency comes into play even when the circumstances may indicate we need to confront the situation. For example:

- A couple senses that their marriage is developing some serious problems. They harbor these concerns but say or do nothing. It seems less painful to pretend that the problems do not exist.
- An employee senses his boss is becoming dissatisfied with his work. He intends to do something about it later. For now, it seems easier to just ignore the warning signs and hope the problems will resolve themselves.
- A happy, high-energy person suddenly is struggling with a depression that has lingered for two months. Even friends have suggested professional help. But she waits, hoping that the depression will eventually go away.

This avoidance tendency is reinforced by the fact that occasionally problems do disappear or are resolved without any direct response on our part. In too many cases, however, our avoidance of the unpleasant has negative consequences. We ignore the situation but the fear, anxiety, and depression continue unabated. We may even think these negative feelings are preferable to confronting the problem situation head on, but by avoiding the situation, the negative emotions seem to linger on and on and on. The feelings persist because the problem persists. The concern over the marital "nothingness" increases, the job situation remains stressful, or the depression deepens.

Soon the long-term emotions, created by avoiding the problems, take a great toll . . . a greater toll than even the most intense short-term emotions, while facing the problems, could ever take. Ulcers, biochemical depression, phobias, migraine headaches, and incapacitating anxiety can come from the long-term stress created by the systematic avoidance. And the longer the avoidance persists, the more we feel helpless to do anything about these situations or the accompanying emotions.

Resolve today to eliminate the avoidance pattern in your relationship, career, or mission by facing the problems directly. A therapist can help when you choose to confront these issues. Having your psychological hand held makes it easier to muster up your emotional courage and mental toughness; you are not alone in this process. Your therapist can help by gently pushing you when you bog down, slow you down when the pace is too accelerated, and keep a nice balance of encouragement, support, and objectivity. He or she may even help by reminding you that the process is worth it. The increase in short-term stress is bearable because it will soon be replaced by long-term solutions.

Facing the problems directly also means taking an inward look at yourself. Socrates, the ancient Greek philosopher, uttered one of the world's most profound statements. His powerful message required only two words: "Know thyself."

People often hesitate to look too closely at themselves. They are afraid some negative psychological truths exist that are ready to spring out and consume them. Often a close look at oneself is attempted only when the personal pain, anxiety, and depression become too intense.

Fortunately, this fear is generally unfounded. Usually the truths people discover about themselves are not as negative as they have feared, and even when painful, repressed material surfaces, people usually feel better once they have directly confronted these inner emotions.

3. Counseling helps you use the psychological strategies. Your therapist can help you (a) uncover deeper problems, (b) face the truths, and (c) be a friend, guide, and mentor in helping you apply the strategies mentioned in this book to your unique situation. He or she can be a coach as well as a counselor.

I am always amused by the way some people assess new psychological techniques. (I am not being critical here because I have a tendency to do the same thing!) As they mentally examine a new approach, there is the initial thought or comment that sounds like one of the following:

- "I know this would never work for me." (No reason is given, but there still is an emphatic rejection.)
- "I tried that back in 1994 and it made no difference." (Ignoring that circumstances and motivation may be quite different now.)
- "That is too difficult." (Assessing the difficulty level before, not after, one gives it a try.)
- "I am not sure I could ever do that." (Determining other people's reactions *before* using the strategy.)
- "Susie tried that approach, and it didn't work for her." (Yes, but you are not Susie!)

I do know that each of the suggestions mentioned in this book has worked for many people. Each is a sound strategy devised by highly competent professional people or self-discovered by creative individuals who have made impressive changes.

Some of the strategies may not work for you, but can you truly make that determination before you test the strategies? One theory is that it takes twenty-one days for a behavior to become a habit. It is easy to give up, but a properly timed, encouraging word from your counselor suggesting that your struggle is a natural part of the process can be uplifting.

Your counselor can also help you customize the strategies. Each person is unique and each situation is unique. Devising little techniques for applying the strategies can make the difference between success and failure. And your counselor has a whole arsenal of other strategies that can come into play in a powerful way because he or she has an intimate knowledge of your unique situation.

Once you combine the psychological strategies in this book with your therapist's strategies—and do not forget your own creative strategies—you will have created a winning recipe. You will have a well-honed, customized, specifically tailored, well-rehearsed set of strategies for putting psychological power in your life.

How do you find the right counselor or therapist? Following are three guidelines.

1. *Is your therapist competent?* Most people are careful in selecting a dentist, physician, or attorney. They ask other professional people or friends for recommendations. They want to ensure they have selected a good one because they know that professionals in any field come in mediocre, good, better, and best packages. Some of these same people, unfortunately, will pick a therapist out of the yellow pages. The explanation is usually that they did not want anyone else to know they had personal problems.

Select your therapist in the same careful manner you use in selecting other professional people. Ask your physician, minister (priest, rabbi), or attorney for a referral. They are in the best position to know because they have referred many other people and have received a broad base of feedback from their patients or clients. They have a track record on these therapists. And they will not be shocked when you inquire. They have been asked this question many times before and will not even give it a second thought. In fact, they will feel complimented that you trusted their judgment.

Friends are a second possibility, but their base of experience is more limited (to the therapist they saw) and may be influenced by factors such as, "The counselor was so sympathetic," or "The therapist said there was nothing wrong with me."

2. *Do you sense a "rapport" with your therapist?* Always try to work with someone you feel good about. If you have a negative reaction to your therapist after the initial session, you may want to consider shifting to another therapist. It is important to have a rapport with your therapist—a gut-level respect and trust. It is hard to open up to a "stone wall" or to someone you do not like.

You want a therapist with whom you can be totally open and honest. Remember, if you hold back from him or her, you will be holding back from yourself. You are seeking help because you could not sort through the murky mess by yourself. Your therapist can only help to the degree that you allow him or her to see the true you. (One note of caution: Good initial rapport is necessary. If after ten sessions, however, you suddenly "lose the rapport," you should not automatically change therapists. You should first consider, "Has he or she brought up a sensitive topic that is making me feel defensive? Perhaps I should look at my personal dynamics before I react negatively.") Rapport is established by a therapist's warmth, genuine caring, and enthusiastic involvement. But it also moves beyond that to a dimension of full acceptance.

Be cautious of any therapist who takes too strong a position on social issues such as divorce, abortion, or religion. Naturally, therapists are entitled to (and should have) well-defined personal value systems, but the key issue is whether they feel a need to impose their value system on you. This is how counseling is different from preaching, teaching, guidance, and persuasion. And it does not make any difference whether you believe divorce is a sin, abortion is murder, or God is the answer; or if you believe abortion is a woman's right, divorce is an acceptable alternative, and religion is not a high priority. Your therapist should always operate out of the principle that you have the total right to use *your* value system in making the critical decisions. After all, it is *your* life!

If your counselor cannot abide by this principle, it should be clearly stated ahead of time rather than covertly and subtly worked into the counseling.

3. *Is your therapist specialized to work in your area of concern?* A heart surgeon could legally give you medical advice on a knee condition, but you may hesitate. It's far better to contact an orthopedic surgeon. Likewise, you may hesitate in talking to a corporate attorney about a divorce issue. He or she could probably give you legal advice, but it would not be as precise, refined, or current as the attorney who practices family law full-time.

The same is true in selecting a therapist. Therapists can legally counsel in many areas, but they often have formal or informal areas of specialization. One therapist could be highly skilled in treating depression but rather inept in dealing with the subjective complexities of a marital problem. A second therapist could be highly experienced in helping a client make good career decisions but totally inexperienced in handling an acute sexual abuse flashback.

Therapists attempt to stay in their areas of expertise, but you can ensure that by selecting a therapist who not only is competent but also spends a sizable portion of his or her professional time working in your problem area. This ongoing experience keeps him or her on the cutting edge, a fine-tuning that you want in the person you see.

You can help ensure a good therapist selection by making certain that your counselor refers clients to other therapists and treatment groups. If you have issues that fall outside his or her areas of specialization, he or she should be quick to refer you to someone else. If your counselor hesitates in this area, watch out! You do not want a possessive therapist.

Find a therapist who is competent, establishes a rapport with you, and frequently works in your area of concern, and you will have taken another giant step toward maintaining an intimate relationship, finding career fulfillment, having a mission for your life, and/or resolving any other problems that surface.

Make six telephone calls today. The first five will be to ask people for recommendations; the sixth call will be to set up your first appointment. You may want to reread the first portion of chapter 36 to prepare yourself psychologically for this scary but exciting adventure.

CHAPTER 39

Persistence

The first strategy in this section was the three magical questions and the second going for counseling. The third strategy is the shortest, yet one of the most powerful. It contains a secret that will give you the winning edge.

> **Persistence**
> Nothing in the world can take the place of persistence. Talent will not, nothing is more common than unsuccessful men with talent. Genius will not, unrewarded genius is almost a proverb. Education will not, the world is full of educated derelicts. Persistence and determination alone are important.
> Calvin Coolidge

Failure is a very positive thing; it is an excellent indicator that you are expanding your potential and going for the big prize. You'll rarely fail if you never take a risk. The only problem is that these minimal efforts lead to such unimpressive personal victories. Always remember that the bigger the win, the greater the danger of losing. If you maximize your potential, you will increase the number of failures and increase the number of spectacular relationship, career, and mission victories!

Thomas Edison failed many times before he perfected the incandescent lamp. Edison viewed these experiences not as failures but as opportunities for learning and self-correction. If he had viewed each event as a failure, he would have given up.

A proper attitude toward failure will keep you persevering. When you do not immediately reach your relationship, career, or mission goal, you have not failed. You have just been provided with valuable information to help you self-correct and pursue the goal (or a modified goal) with renewed energy, knowledge, and enthusiasm. The alternative of safe little goals (and thus no failures) is a sad choice that you never want to make. This is why you want to persevere in getting on one or more of the three magical paths.

If you want to find personal happiness, you will *persevere* until you reach the emotional state that you so richly deserve!

Read the persistence poem again—more carefully this time—and etch it deeply into your mind, heart, and soul. Persistence will have even more power when it is channeled along the three magical paths to your personal happiness.

I hope and pray that you find at least one of them.

REFERENCES AND HELPFUL READING

Alberti, Robert E. and Michael L. Emmons. *Your Perfect Right: A Guide to Assertive Living*. San Luis Obispo, CA: Impact Publishers, 1986.

Bandura, A.L. *Principles of Behavior Modification*. New York: Holt, Rinehart, and Winston, 1969.

Beattie, Melody. *Codependent No More*. San Francisco: Harper/Hazelden, 1987.

Beck, Aaron T., M.D. *Love is Never Enough*. New York: Harper and Row, 1988.

Benson, Herbert and Miriam Z. Klipper. *The Relaxation Response*. New York: Morrow, 1975.

Berne, Eric, M.D. *What Do Your Say After You Say Hello*. New York: Bantam Books, 1971.

Bolles, Richard N. *What Color is Your Parachute?* Berkley, CA: Ten Speed Press, 1993.

Brandon, Nathaniel. *The Psychology of Romantic Love*. Los Angeles, CA: J.P. Tarcher, Inc., 1980.

Brandon, Nathanial. *How to Raise Your Self-Esteem*. New York: Bantam Books, 1987.

Brown, H. Jackson. *Life's Little Instruction Book*. Nashville, TN: Rutledge Hill Press, 1991.

Burns, David D. *Feeling Good: The New Mood Therapy*. New York: Signet, 1981.

Burns, David D. *Intimate Connections*. New York: William Morrow & Co., 1985.

Colgrove, Melba, Harold Bloomfield, and Peter McWilliams. *How to Survive the Loss of a Love*. New York: Bantam Books, 1976.

Covey, Stephen R. *The Seven Habits of Highly Effective People*. New York: Simon and Schuster Inc., 1989.

Ellis, Albert and Robert A. Harper. *A New Guide to Rational Living*. North Hollywood, CA: Wilshire Book Co., 1975.

Festinger, L. *A Theory of Cognitive Dissonance*. Stanford, CA: Stanford University Press, 1957.

Fromm, Erich. *The Art of Loving*. New York: Harper and Row, 1974.

Gibran, Kahlil. *The Prophet*. New York: Alfred A. Knopf, 1985.

Gray, John. *Mars and Venus in the Bedroom*. New York: Harper Collins Publishers, 1995.

Gray, John. *Men are From Mars, Women are From Venus*. New York: Harper Collins Publishers, 1992.

Hendrix, Harville. *Getting the Love You Want*. New York: Henry Holt and Company, Inc., 1988.

Houck, Catherine. "How to Beat a Bad Mood." *Reader's Digest* Volume 134 (January 1989): 93-95.

Johnson, Caesar. *Something to Love*. Norwalk, CT: C.R. Gibson Co., 1970.

Kinder, Melvyn and Connell Cowan. *Husbands and Wives.* New York: Clarkson N. Potter, Inc., 1989.

Kowalski, Robert E. *The 8-Week Cholesterol Cure.* New York: Harper and Row Publishers, 1987.

Kubler-Ross, Elisabeth. *On Death and Dying.* New York: Macmillan Publishing Co., 1969.

Kushner, Harold S. *When Bad Things Happen to Good People.* New York: Schocken Books, 1981.

Luks, Allen. "Helper's High." *Psychology Today* Volume 22, No. 10 (October 1988): 39-42.

Masters, William H. and Virginia E. Johnson. *Human Sexual Response.* Boston: Little, Brown, 1969.

Masters, William H. and Virginia E. Johnson in association with Robert J. Levin. *The Pleasure Bond.* New York: Bantam, 1976.

Norwood, Robin. *Women Who Love Too Much.* Los Angeles: Tarcher/St. Martin Press, 1985.

Peale, Norman Vincent. *The Power of Positive Thinking.* Englewood Cliffs, NJ: Prentice Hall, 1952.

Peck, M. Scott, M.D. *The Road Less Traveled.* New York: Simon & Schuster, 1978.

Pines, Maya. "Psychological Hardness: The Role of Challenge in Health." *Psychology Today* Volume 14, No. 12 (December 1980): 34-44.

Rogers, Carl R. *A Way of Being.* Boston: Houghton Mifflin, 1980.

Satir, Virginia. *Conjoint Family Therapy.* Palo Alto, CA: Science and Behavior Books, Inc., 1967.

Scarf, M. *Intimate Partners: Patterns in Love and Marriage.* New York: Random House, 1987.

Schuller, Robert H. *The Be-Happy Attitudes: Eight Positive Attitudes That Can Transform Your Life.* Waco, TX: Word Books, 1985.

Skinner, B.F. *The Behavior of Organisms.* New York: Appleton-Century-Croft, 1938.

Smith, Marcell J. *When I Say No I Feel Guilty.* New York: Bantam Books, 1975.

· INDEX ·

A

A-B-C formula 211
   activating event 211
   belief system 211
   consequences 211
   illustration 214
Acceptance 23, 26, 37, 72, 181, 271, 272, 287. *See also* Caring
   changing behaviors 48
   cornerstone of deep friendship 47
   of spouse 50
   lack of 74
   negative feedback 48
   quiz 49
   unconditional 48
   underestimated value 46
   within marriage 48
Active listening 69
   acceptance 72
   body language 184
   clarifying response 179
   confidentiality 71
   developing skills 70
   empathy 71
   evaluation response 178
   information-giving response 178
   power of 178
   response patterns 180
   three qualities of 71
   understanding response 179
Addison, Joseph 2
Aerobic exercise 191
Affirmation 88, 89, 169
Agape 228

Alcoholics Anonymous 240
Argument 51-60, 110
   codependency 53
   dominance 53
   extramarital affairs 52
   passive-aggressive behavior 54
   physical attack 52
   sarcastic comments 54
Avoidance 190, 269, 294
Avoidance tendency 294

B

B 211-215
   belief system 211
   intervening variable 211
Bandura, A.L. 208
Bear Bryant syndrome 255
Body language. *See* communication: nonverbal
Burnout 159, 237
Burns, George 138

C

Career path 1, 10-11, 91, 99, 112, 117, 126, 135-217, 233, 275
   being well-matched 140
   critical factor to happiness 137
   job stress 139
   positive relationships on job 140
   typical daily schedule 137
Career matching 157-170
   career mismatch 168

data, things, or people 159
interaction with people 162
motivation 165
personal needs 167
seven questions for 159
working with other coworkers 163
Career mismatch, resolving 148
challenge of career 164
Caring 20, 26, 33, 35, 45-50, 75, 77, 85, 93-95, 104, 174, 229, 263-264, 268
excitement of chemistry/comparison 46
in a romantic relationship 45
value of 46
Carson, Johnny 138
Change
29, 33, 43, 47, 48, 49, 50, 74, 76, 79, 87, 88, 90, 151, 292
five-step approach 68
positive attitude toward 10
systematic approach 68
Chemistry 20-21, 23-39, 85, 94, 172
essential quality 27
electricity, flow of 23
illustration 24
imagery 32
sexual security 35
sexual turn-ons 31
without love 28
Churchill, Winston 251
Codependency 2, 53
Cognitive dissonance 207
Commitment 19-95, 98, 101, 228, 266, 287
and unreasonable expectations. *See* Expectations
five C's 92
goal setting 86
quiz 91
shaped by 85
the little things 92
three C's 85
value system 86
ways to strengthen 90
Communication 20, 43, 61-72, 63, 73, 76, 79, 85, 178, 287
and criticism. *See* Criticism

honesty, degree of 61
nonverbal 181
not measured by talking 61
positive 82
sharing ideas, feelings, emotions 61
soul to soul 64
verbal, nonverbal 181
Competency 20, 94, 103-121, 123, 287
happy marriages 104
insecurity 111
jealousy 114
Complacency 235
Compliments/criticisms ratio 177
Confidentiality 71
Conflict 24, 27, 104, 105, 168, 173
personal, relationship 106
Confrontation 192
Connection
emotional 16
intellectual 16
sexual 16
spiritual 16
Coolidge, Calvin 299
Coping 139, 191, 285
strategies for 3
Counseling
2, 47, 54, 97, 106, 113, 146, 191, 241, 283, 293, 297
deeper psychological problem 293
face the truth 293
psychological strategies 295
Counselor 71, 106, 111, 279, 293, 296.
finding a competent one 293-298
Covey, Stephen R. 268
Critical attitude, reasons for 78
Criticism 25, 73-84, 177, 196, 198-199, 203
analyze your messages 81
art of handling 199
cancerous growth 73
conditional, unconditional messages 79
emotional distance 77
empty bucket approach 200
four common reasons for 74
increased stress level 197

low self-image 77
marital communication 73
modeling 75
negative messages 73
protection from 79
rejection of spouse 74
valid 75

D

Dallas Cowboys 251
Dating Mentality. *See* Chemistry
Defensive behavior 108
Depression 64, 116-117, 119-120, 128, 157, 243, 255, 257, 269
    causes for 117
    deeper problems 117
    personal worth 119
    poor marriage 120
    repressed emotions 118
Dominance 53

E

Edison, Thomas 299
Eliot, George 61
Ellis, Albert 107, 211
Emotions 16, 26, 35, 37, 47, 55, 61-62, 67, 71, 89, 105, 117-118, 128-129, 182, 183, 189, 267, 294
    assume responsibility for 212
Emotional blues 205
    diet 205
    music 205
    naps 205
    positive thinking 205
Emotional bonding 166
Emotional connection 16, 62
Emotional distance 77
Emotional intimacy, without risk 76
Emotional responses 37
Empathy 71
Endorphin fix 205-209
    biochemical changes 206
    motivational program 207
Erection, failure to sustain 41, 77
Eros 228
Expectation 36, 48, 86, 95, 98, 227

    and commitment 101
    happiness 96
    love 99
    needs chart 100
    personal needs 98
    rights 96
    security 99
    self-actualization 100
    self-esteem 99
    sense of belonging 99
Expectations, unreasonable 95-101
Extramarital affairs 52

F

Fame 165
Financial frustrations, reducing 147
First Magical Path 13-133
Five C's 17, 19-21, 90, 103, 172, 287
    caring 20, 92
    chemistry 20, 93
    commitment 20, 93
    communication 20, 92
    competency 20, 93
    psychological strategies 94
Ford, Henry 130
Forgiveness 58, 262
    ask for 59
    extramarital affair 59
    initiating 60
    physical beating 59
    to your partner 59
Fortune 165
Freudian psychoanalysis 127

G

Gambler 158
Gibran, Kahlil 15
Gibson, Kurt 251
GIGO (garbage in, garbage out) 196
Goal setting 86-87, 169
    personal affirmation 88
Goal, vs. affirmation 88
Goals, pursuing vs. reaching 248
Golden Rule 264
Good Samaritan 264

Good-feelings ticket 202
  filter the feedback 202
  punch your own ticket 202
Great Warrior 261
Greek gods 261
Grief counseling 238

H

Happiness 1-3, 9, 19, 47, 96, 101, 104, 127, 138, 146, 159, 232, 242, 256, 275
Helper's high 222. *See also* Mission
Hill, Ron 92

I

Imagery 32-33, 88, 127, 130, 132, 207, 209, 251-254. *See also* Chemistry
  four-step process 253
  inspiration 251
  maximize ability 251
  subconscious mind 129
Incompatibility in marriage 104
Indians 261
Information method 207
Inner being 66
Inner satisfaction 165
Inner voice 106-108, 111
  avoiding pain 108
  distortion of 107
Insecurity 16, 20, 104, 107, 111, 113-114, 117, 121
  and dependency 112
  jealousy 114
Intellectual connection 16
Intimacy 23, 26, 44, 61-64, 72, 76, 127, 152, 272
  without risk 76
Intimate relationship
  maintaining an 19
Introspective look 1-8, 279-281

J

Jealousy 16, 20, 104, 106-107, 111, 114, 116-117, 121
  insecurity 114
  projection 115
  reality 116
Job failure 143
  ways to reduce 147
Job insecurity, reducing 148
Job stress 60, 139, 141, 143-148, 187, 193, 205
  job failure 143
  job insecurity 145
  job mismatch 145
  lack of money 145
  personality conflicts 144
  pet solution 143
  reasons for 143
  reducing workload 147
  too much to do 144

K

Kentucky Fried Chicken 164
King, Dr. Martin Luther 251
Kissinger, Henry 56

L

Landers, Ann 67
Learning theories, five 208
Listening 71, 72, 108, 110, 152, 178, 181, 184, 185, 186, 189, 191, 243. *See also* Active Listening
Listening, active. *See* Active Listening
Love 2, 15-16, 20, 26-28, 37, 45, 57, 75, 77, 82, 92, 97, 99, 104, 126, 138, 228
  essential quality 27
  magic of 15-17
Love and lust
  distinction between 26
  essential qualities 27
Loving relationship 13
Lust 26, 32
  and love, distinction between 26
  essential quality 27

M

M.E. (mind's eye) 121, 123-132. *See also* Mind's eye
  and self-image 127
  and self-talk 129
  controlling force 125
  impact on marriage 124
Magical Paths, three 9-12
Magical questions 283-292
Marital commitment 19
Marital intimacy 89
  goal setting 89
  specific commitments 89
Marriage
  protected in 76
  without criticism 76
Masculinity and sexuality 235
Maslow 98
Masters and Johnson 36
Mental toughness 191
Midlife crisis 232
Midlife slump 247
Midlife transition 231-236
  biological clock 234
  career plateau 233
  empty nest 233
  fear of dying 234
  goals, too few 235
  self-fulfilling prophecy 233
  sexual adequacy, loss of 235
  signs of aging 234
Mind's eye. *See also* M.E.
  quiz to determine 125
  three steps to change 130
Mission 10-12, 221-223
  behind the scenes 242
  community needs 244
  congruent 228
  established talent 243
  fund-raising 242
  hands-on 241
  having a cause 240
  inspiring challenge 239
  managerial 241
  religious faith 245
  selection of 237-245
  seven questions to ask 239
  specialist or generalist 243
  spiritual 228
  time 242
  unselfish 227
  vision 227
  what is it 225-229
Mission goals 247-250
  five goal-setting strategies 248
  pursuing vs. reaching 248
Mission path 12
Modeling 75, 208,-209
Motivation, six ways 165

N

Navratilova, Martina 251
Negative conditional message 80
Negative unconditional message 80
Nonverbal messages 181
Nothingness 116. *See also* Depression

O

O'Hair, Madelyn Murray 261
Overcoming obstacles 277-300

P

P + E = R 129-130, 252
Peale, Norman Vincent 256
Persistence 271, 299-300
Personality conflicts on job
  ways to reduce 147
Philo 228
Physical attack 52
Physical health 9
Positive changes, five ways to create 207
Positive conditional message 79
Positive focus 65
Positive qualities 65
Positive unconditional message 79
Praising, power of 175
  assignment 177
  compliments/criticisms ratio 177
Projection 115
Psychological cocktails 30

Psychological paths, three 10
  heart 10
  mind 10
  soul 10
Public self 7, 61-64. *See also* Real self
  1 to 10 scale 63
  activity with spouse 66
  social image 61

Q

Quizes
  commitment 91
  mind's eye 125
  self-assessment 3
  self-talk 193

R

Rational emotive therapy 211
Real self 61-64, 67, 69, 127
  exposing 67
  sharing of 62
  true you 62
Reinforcement theory 207
Relationship 10-11, 15, 19, 21, 23, 43, 45-46, 48, 52, 54, 64, 73, 75, 82, 86-87, 96-99, 104, 111, 118-120, 124, 127, 140, 168, 171, 177-178, 245, 267
  emotional component 37
  establishing positive 175-186
  expectation guidelines 69
  goals 87
  guidelines 87
  intimate, maintaining an 19
  path 11
Relationships on the job 171-174
  genuine caring 174
  how to form positive 172
Relaxation techniques 191
Responsibility 60, 108, 154, 212
  taking 60
Retirement 120, 237, 255-259
  demands on marriage 255
  depression 255
  easy transition, three reasons 256
  how much free time 257
  need to plan 255
  worthlessness 255
Rodgers, Pat 234
Rogers, Kenny 158
Roosevelt, Eleanor 215

S

Satir, Virginia 132
Schaeffer, Nathan C. 228
Second magical path 135-217
Security 26, 85, 126, 146, 165
Self-esteem 2, 10, 20, 78, 99, 121, 173, 263
  negative 9
  positive 9
Self-image
  47, 77, 121, 125, 127, 129, 272
Self-talk 99, 104, 107, 127, 129-130, 193, 194, 195, 199
  and job stress 193-203
  experiment 128
  impact of 199
  quiz 193
Sex
  anxiety over 36
  as an achievement 37
  emotional and sexual expression 37
Sex after forty 41-44
  changes 43
  ejaculation 43
  erection 43
  frequency 43
  impotency 43
  physical fatigue 43
  recovery time 43
Sexual connection 16
Sexual expectations 35
Sexual imageries, negative/positive 34
Sexual imagery. *See* Imagery
Sexual inadequacy 42
Sexual performance
  absence of concern about 36
Sexual response
  external signs 37
  fluctuating 35
  forced 35

Index • 311

preoccupation with 37
Sexual response, weak 33
Sexual security. *See* Chemistry
Sexual turn-ons 31. *See also*
  Chemistry
Sharing feelings 191
Simonson, Dr. Carl 251
Skinner, B.F. 207
Socrates 295
Soul-to-soul 62, 64
Spectator role 36
Spiritual connection 16, 229
Spiritual faith
  accept what is 271
  caring 263
  commitment 264
  coping with stress 268
  enriching one's mission 272
  forgiveness 267
  never give up 270
  overcoming tragedy 270
  positive impact 263
  positive job relationships 268
Spiritual force 261-274
Spouse, reading your 67
St. Augustine 262
Stress 29, 43, 143, 145-146, 149-155,
    189, 190, 192, 195, 211, 248, 268
  change 151
  common advice 150
  control 153
  coping with 3-7, 9, 187-192
  criticism 197
  developing qualities to fight 154
  early warning signs 150
  involvement 152
  qualities that help fight 151
  signs of 149
Stress strategies 187-192
  aerobic exercise 189
  confrontation 190
  five categories 189
  mental toughness 190
  relaxation techniques 189
  sharing feelings 189
Subconscious mind. *See* Imagery

T

Ten Commandments 264
Ten Commandments for Arguing. *See*
    Arguments
Therapist 279. *See also* Counselor
Third magical path 219-275
Three magical questions 283-292
  alternatives 286
  consequences 290
  problem 284
Tragic losses, recovery from 239
True intimacy 62

U

Understanding 60, 71, 78, 94

W

Work ethic 166

Give the Gift of
FINDING PERSONAL HAPPINESS
to Your Friends and Colleagues

CHECK YOUR LEADING BOOKSTORE OR ORDER HERE

❑ **YES,** I want ___ copies of *Finding Personal Happiness* at $22.95 each, plus $3 shipping per book (Texas residents please add $1.49 state sales tax per book). Canadian orders must be accompanied by a postal money order in U.S. funds. Allow 15 days for delivery.

My check or money order for $_____ is enclosed.

Please charge my ❑ Visa ❑ MasterCard

Name _____

Phone _____

Organization _____

Address _____

City/State/Zip _____

Card #_____ Exp. Date _____

Signature _____

Please make your check payable and return to:
Psychological Insights Press
7500 Callaghan Road, Suite 145
San Antonio, TX 78229

Or call your credit card order to: (800) 694-8060
Fax: (210) 697-8603